Strive for a 5: Preparing for the Macroeconomics Examination

Strive for a 5: Preparing for the AP® Macroeconomics Examination

to accompany

KRUGMAN'S ECONOMICS for AP® Second Edition

and

KRUGMAN'S MACROECONOMICS for AP® Second Edition

Margaret Ray and David Anderson

Margaret Ray
University of Mary Washington

Melanie E. Fox
University of Louisville

BFW/WORTH PUBLISHERS

Strive for a 5: Preparing for the AP® Macroeconomics Examination
By Margaret Ray and Melanie Fox to accompany
Krugman's Economics for AP®, Second Edition
and *Krugman's Macroeconomics for AP®*, Second Edition

ISBN 10: 1-4641-5577-1
ISBN 13: 978-1-4641-5577-2

Third   Printing

Printed in the United States of America

BFW/Worth Publishers
41 Madison Avenue
New York, NY 10010
highschool.bfwpub.com

CONTENTS

Preface   *vii*

Study Guide

Section 1   Basic Economic Concepts   1

    Module 1   The Study of Economics..2
    Module 2   Introduction to Macroeconomics 7
    Module 3   The Production Possibilities Curve Model............................12
    Module 4   Comparative Advantage and Trade....................................17

Section 2   Supply and Demand   33

    Module 5   Supply and Demand: Introduction and Demand......................34
    Module 6   Supply and Demand: Supply...39
    Module 7   Supply and Demand: Equilibrium......................................43
    Module 8   Supply and Demand: Price Controls...................................48
    Module 9   Supply and Demand: Quantity Controls...............................52

Section 3   Measurement of Economic Performance   71

    Module 10   The Circular Flow and Gross Domestic Product.......................72
    Module 11   Interpreting Real Gross Domestic Product............................78
    Module 12   The Meaning and Calculation of Unemployment......................81
    Module 13   The Causes and Categories of Unemployment........................85
    Module 14   Inflation: An Overview...88
    Module 15   The Measurement and Calculation of Inflation........................92

Section 4   National Income and Price Determination   109

    Module 16   Income and Expenditure..110
    Module 17   Aggregate Demand: Introduction and Determinants..................114
    Module 18   Aggregate Supply: Introduction and Determinants...................118
    Module 19   Equilibrium in the Aggregate Demand-Aggregate Supply Model...122
    Module 20   Economic Policy and the Aggregate Demand-Aggregate Supply
                 Model...127
    Module 21   Fiscal Policy and Multiplier Effects....................................131

Section 5   The Financial Sector   149

    Module 22   Saving, Investment, and the Financial System........................150
    Module 23   The Definition and Measurement of Money..........................156
    Module 24   The Time Value of Money...160
    Module 25   Banking and Money Creation..163
    Module 26   The Federal Reserve System: History and Structure..................167
    Module 27   The Federal Reserve System: Monetary Policy.......................170
    Module 28   The Money Market..173
    Module 29   The Market for Loanable Funds.......................................176

Section 6   Inflation, Unemployment, and Stabilization Policies   195

Module 30   Long-Run Implications of Fiscal Policy: Deficits and the Public Debt...196
Module 31   Monetary Policy and the Interest Rate.................................200
Module 32   Money, Output, and Prices in the Long Run.........................204
Module 33   Types of Inflation, Disinflation, and Deflation.......................207
Module 34   Inflation and Unemployment: The Phillips Curve....................211
Module 35   History and Alternative Views of Macroeconomics.................216
Module 36   Consensus and Conflict in Modern Macroeconomics.................221

Section 7   Economic Growth and Productivity   237

Module 37   Long-Run Economic Growth 238
Module 38   Productivity and Growth..242
Module 39   Growth Policy: Why Economic Growth Rates Differ.................246
Module 40   Economic Growth in Macroeconomic Models.........................249

Section 8   The Open Economy: International Trade and Finance   261

Module 41   Capital Flows and the Balance of Payments..........................262
Module 42   The Foreign Exchange Market...266
Module 43   Exchange Rate Policy and Macroeconomic Policy....................269
Module 44   Barriers to Trade...274
Module 45   Putting It All Together..278

Preparing for the AP® Macroeconomics Exam................................293

PREFACE

This book, *Strive for a 5: Preparing for the AP® Macroeconomics Examination,* is designed for use with a main textbook: *Krugman's Economics for AP®,* **Second Edition,** or *Krugman's Macroeconomics for AP®,* **Second Edition,** by Margaret Ray and David Anderson. It is intended to help you evaluate your understanding of the material covered in the textbook, reinforce the key concepts you need to learn, and get you comfortable in applying these concepts to problems, all of which will prepare you to take the AP® Macroeconomics exam. This guide is divided into two sections: a study guide section and a test preparation section.

The Study Guide Section

The study guide section is designed for you to use throughout your AP® course. As each module is covered in your class, you can use the study guide to help you identify and learn the economic models, concepts, and terms that are important for your course. After you read the modules in each section, this guide provides practice problems and review questions to help you master the material and verify your understanding before moving on to the next section.

Each **Section** is organized as follows:

Overview: An overview of the section content that provides an orientation to the material covered in the section and modular material.

Featured model/graph: Each section focuses on an important economic model. At the beginning of each section, the economic model developed within the section is identified and described.

Listing of modules: Each section is broken into 4 – 8 modules. This list identifies each of the modules within the section.

Module content: Each section includes a module-by-module presentation of the important content in that section. The module content serves as your guide before you read the corresponding module in the text, while you read the corresponding module in the text, and after you have read the corresponding module in the text.

Before You Tackle the Test: When you have completed all of the modules for a section, this feature allows you to apply your new knowledge.

- **Draw the Featured Graph**: For each section, a framework is provided to help you practice the featured graph.

- **Complete the Exercise**: Each section includes an exercise designed to illustrate how to apply the economic content developed in that section.
- **Problems**: A set of comprehensive practice problems help you learn to apply economic concepts.
- **Review Questions**: A set of multiple-choice questions focus on the key concepts from the text. These questions are designed for quick exam preparation.
- **Answer Key**: Your teacher has access to the answers to all questions within this text and may provide them to you upon request. Because some teachers like to assign portions of the Strive for a 5 guide for a grade, we chose to restrict answer access to instructors only. Answers to all questions and problems in the study guide include thorough explanations, including examples of common student errors. You might be tempted to read questions, and then read the answers to those questions in the Answer Key, or to simply use the Answer Key to check that you got a question correct without considering the explanations. To get the most value out of this, we caution you to pay more attention to the explanation. Knowing *why* an answer is correct is just as important as getting the answer correct. In economics, the reasoning used in coming to conclusions and correctly modeling the problems are as important as coming to an accurate answer, and will enable you to apply that reasoning to other questions.

Each **Module** is organized as follows:

Before You Read the Module – Use this section to gain a basic understanding of module content and learning objectives BEFORE you start to read.

- **Summary**: An opening paragraph provides a brief overview of the Module.
- **Module Objectives**: This list outlines and describes the material that you should have learned in the Module with a space to check as you master each one.

While You Read the Module – Use this section to actively engage with module content to ensure you understand and remember what you read.

- **Key Terms**: A list of key terms from the module includes room to write definitions.
- **Practice the Model** exercises allow you to get familiar with an important graph and diagram within each module.
- **Questions**: Note any questions that you have as you read the module.

After You Read the Module – Use this section to identify areas where you need to spend more time reading and studying the material in the module.

- **Fill-in-the-Blanks** and **Multiple-Choice Questions** help identify important topics in the module.
- **Helpful Tips** and **Module Notes** discuss common difficulties with the module material and provide tips for mastering the module content.

The Test Preparation Section

Preparing for the AP® Macroeconomics Exam, the test preparation section of this guide, is written by AP® Economics teachers and exam readers with a wealth of experience preparing students to successfully show their mastery of economic principles on the AP® Macroeconomics exam. Use this part of this book to help you better understand how the AP® Macroeconomics exam is constructed and scored, how best to study for the exam, and how to make sure you convey what you have learned when answering exam questions. It is a good idea to read through the test preparation section early in the course so that you have a solid understanding of what you are preparing for from the start and understand how to best communicate your understanding on the AP® Macroeconomics exam.

The study of economics has the potential to alter the way you evaluate and understand the world. We hope that your use of *Strive for a 5: Preparing for the AP® Macroeconomics Examination*, Second Edition, will help you in your study of basic macroeconomics principles and will provide a jumping-off point for further study in economics.

Margaret A. Ray

Melanie Fox

Section ① Basic Economic Concepts

Overview

This section provides an introduction to the study of economics. It presents the definition of economics and the difference between the two main branches of the discipline, microeconomics and macroeconomics. In addition, it introduces the business cycle, a major focus of macroeconomics, and three important measures economists use when they study it: unemployment, inflation, and aggregate output. Finally, this section develops the production possibilities curve model and uses it to explain basic economic activity, including trade between countries. Because the study of economics relies heavily on graphical models, an appendix on the use of graphs follows this section.

Economics is a social science, and therefore, like history or geography, it is concerned with the study of people. However, learning the economic way of thinking can be different from learning about other social sciences. Often, how you study math or statistics will be the best approach to studying economics. As you begin your study of economics, keep in mind that you need to adapt your approach to fit the unique nature of the discipline. Blend your approach to learning other social sciences with your approach to learning math or statistics.

Featured Model/Graph: The Production Possibilities Curve

This section presents the first of many economic models in the course, the production possibilities curve, or *PPC*. The *PPC* is a basic macroeconomic model that illustrates the alternative production choices (i.e. possibilities) from which an economy can choose. The model is used to illustrate the basic economic concepts presented in this section, as well as to introduce the use of models in economics.

MODULES IN THIS SECTION

Module 1   **The Study of Economics**

Module 2   **Introduction to Macroeconomics**

Module 3   **The Production Possibilities Curve Model**

Module 4   **Comparative Advantage and Trade**

BEFORE YOU TACKLE THE TEST

Draw the Featured Model

Complete the Exercise

Problems

Review Questions

MODULE 1   THE STUDY OF ECONOMICS

BEFORE YOU READ THE MODULE

Summary

This module presents economics as the study of the production, distribution and consumption of goods and services. It focuses on scarcity and the need to make choices about the production, distribution, and consumption of goods and services, and the resulting importance of opportunity costs. The distinction between positive and normative economics and the two main branches of economics, microeconomics and macroeconomics, are also explained.

Module Objectives

Review these objectives before you read the module. Place a "√" on the line when you can do each of the following:

_____**Objective #1.** Explain how scarcity and choice are central to the study of economics

_____**Objective #2.** Discuss the importance of opportunity cost in individual choice and decision making

_____**Objective #3.** Explain the difference between positive economics and normative economics

_____**Objective #4.** Identify areas of agreement and disagreement among economists

_____**Objective #5.** Distinguish between microeconomic concepts and macroeconomic concepts

WHILE YOU READ THE MODULE

Key Terms

Define these key terms as you read the module:

Economics:

Individual choice:

Economy:

Market economy:

Command economy:

Incentives:

Property rights:

Marginal analysis:

Resource:

Land:

Labor:

Capital:

Entrepreneurship:

Scarce:

Opportunity cost:

Microeconomics:

Macroeconomics:

Economic aggregates:

Positive economics:

Normative economics:

Practice the Model

Identify each of the following statements as being positive statements or normative statements in the space provided.

1) Prices of goods are expected to rise.

2) Workers should earn higher wages.

3) Workers should earn lower wages.

4) Consumers are negatively impacted when prices increase but wages do not.

List questions or difficulties from your initial reading of the module.

AFTER YOU READ THE MODULE

Fill-in-the-Blanks

Fill in the blanks to complete the following statements. If you find yourself having difficulties, please refer back to the appropriate section in the text.

- At its most basic level, economics is about **1)**_____.

- Even though individuals may have unlimited alternatives to choose from, **2)**_____

  means that individuals cannot always get what they want. The activities that create the goods and

  services people want, and get them to the people who want them form the system that we know as the

  3)_____. A **4)**_____ is anything that can be used to produce

  goods and services.

- If a country has a central authority that makes choices about the use of resources to produce goods and services, and also makes choices about the distribution of those goods and services, it has a(n) 5)_____ economy.

- The United States has a 6)_____ economy, in which production and consumption are largely the result of decentralized decisions made by many firms and individuals. For instance, a firm deciding to produce a good determines which of the four types of 7)_____, including 8)_____, _____ , _____ , and _____ to use to produce those goods and services. Because economics is concerned with choices, it is important to consider what you must give up when you make a choice. This is known as the 9) _____ cost of a choice.

- Economics is divided into two main branches. Microeconomics studies the choices made by 10)_____ while macroeconomics focuses on data that summarizes measures across many markets, called economic 11)_____.

- When economic analysis is used to answer questions about the way the world works that have definite right and wrong answers, it is known as 12)_____ economics. In contrast, economic analysis that involves saying how the world should work is known as 13)_____ economics. An economist who tells you that a certain policy is "good" or "bad" is engaging in 14)_____ economics.

Multiple-Choice Questions

Circle the best choice to answer or complete the following questions or incomplete statements. For additional practice, use the space provided to explain why one or more of the incorrect options do not work.

15. Which of the following is not an economic resource?
    a. land
    b. labor
    c. capital
    d. entrepreneurship
    e. money

Helpful Tips

- Many students assume economics is "about money." But the driving force behind the study of economics is scarcity and choice: because resources are scarce, we must choose how to allocate those resources.

- Positive analysis is stating how things "are." Normative analysis is stating how things "should be." An easy way to keep these straight is to think about social norms, the way you should behave in a given context. Positive analysis is absent of value statements.

- The opportunity cost of one choice is not the cost of all foregone opportunities; it is the cost of the *next best* foregone opportunity. For instance, if I decide to spend an hour babysitting and make $20, when I could have spent the same hour mowing a lawn for $15 or wash windows for $10, the opportunity cost of babysitting is only the value of mowing lawns.

Module Notes

John Maynard Keynes, considered by many to be the father of modern macroeconomics, wrote that "[Economics] is a method rather than a doctrine, an apparatus of the mind, a technique of thinking which helps its possessor to draw correct conclusions." Similarly, the influential microeconomist Alfred Marshall described economics as a study of the "ordinary business of life" and wrote that "[Economics] is not a body of concrete truth, but an engine for the discovery of concrete truth." Each of these important economists was pointing out that economics is a valuable way of thinking about the world rather than just an established body of knowledge.

You will be expected to solve new and varied problems not by providing memorized definitions or explanations, but by using this "technique of thinking." Knowing the definitions and equations are a necessary first step, but this is not sufficient to demonstrate that you can use this "technique of thinking."

Use the Problems and Review Questions in your textbook to determine if you have learned what you need to know. At the beginning, try all of the sample questions, problems, and approaches that you and your instructor can find, and determine which ones work best to help you master the material. Keep the following in mind as you continue:

- The study of economics is cumulative. You should master each topic as it is presented since later topics build on earlier topics.

- Pay attention to new vocabulary and make sure you know, understand, and can apply these terms. You will be expected to do more than just define the terms: you must also be able to indicate through your work an ability to apply these terms in a meaningful manner.

- Plan to spend time every day studying economics. Review your lecture notes, review the vocabulary, work on the practice questions, and identify questions you have about the material. Once you identify your questions, seek out answers by returning to your text, your lecture notes, your classmates, or your teacher. If you find you have made a mistake, focus on discovering the error in reasoning that led to that mistake, rather than simply memorizing the correct answer.

MODULE 2 INTRODUCTION TO MACROECONOMICS

BEFORE YOU READ THE MODULE

Summary

This module introduces the business cycle in an economy. It also presents three important related macroeconomic concepts: unemployment, inflation, and economic growth. Measures of employment, the price level, and aggregate output are used to evaluate the performance of the macroeconomy. The basic concepts are presented here and developed in greater detail in Section 3. These topics will be used in the models we build throughout the course.

Module Objectives

Review these objectives before you read the module. Place a "√" on the line when you can do each of the following:

_____ **Objective #1.** Explain what a business cycle is and why policy makers seek to diminish the severity of business cycles

_____ **Objective #2.** Describe how employment and unemployment are measured and how they change over the business cycle

_____ **Objective #3.** Define aggregate output and explain how it changes over the business cycle

_____ **Objective #4.** Define inflation and deflation and explain why price stability is preferred

_____ **Objective #5.** Explain how economic growth determines a country's standard of living

_____ **Objective #6.** Summarize the crucial role of models--simplified representations of reality--in economics

WHILE YOU READ THE MODULE

Key Terms

Define these key terms as you read the module:

Business cycle:

Depression:

Recessions:

Expansions:

Employment:

Unemployment:

Labor force:

Unemployment rate:

Output:

Aggregate output:

Inflation:

Deflation:

Price stability:

Economic growth:

Model:

Other things equal assumption (*ceteris paribus*):

Practice the Model

Figure 2.1 in the text shows the unemployment rate and the timing of business cycles between 1989 and 2013. For each of the time frames below, indicate what was happening to Unemployment and GDP. The first one has been done for you.

Time period	Unemployment and GDP
1989 - 1992	Unemployment was increasing; therefore, GDP was decreasing.
1993 - 2000	
2001 - 2004	
2005 - 2007	
2008 - 2010	
2011 - 2013	

List questions or difficulties from your initial reading of the module:

AFTER YOU READ THE MODULE

Fill-in-the-Blanks

Fill in the blanks to complete the following statements. If you find yourself having difficulties, please refer back to the appropriate section in the text.

- The upturns and downturns in the macroeconomy are known as the **1)**_____.

    Economic downturns are known as **2)**_____, and economic upturns are known as

    3)_____. During an economic downturn, employment and aggregate output both

    4)_____ while unemployment **5)**_____.

Multiple-Choice Questions

Circle the best choice to answer or complete the following questions or incomplete statements. For additional practice, use the space provided to explain why one or more of the incorrect options do not work.

6. Unemployment is best described as
    a. a rise in the overall price level.
    b. the total number of people who are not currently employed.
    c. the total number of people who are not currently employed but are actively looking for work.
    d. the labor force plus the total number of people looking for pay.
    e. what is experienced by anyone who is looking for a job.

7. Economists believe that which of the following is a desirable goal for an economy?
  a. deflation
  b. inflation
  c. depressions
  d. price stability
  e. recessions

Helpful Tips

- Inflation is undesirable, but that does not mean that its opposite, deflation, is desirable either. Both have negative consequences for the economy.

- Not all economic downturns are recessions. The term recession is generally reserved for a downturn that lasts two quarters (six months) or more.

- Not all economic expansions (or recoveries) are economic growth. Economic expansions may be temporary, but economic growth is a permanent increase in the amount of goods and services that can be produced. Economic growth can only occur when there is an increase in one or more of the four economic resources.

- Aggregation of data is at the heart of macroeconomics. This module briefly describes the meaning of aggregation and gives examples of aggregated measures like employment, real GDP, and the overall price level.

Module Notes

A model is a simplified representation of reality used to better understand the world. An important part of economics is working with models. Very often, economic models use graphs to simplify reality and facilitate understanding. Graphs can make it much easier to understand verbal descriptions, numerical information, or ideas. To understand economics, you must learn how to interpret and manipulate graphs. A picture may be worth a thousand words, but a graph is even more valuable. Graphs are used not just to depict something, but they can be used to predict what might happen as well.

As you study economics, make sure that you are able to not only read and understand the graphs that you see, but also that you are able to construct and explain graphs on your own. The ability to represent an economic idea using a graph is different than the ability to look at and understand an existing graph and you should be able to do both. The appendix to this section explains how graphs are constructed and interpreted and how they are used in economics. The appendix, and lots of practice drawing graphs, will help you to master the material.

Graphs are a way of describing the relationship between two variables (in other words, two things that might vary with each other). For instance, how does the quantity people buy vary with the price that they pay, how does aggregate output vary over time, etc.? Each of the variables being compared will be one of the two axes on a graph.

To get used to the idea of drawing graphs in economics, begin by drawing your own graph of the business cycle. You can use the one in this module as a guide to the labels and information you will need on your graph. Labeling your graph is critical: without labels, nobody else reading your graph can tell what you are trying to show.

Many of the models you will encounter in this course make the other things equal assumption (also known as *ceteris paribus*), which means that the model considers only one change at a time while holding everything else constant. Make sure you understand this basic assumption before working with the models introduced in the module.

MODULE 3 — THE PRODUCTION POSSIBILITIES CURVE MODEL

BEFORE YOU READ THE MODULE

Summary

This module introduces the concept of model building by presenting the production possibility curve model. The *PPC* provides a simplified framework for discussing the concept of opportunity cost, trade-offs, scarcity, efficiency, and (in the next module) gains from trade.

Module Objectives

Review these objectives before you read the module. Place a "√" on the line when you can do each of the following:

_____ **Objective #1.** Explain the importance of tradeoffs in economic analysis

_____ **Objective #2.** Describe what a production possibilities curve model tells us about efficiency, opportunity cost, and economic growth

_____ **Objective #3.** Explain why increases in the availability of resources and improvements in technology are the two sources of economic growth

WHILE YOU READ THE MODULE

Key Terms

Define these key terms as you read the module:

Trade-off:

Production possibilities curve:

Efficient:

Productive efficiency:

Allocative efficiency:

Technology:

Practice the Model

Consider an economy that can produce two goods, A and B. In the space below, sketch a correctly labeled graph of a bowed-out production possibilities curve with A on the vertical axis and B on the horizontal axis.

List questions or difficulties from your initial reading of the module:

AFTER YOU READ THE MODULE

Fill-in-the-Blanks

Fill in the blanks to complete the following statements. If you find yourself having difficulties, please refer back to the appropriate section in the text.

- A graph that shows the trade-off between the production of two goods is called a

  1)_____ curve. If a production point lies on this curve, it is feasible and

  2)_____ . If a production point lies inside this curve, it is feasible, but

  3)_____ . If a production point lies **4)**_____ this curve, it is not

  feasible.

- There are missed opportunities if a production point lies **5)**_____the production

  possibilities curve. Because the *PPC* has a negative slope, producing more of one good means less of

  the other good can be produced. Therefore, a movement from one point on the *PPC* to another point

  on the same *PPC* illustrates the concept of **6)**_____cost.

Multiple-Choice Questions

Circle the best choice to answer or complete the following questions or incomplete statements. For additional practice, use the space provided to explain why one or more of the incorrect options do not work.

Questions 7 and 8 refer to the following graph:

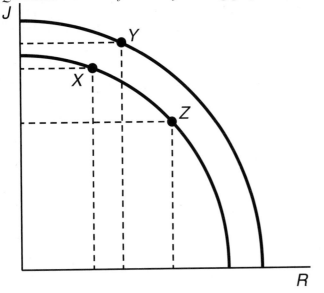

7. If an economy moves from _____, it is experiencing economic growth.
   a. X to Z
   b. Y to Z
   c. X to Y
   d. Y to X
   e. Z to X

8. Which of the following could produce a movement from X to Z?
   a. an increase in the total amount of capital available
   b. moving some capital that was being used to produce good R to produce good J instead
   c. moving some capital that was being used to produce good J to produce good R instead
   d. an increase in the total amount of labor available
   e. an increase in the technology used to produce good R

Helpful Tips

- A movement along a production possibilities curve is not economic growth. Remember that economic growth occurs when there is more of any of the economic resources. A common error is to mistake being able to produce more of one good as growth. Economic growth means being able to produce more of one of the two goods, without reducing the amount of the other good available.

- Make sure you understand how to calculate opportunity cost based on a linear *PPC*, which is important for determining comparative advantage in the next module. First, graph the *PPC* and calculate its slope. Since the *PPC* is linear, the slope is the same anywhere along the *PPC* (recall that "rise over run" is used to calculate slope). You can use the slope to find the opportunity cost for both goods. The opportunity cost of producing one more unit of the good on the *x*-axis is the slope. The opportunity cost of producing one more unit of the good on the *y*-axis is the reciprocal of the slope.

- Another way to calculate opportunity cost based on a linear *PPC* shown in a graph or a table of data is to use the intercepts. Suppose Tom has a linear *PPC*, and he can produce 30 coconuts (C) if he spends all of his time on coconuts (this is the *y*-intercept) or produce 40 fish (F) if he spends all of his time on fish (this is the *x*-intercept). Since Tom can use his time to produce either 30 C OR 40 F, 30C = 40F

  To solve for the opportunity cost of each good, solve for *that* good. For instance, to find the opportunity cost of 1 coconut, solve for C:
  30C = 40 F
  C = 40/30 F
  C = 4/3 F

  Then solve for F to get the opportunity cost of a fish:
  30C = 40 F
  30/40 C = F
  3/4 C = F

  In other words, the opportunity cost of one fish is 3/4 of a coconut and the opportunity cost of one coconut is 4/3 of a fish. Note that this method only works when you have a linear *PPC*: a linear *PPC* implies that there is a constant trade-off (so 1 fish is always worth 3/4 of a coconut). A bowed out *PPC* implies that the trade-off will vary along the curve, so the slope, and therefore the opportunity cost, will be different at different points along the curve.

Module Notes

The production possibilities curve is the first model presented in this book. It is important that you identify what the *PPC* illustrates and how it is used to understand the choices facing any economy. The *PPC* model is a graphical representation of an economy that illustrates trade-offs, scarcity, opportunity cost, efficiency, and economic growth. Notice that each axis represents the *quantity* of a good being produced. For instance, the horizontal axis in the Crusoe example represented the quantity of fish, and the vertical axis represented the *quantity* of coconuts. Each point on the production possibility curve shows the amount of coconuts that could be produced when a given amount of fish was produced. For instance, with Crusoe's initial resources and technology, whenever he caught 20 fish, he could also pick 25 coconuts.

You will need to understand how these concepts are illustrated on a *PPC* graph (i.e. movements along the curve, points on the curve, and shifts of the curve). You also need to be able to draw a *PPC* graph and use it to illustrate and explain these concepts. Finally, you will need to understand how these concepts are illustrated on a *PPC* with enough depth to answer questions in examples and contexts that you have not seen before. Achieving this level of understanding requires practice with drawing and interpreting graphs and applying the *PPC* model to different real-world and hypothetical examples. The ability to use economic models to analyze situations and answer questions is an essential part of mastering introductory economics.

Economic models can be described verbally, but they can also be represented by graphs or equations. Another way to think about economic models is that they involve math and/or a graph to tell a story. You will want to be comfortable working with all three types of representations. You may find it helpful to be able to sketch graphs to illustrate the ideas you are analyzing. Even if you are just doing a quick sketch of a graph, it is important that you *always* take the time to correctly label both axes and any curves.

Practice making precise graphs using any specific values given, but also practice graphs that sketch the general relationship between variables without numbers. For instance, when graphing a production possibilities curve for two goods that could be produced, include values of each good that can be produced if they are given. If they are not, be able to show a production possibilities curve that shows that there is an opportunity cost to producing more of one of those goods.

Opportunity cost can be measured using the production possibilities curve model. To do this calculation, pick a point on the *PPC* and identify how much of each good is being produced. Then pick a second point on the *PPC* and identify the new levels of production. The opportunity cost is measured as the number of units of the good you must give up to get more of the other good.

Make sure you understand how to interpret the shape of the curves in the *PPC* model. In particular, make sure you can draw and understand what is shown by both a linear and a "bowed out" *PPC*. Know the assumption that leads to a linear or bowed out *PPC*. Make sure you can identify and indicate feasible and infeasible points as well as efficient and inefficient points. Know what two factors can shift the *PPC* out in the future.

MODULE 4   COMPARATIVE ADVANTAGE AND TRADE

BEFORE YOU READ THE MODULE

Summary

This module introduces the concepts of comparative and absolute advantage, and explains the benefits of specialization and trade. It shows how the *PPC* model can be used to illustrate gains from trade based on comparative advantage, and presents the basic economic argument in favor of international trade by showing that total world output can increase when countries specialize and trade.

Module Objectives

Review these objectives before you read the module. Place a "√" on the line when you can do each of the following:

_____**Objective #1.** Explain how trade leads to gains for an individual or an economy

_____**Objective #2.** Explain the difference between absolute advantage and comparative advantage

_____**Objective #3.** Describe how comparative advantage leads to gains from trade in the global marketplace

WHILE YOU READ THE MODULE

Key Terms

Define these key terms as you read the module:

Trade:

Gains from trade:

Specialization:

Comparative advantage:

Absolute advantage:

Terms of trade:

Practice the Model

Use the data from the following table to construct correctly labeled graphs showing the production possibilities curves for Portugal and the United States. Assume that both countries have constant opportunity costs.

	Olive oil	Textiles
United States	20	30
Portugal	50	50
Total	70	80

List questions or difficulties from your initial reading of the module:

AFTER YOU READ THE MODULE

Fill-in-the-Blanks

Fill in the blanks to complete the following statements. If you find yourself having difficulties, please refer back to the appropriate section in the text.

• When people divide tasks among themselves and each person provides a good or service that other

people want in return for different goods and services that he or she wants, it is called

1)_____. This is a key to a much better standard of living for everyone because it

allows a division of tasks based on what each person is better at producing, called

2)_____.

- If the opportunity cost of production is lower for one person (or country) than it is for other people (or countries), then that person (or country) has a(n) **3)**_____ advantage. If an individual (or country) can produce more output with a given amount of input than another person (or country), then that person (or country) has a(n) **4)**_____ advantage.

- **5)**_____ advantage is the basis for mutual gains from trade. In an example in which two countries can each produce the same two goods, it is possible for a country to have a(n)

  6)_____ advantage in both goods, but it is not possible for a country to have a(n)

  7)_____ advantage in both goods.

Multiple-Choice Questions

Circle the best choice to answer or complete the following questions or incomplete statements. For additional practice, use the space provided to explain why one or more of the incorrect options do not work.

Use the following information to answer questions 8 and 9.
Suppose that two countries, Texia and Urbania, produce food and clothing, and currently do not trade. Both countries have linear *PPC*s. If Texia devotes all of its resources to food production, it can produce 1,000 units of food this year and 0 units of clothing. If it devotes all of its resources to clothing production, it can produce 500 units of clothing and 0 units of food. Urbania can produce either 900 units of food and 0 units of clothing or 300 units of clothing and 0 units of food.

8. _____ has the absolute advantage in the production of clothing, and _____ has the absolute advantage in the production of food.
   a. Texia; Texia
   b. Texia; Urbania
   c. Urbania; Texia
   d. Urbania; Urbania
   e. Neither country, neither country

9. _____ has the comparative advantage in the production of clothing, and _____ has the comparative advantage in the production of food.
   a. Texia; Texia
   b. Texia; Urbania
   c. Urbania; Texia
   d. Urbania; Urbania
   e. Neither country, neither country

10. Specialization and trade benefit
   a. usually only one of the trading partners.
   b. the wealthier country more than the poorer country.
   c. the poorer country more than the wealthier country.
   d. both countries if they specialize according to their respective comparative advantages.
   e. neither country when one country is better at producing both goods.

Helpful Tips

- Gains from trade come from differences in opportunity cost (and therefore comparative advantage), not absolute advantage.

- It is not possible to have comparative advantage in more than one good.

- A common misperception is that trade will always make one trading partner worse off. Both will be better off with trade than they were without trade as long as there are differences in opportunity costs between the two. It is possible, however, that one country is made better off more than another country is made better off depending on the *terms of trade* (the trading prices), but they will still both be better off than they were before. The only possible other situation is that nobody is made better off, which would only occur when two countries have identical opportunity costs, in which case there would not be any point in trading.

- Gains from trade will occur when the terms of trade are between the opportunity costs for the traders. Recall from the text that Tom and Hank were made better off from trading 10 coconuts for 10 fish, which made the terms of trade 1C = 1F. Tom's opportunity cost for fish was 3/4 of a coconut and Hank's opportunity cost for a fish was 2 coconuts. One coconut is between 3/4 coconut and 2 coconuts. *Any* price of fish between 3/4 of a coconut and 2 coconuts results in both Tom and Hank benefitting (for example, 1 F = 1 1/2 C or 1 F = 8/10 C).

Module Notes

Students do it, pundits do it, and politicians do it all the time: they confuse *comparative* advantage with *absolute* advantage. For example, back in the 1980s, when the U.S. economy seemed to be lagging behind that of Japan, commentators warned that if we didn't improve our productivity, we would soon have no comparative advantage in anything. What those commentators meant was that we would have no *absolute* advantage in anything—that there might come a time when the Japanese were better at producing everything than we were. And they had the idea that if that were to happen, Japan would no longer be able to benefit from trade with the United States. But just as Hank is able to benefit from trade with Tom (and vice versa) despite the fact that Tom is better at everything, nations can still gain from trade even if they are less productive in all industries than the countries they trade with.

Once you can calculate the opportunity cost of producing good X or good Y, as explained in the previous module, you can compare the opportunity costs faced by two countries. The model of comparative advantage illustrates that countries will benefit from trade when they specialize and produce the good that has the lowest opportunity cost of production relative to the other country. More simply: the country with the lower opportunity cost of a good has comparative advantage in that good.

BEFORE YOU TACKLE THE TEST: SECTION ①

Draw The Featured Graph: Production Possibilities Curve

1) The following table gives the amount of two goods that a single person can produce in a single day. Graph the *PPC* corresponding to the data provided in the table.

<u>y-axis label</u>

Fish	Coconuts
0	8
2	6
4	4
6	2
8	0

<u>x-axis label</u>

2) Using the graph you created above, give an equation that represents the amount of fish and coconuts that this person can produce in a single day, and then solve for the opportunity cost of each good.

3) Graph a *PPC* showing the trade-off between two goods, good A and good B. Draw your *PPC* so that it illustrates increasing opportunity costs.

<u>y-axis label</u>

<u>x-axis label</u>

Complete the Exercise

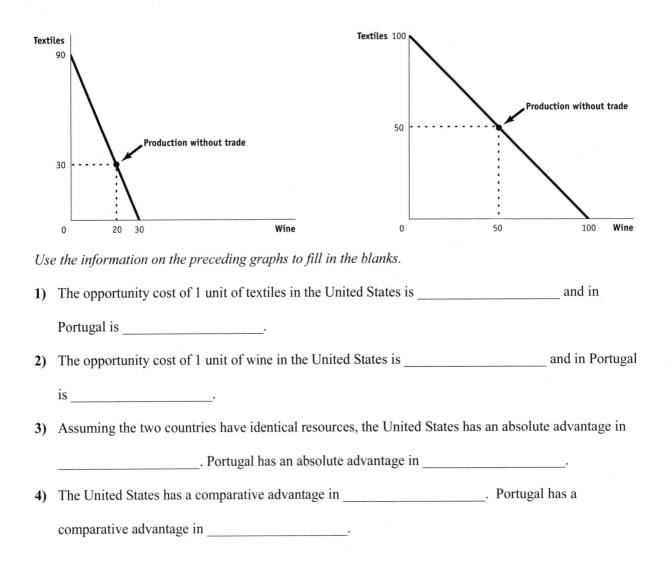

Use the information on the preceding graphs to fill in the blanks.

1) The opportunity cost of 1 unit of textiles in the United States is _____ and in

    Portugal is _____.

2) The opportunity cost of 1 unit of wine in the United States is _____ and in Portugal

    is _____.

3) Assuming the two countries have identical resources, the United States has an absolute advantage in

    _____. Portugal has an absolute advantage in _____.

4) The United States has a comparative advantage in _____. Portugal has a

    comparative advantage in _____.

*Fill in the following table. Assume that with trade, each country specializes and exports ½ of its production. Also assume
that the terms of trade are 1 wine for 2 textiles.*

	Without Trade		With Trade (Production)		With Trade (Consumption)	
	Wine	Textiles	Wine	Textiles	Wine	Textiles
Portugal						
United States						
Total						

5) What happens to total world output when the countries specialize and trade?

6) What is this called?

7) Are both of the countries better off? Explain.

Problems

1. For each of the following situations, describe the opportunity cost of each decision.

   a. Sarah considers two options for Saturday night: she can attend a concert that costs $10 per ticket or she can see a free movie. She attends the concert.

   b. A new firm in town must decide between paying $20,000 for a prime location versus $12,000 for another less desirable location. The firm estimates that it will eventually serve the same number of customers in either location, but that it will take six months before the less desirable location provides the same number of customers as the prime location. The firm decides to purchase the $12,000 property.

   c. Jamie can either be an unpaid intern at a company or he can earn $2,000 working as a camp counselor. He takes the internship.

2. The following table presents the possible combinations of study time available to Roberto this week as he prepares for his two midterms: economics and chemistry. Assume Roberto has 20 hours to study and that he will use all 20 hours studying economics and chemistry. Roberto currently plans to study 10 hours for economics and 10 hours for chemistry.

Hours of study time spent on economics	Hours of study time spent on chemistry	Grade in economics	Grade in chemistry
0	20	60	90
5	15	70	85
10	10	80	75
15	5	86	73
20	0	90	70

   a. If he changes his plan and studies 15 hours for economics, what is his opportunity cost?

   b. If he changes his plan and studies 15 hours for chemistry, what is his opportunity cost?

   c. If he changes his plan and studies 20 hours for economics, what is his opportunity cost?

3. Decide whether each of the following statements is a normative statement or a positive statement. Explain.

   a. The gasoline tax is projected to yield $10 million in tax revenue next year.

   b. If the gasoline tax was raised by 10 cents per gallon, tax revenue would increase by 4%.

   c. The state should raise the gasoline tax for the coming year. An increase in the tax will reduce congestion and smog, which is more important than the cost to commuters if they shift from private car transportation to public transportation.

4. Economists sometimes disagree about positive economics, but more often they disagree about normative economics. Define each of these terms, and explain why economists do not always agree.

5. This section distinguishes between an economic expansion as part of the business cycle and long-run economic growth. Concisely explain the difference between these two terms.

6. In the beginning of 2011, suppose the population in Funland was 2 million people and the level of real GDP, or aggregate output, was $40 million. During 2011, population increased by 3%, while real GDP increased by 3%. During 2012, population increased by 4%, while real GDP increased by 3%. During 2013, population increased by 5%, while real GDP increased by 3%.

   a. Fill in the following table using the given information. (Round to two decimal places.)

	Beginning of 2011	**Beginning of 2012**	**Beginning of 2013**	**Beginning of 2014**
Real GDP				
Population				
Real GDP/person				

   b. What do you know about this country's standard of living between the beginning of 2011 and the beginning of 2014? Explain how you know.

7. The country of Utopia produces two goods from its available resources and technology. The only resource that Utopia has is labor. It takes 3 hours of labor to produce 2 widgets and 4 hours of labor to produce 1 gadget. For this question assume that the *PPC* for Utopia is a straight line.

   a. Sketch the *PPC* for the country of Utopia. (Hint: choose a relevant time period, e.g. 20 hours, as your labor constraint, and sketch your *PPC* based on this amount of time and labor.) Graph widgets on the *y*-axis and gadgets on the *x*-axis.

   b. What is the slope of your *PPC*?

   c. What is the opportunity cost of producing an additional widget in Utopia?

   d. What is the opportunity cost of producing an additional gadget in Utopia?

8. The country of Jonesville produces two goods from its available resources and technology. The only resource that Jonesville has is labor. It takes 2 hours of labor to produce a gadget and 5 hours of labor to produce a widget. For this question assume that the *PPC* for Jonesville is linear.

   a. Suppose that you want to draw a *PPC* for Jonesville. What must you do first?

   b. Sketch the *PPC* for Jonesville assuming that Jonesville has 120 hours of labor available. Place gadgets on the *x*-axis and widgets on the *y*-axis.

   c. What is the slope of the *PPC*?

d. What is the opportunity cost of producing an additional gadget?

e. What is the opportunity cost of producing an additional widget?

f. Suppose that Jonesville has 240 hours of labor instead of 120 hours of labor. Does this affect the opportunity cost of producing widgets or gadgets? Explain your answer.

9. The following table provides six possible production combinations that Smithtown can produce from its available resources and technology during this year. Assume that Smithtown only produces bicycles and tents from its available resources.

Combination	Bicycles	Tents
A	100	0
B	90	10
C	70	25
D	40	36
E	10	42
F	0	44

a. Sketch Smithtown's *PPC*. Measure bicycles along the *x*-axis and tents along the *y*-axis.

b. Suppose Smithtown is currently producing at combination *C*. If Smithtown chooses to produce at combination *B*, what is the opportunity cost of moving from combination *C* to *B*?

c. Suppose Smithtown is currently producing at combination *C*. If Smithtown chooses to produce at combination *D*, what is the opportunity cost of moving from combination *C* to *D*?

d. Smithtown's *PPC* is not linear. Explain why not.

10. There are two islands in the middle of the ocean, and these two islands produce fish and baskets. Big Island can produce either 100 fish and 0 baskets per day or 0 fish and 200 baskets per day. Big Island can also produce any combination of fish and baskets that lies on its linear *PPC*. Small Island can produce either 80 fish and 0 baskets per day or 0 fish and 80 baskets per day. Like Big Island, Small Island has a linear *PPC*.

a. Sketch two graphs. Sketch Big Island's *PPC* on the first graph and Small Island's *PPC* on the second graph. Place fish/day on the *y*-axis and baskets/day on the *x*-axis.

b. What is the slope of Big Island's *PPC*?

c. What is the slope of Small Island's *PPC*?

d. Express the production of Big Island as an equation showing that one day can be used to produce 100 fish or 1 day can be used to produce 200 baskets. Use this equation to solve for the opportunity cost of baskets, and then solve for the opportunity cost of fish. Then describe the opportunity cost for each (see the helpful tips in this module).

e. Express the production of Small Island as an equation showing that one day can be used to produce 80 fish or 1 day can equivalently be used to produce 80 baskets. Use this equation to solve for the opportunity cost of baskets, and then solve for the opportunity cost of fish.

f. Which island can produce baskets at lower opportunity cost?

g. Which island can produce fish at lower opportunity cost?

h. What good should Big Island specialize in producing? Explain.

i. What good should Small Island specialize in producing?

Review Questions

Circle your answer to the following questions.

1. Scarcity of resources implies that
   a. people can do whatever they want and do not need to worry about making choices.
   b. life involves making choices about how to best use scarce resources.
   c. societies should invest time and money to discover more resources.
   d. only very wealthy individuals are not constrained by limited resources.
   e. only some resources are finite.

2. Camillo is offered two jobs: one pays a salary of $30,000 per year and offers three weeks of vacation, and the other job pays a salary of $32,000 per year and offers two weeks of vacation. What is the opportunity cost for Camillo of taking the job offering $32,000 per year?
   a. $2,000 plus two weeks of vacation per year
   b. $2,000 per year
   c. one week of vacation per year
   d. $30,000 plus two weeks of vacation per year
   e. three weeks of vacation per year

3. Which of the following statements describes positive economics?
   a. It is descriptive.
   b. It recommends a course of action.
   c. It is prescriptive.
   d. It is subjective.
   e. It is value oriented.

4. Which of the following statements is an example of normative economics?
   a. The United States should pass a value-added tax, since this is a tax that will work best.
   b. A value-added tax will add $10 billion to the administrative costs of the U.S. tax system.
   c. It can be demonstrated that value-added taxes increase the tax burden on less wealthy households.
   d. A value-added tax would generate $200 billion in revenue each year.
   e. Two other countries have value-added tax systems.

5. Macroeconomics, unlike microeconomics,
   a. considers the behavior of individual firms and markets.
   b. focuses on the production and consumption of particular goods.
   c. tries to explain increases in living standards over time.
   d. finds that the behavior of individuals is more important than its aggregate summation.
   e. considers the efficiency of markets.

6. Economic growth
   a. refers to increases in real GDP per capita over the long run.
   b. refers to short-term fluctuations in real GDP per capita.
   c. is best measured using the employment rate.
   d. is of little importance to economists.
   e. is best measured using inflation rates.

7. Which of the following statements is true?
   a. An economy in a recession will have lower unemployment than during an expansion.
   b. In an economic expansion, the unemployment rate decreases while aggregate output increases.
   c. An economy's output level and employment rate move in opposite directions.
   d. During recessions output decreases as well as unemployment.
   e. In a recession, employment increases and output increases.

8. Inflation means that
   a. the aggregate level of output increases.
   b. the unemployment rate increases.
   c. the aggregate price level rises over time.
   d. consumers' purchasing power increases over time.
   e. workforce participation increases.

9. An economic contraction
   a. is another term for an economic boom.
   b. indicates that the economy is experiencing an increase in the level of employment.
   c. is not part of the business cycle.
   d. occurs when output is falling.
   e. always occurs after the trough in the business cycle.

10. An economic expansion
   a. is associated with an increase in the unemployment rate.
   b. indicates that the economy is experiencing a decrease in the level of unemployment.
   c. is that part of the business cycle between the peak and the trough.
   d. is not part of the business cycle.
   e. is associated with a decrease in the employment rate.

11. When the economy is in a recession, what is true about output, the unemployment rate, and overall level of prices?

	Output	*Unemployment rate*	*Aggregate price level*
a.	increases	increases	rise
b.	decreases	decreases	rise
c.	increases	decreases	fall
d.	decreases	decreases	fall
e.	decreases	increases	fall

12. A recession is best described as
   a. a decrease in the price level.
   b. that part of the business cycle between the trough and the peak.
   c. any decrease in output and unemployment.
   d. that part of the business cycle between the peak and the trough.
   e. an increase in employment and a decrease in output.

13. Suppose Mike has a linear *PPC* in the production of potatoes and tomatoes. If Mike devotes all his time to the production of potatoes, he can produce 1,000 pounds of potatoes a year; if he devotes all his time to the production of tomatoes, he can produce 2,000 pounds of tomatoes a year. Which of the following combinations of potatoes and tomatoes are feasible for Mike in a year?
    a. 1,000 pounds of potatoes and 2,000 pounds of tomatoes
    b. 1,000 pounds of potatoes and 100 pounds of tomatoes
    c. 100 pounds of potatoes and 2,000 pounds of tomatoes
    d. 500 pounds of potatoes and 1,200 pounds of tomatoes
    e. 500 pounds of potatoes and 1,000 pounds of tomatoes

14. Utopia has a linear *PPC* in the production of widgets and gadgets. It can produce three gadgets per hour of labor time or four widgets per hour of labor time. What is the opportunity cost of producing one widget in Utopia?
    a. 3 gadgets
    b. 4 widgets
    c. 0.75 gadget
    d. 1.33 gadgets
    e. 1 gadget

Refer to the following scenario to answer questions 15 through 18:

Jonesville produces widgets and gadgets, and its *PPC* is linear. It takes 5 hours of labor to produce a gadget and 10 hours of labor to produce a widget.

15. Suppose that Jonesville has 100 hours of labor. What is the maximum number of widgets it can produce?
    a. 10 widgets
    b. 20 widgets
    c. 1 widget
    d. 100 widgets
    e. 50 widgets

16. How many widgets and gadgets can Jonesville produce if it devotes half of its 100 hours of labor time to the production of gadgets and half to the production of widgets?
    a. 20 gadgets and 5 widgets
    b. 10 gadgets and 5 widgets
    c. 5 gadgets and 20 widgets
    d. 5 gadgets and 10 widgets
    e. 5 widgets and 10 gadgets

17. What happens to the opportunity cost of producing a widget if Jonesville's labor resource increases to 200 hours of labor?
    a. The opportunity cost of producing a widget will double.
    b. The opportunity cost of producing a widget will increase, but not double.
    c. The opportunity cost of producing a widget will not change.
    d. The opportunity cost of widgets and gadgets will decrease by one half.
    e. The opportunity cost of widgets will decrease by less than one half.

18. If Jonesville has 100 units of labor, which of the following combinations of gadgets and widgets is both feasible and efficient?
    a. 4 gadgets and 18 widgets
    b. 6 gadgets and 0 widgets
    c. 8 gadgets and 6 widgets
    d. 2 gadgets and 10 widgets
    e. 8 gadgets and 1 widget

Refer to the following scenario to answer questions 19 and 20:

Suburbia has a *PPC* bowed out from the origin for two goods, guns and butter, that Suburbia produces from its available resources and technology. The following table describes six points that lie on Suburbia's *PPC*:

Combination	Number of guns	Pounds of butter
A	0	80
B	10	75
C	20	65
D	30	50
E	40	30
F	50	0

19. Suppose that Suburbia initially produces at point *D*. What is the opportunity cost of moving to point *E*?
    a. 10 guns
    b. 40 guns
    c. 20 pounds of butter
    d. 30 pounds of butter
    e. 70 pounds of butter

20. Suppose that Suburbia initially produces at point *D*. What is the opportunity cost of moving to point *B*?
    a. 25 pounds of butter
    b. 20 guns
    c. 10 guns
    d. 75 pounds of butter
    e. 50 pounds of butter

21. Assume there are two countries, country A and country B, that produce two goods, slosh and glem. Country A can produce 20 units of slosh or 40 units of glem in a day. Country B can produce 30 units of slosh or 60 units of glem in a day. Which of the following is true?
    a. Neither country has an absolute advantage in either good.
    b. Both country A and country B should specialize in slosh.
    c. Country A should specialize in slosh and country B should specialize in glem.
    d. There is no potential for gains from trade in this situation.
    e. Country A should specialize in slosh, but country B should not specialize in glem.

Section ② Supply and Demand

Overview

This section first presents the two sides of the market, demand and supply, individually. Once the supply and demand sides of the market have been presented, it puts them together to show how the supply and demand model can be used to understand markets. Variations on the supply and demand model, such as the market for loanable funds, aggregate supply and aggregate demand, and the money market will appear throughout the remainder of the course.

Featured Model/Graph: Supply and Demand

This section presents the supply and demand model, which is probably the best known and perhaps the most important economic model. The basic supply and demand model provides the framework for the macroeconomic models presented in later sections. There are five key elements in this model: the demand curve, the supply curve, the set of factors that cause the demand curve to shift, the set of factors that cause the supply curve to shift, and the market equilibrium (the price and quantity associated with a market clearing).The supply and demand model is used to determine the change in the market equilibrium when supply and/or demand changes.

MODULES IN THIS SECTION

Module 5   **Supply and Demand: Introduction and Demand**

Module 6   **Supply and Demand: Supply**

Module 7   **Supply and Demand: Equilibrium**

Module 8   **Supply and Demand: Price Controls (Ceilings and Floors)**

Module 9   **Supply and Demand: Quantity Controls**

BEFORE YOU TACKLE THE TEST

Draw the Featured Model

Complete the Exercise

Problems

Review Questions

MODULE 5   SUPPLY AND DEMAND: INTRODUCTION AND DEMAND

BEFORE YOU READ THE MODULE

Summary

This module introduces the supply and demand model and presents the demand side of the model. It develops the concept of demand and presents demand schedules (tables) and curves. The module explains the difference between a change in demand and a change in quantity demanded and presents the factors that will shift a demand curve (i.e. increase or decrease demand).

Module Objectives

Review these objectives before you read the module. Place a "√" on the line when you can do each of the following:

_____**Objective #1.** Explain what a competitive market is and how it is described by the supply and demand model

_____**Objective #2.** Draw a demand curve and interpret its meaning

_____**Objective #3.** Discuss the difference between movements along the demand curve and changes in demand

_____**Objective #4.** List the factors that shift the demand curve

WHILE YOU READ THE MODULE

Key Terms

Define these key terms as you read the module:

Competitive market:

Supply and demand model:

Demand schedule:

Quantity demanded:

Demand curve:

Law of demand:

Change in demand:

Movement along the demand curve:

Substitutes:

Complements:

Normal good:

Inferior good:

Individual demand curve:

Practice the Model

In the space below, sketch a correctly labeled graph of demand showing the effect of an increase in the number of buyers. Be sure to fully label your graph including all axes and curves. Label the demand curve before the change D_1 and the demand curve after the change D_2. Your graph should resemble the graphs in Table 5.1 in your textbook that show a decrease in demand.

List questions or difficulties from your initial reading of the module:

AFTER YOU READ THE MODULE

Fill-in-the-Blanks

Fill in the blanks to complete the following statements. If you find yourself having difficulties, please refer back to the appropriate section in the text.

- A competitive market is one in which there are **1)**_____ sellers each selling a(n)

  2)_____ good or service and individual buyers and sellers **3)** (do/do not)

  _____ have an effect on market price.

- Demand is the relationship between the amount of a good consumers want to purchase and its

  4)_____ . According to the law of demand, people purchase more of a good or

  service when the price is **5)**_____ . As the price of a good or service increases, we

  say that there is an increase in the **6)**_____ of a good. However, whenever

  something changes that causes consumers to want less at any price, we say that there has been a

  decrease in the **7)**_____ for the good.

- An increase in demand will shift the demand curve to the **8)**_____ . The 5 factors

  that will cause the demand curve to shift are; **9)**_____ , _____ ,

  _____ , _____ , and _____ .

Multiple-Choice Questions

Circle the best choice to answer or complete the following questions or incomplete statements. For additional practice, use the space provided to explain why one or more of the incorrect options do not work.

10. Ham and turkey are substitutes for many people. Holding everything else constant, if the price of ham decreases, the demand for
   a. turkey will shift to the left.
   b. turkey will shift to the right.
   c. ham will shift to the left.
   d. ham will shift to the right.
   e. turkey will not change.

11. For an inferior good, an increase in consumer income will
   a. shift the demand curve to the right.
   b. cause a movement to the right along the demand curve.
   c. shift the demand curve to the left.
   d. cause a movement to the left along the demand curve.
   e. not affect demand.

Helpful Tips

- It is easy to confuse a change in demand and a change in quantity demanded. A good's own price is *not* a determinant of demand. It is a determinant of quantity demanded. Because price is on one of the axes (the vertical axis), a change in price moves along a demand curve to a new quantity demanded. A change of the entire demand curve occurs when one of the determinants of demand (which are not on either axis) changes.

- When a demand curve shifts, think of the shift as a shift to the right (an increase in demand), or to the left (a decrease in demand). Avoid thinking of demand curve shifts as shifts "up" or "down," as this can lead to errors when working with supply curves.

- When the price of a good changes, the quantity demanded of *that* good changes, but the demand for its *complement or substitute* also changes. A change in a good's own price causes a movement along the demand curve, because its own price is on the vertical axis. The price of a related good is a determinant of demand and therefore shifts the entire demand curve.

Module Notes

When economists say "an increase in demand," they mean a rightward shift of the demand curve, and when they say "a decrease in demand," they mean a leftward shift of the demand curve—that is, when they're being careful. In ordinary speech, most people, including professional economists, use the word *demand* casually. For example, someone might say "the demand for air travel has doubled over the past 15 years, because of falling air fares" when he or she really means that the *quantity demanded* has doubled.

It is bad enough to be a bit sloppy in ordinary conversation, but when you're doing economic analysis, it's very important to make the distinction between changes in the quantity demanded, which involve movements along a demand curve, and shifts of the demand curve. Sometimes students end up writing something like this: "If demand increases, the price will go up, but that will lead to a fall in demand, which pushes the price down . . ." and then go around in circles. If you make a clear distinction between changes in *demand*, which mean shifts of the demand curve, and changes in *quantity demanded*, you can avoid a lot of confusion.

A full understanding of this section is critical for your study of economics. The model of supply and demand is used repeatedly in a variety of settings throughout this course.

A demand curve illustrates the relationship between the price of the good and the quantity demanded at each specific price. In drawing the demand curve, the other determinants of demand are held constant; this constancy is referred to as the other things equal (or *ceteris paribus*) assumption. In the examples throughout the remainder of the course, we typically consider a single change in a situation while holding the other variables constant. Any time you think, "But what if…", be careful, you may be violating this assumption!

The demand for a good is affected by changes in these factors: income, tastes, expectations, the price of related goods, and the number of consumers. You will need to remember these factors, recognize them in examples, and know how they affect the demand curve.

It can be easier to understand the concepts of substitutes and complements using examples. When the price of a good changes, the quantity demanded of that good will change, but the demand for its substitute will also change. For instance, if the price of hot dogs decreases, people will buy more hot dogs. However, people will need to buy more hot dog buns to go with those hot dogs regardless of the current price of buns, so the demand for buns will increase. Since the quantity demanded of hot dogs increased and the demand for buns also increased, hot dogs and buns are complements.

Whether two goods are substitutes or complements (or are unrelated) depends on individual preferences. When considering whether a good is a complement or substitute, focus on how each responds to changes in the price of the other, rather than making an assumption about the relationship between the goods. For example, you may think apples and peanut butter are complements because you will only eat apples with peanut butter on them, while someone else thinks they are substitutes because they will eat an apple OR have peanut butter as their snack. If you are told that in response to an increase in the price of apples, the demand for peanut butter increased, you know that apples and peanut butter are substitutes.

It can also be easier to understand questions about normal and inferior goods if you think of specific examples. But don't let the terms "normal" and "inferior" mislead you. In economics, the opposite of normal is inferior (not "abnormal") and the opposite of inferior is normal (not "superior"). Whether a good is normal or inferior for a particular individual depends on his or her preferences. A good that is normal for me might be inferior for you! A normal good is a good that you will choose to buy more of as your income increases (demand shifts to the right as income increases). For example, as your income increases you may take more vacations. An inferior good is a good that you will buy less of as your income increases (demand shifts to the left as income increases). For example, as your income increases you may buy fewer fast-food restaurant meals.

MODULE 6   SUPPLY AND DEMAND: SUPPLY

BEFORE YOU READ THE MODULE

Summary

This module presents the supply side of the market. It develops the concept of supply and presents supply schedules (tables) and curves. The module explains the difference between a change in supply and a change in quantity supplied and presents the factors that will shift a supply curve (i.e. increase or decrease supply)

Module Objectives

Review these objectives before you read the module. Place a "√" on the line when you can do each of the following:

_____**Objective #1.**   Draw a supply curve and interpret its meaning

_____**Objective #2.**   Discuss the difference between movements along the supply curve and changes in supply

_____**Objective #3.**   List the factors that shift the supply curve

WHILE YOU READ THE MODULE

Key Terms

Define these key terms as you read the module:

Quantity supplied:

Supply schedule:

Supply curve:

Law of supply:

A change in supply:

Movement along the supply curve:

Input:

Individual supply curve:

Practice the Model

In the space below, sketch a correctly labeled graph of the supply of gasoline today and show the effect if producers today start expecting that the price of gasoline tomorrow will increase. Be sure to label your axes and curves. Your graph should resemble the graphs in Table 6.1 in your textbook.

List questions or difficulties from your initial reading of the module:

AFTER YOU READ THE MODULE

Fill-in-the-Blanks

Fill in the blanks to complete the following statements. If you find yourself having difficulties, please refer back to the appropriate section in the text.

- Supply is the relationship between the amount of a good producers are willing to sell and its

   1)_____. As the price of a good or service increases, we say that there is an

   increase in **2)**_____. However, whenever something changes that causes producers

   to sell less at any price, we say that there has been a decrease in **3)** _____.

- An increase in supply will shift the supply curve to the **4)**_____. The 5 factors that

   will cause the supply curve to shift are **5)**_____, _____,

   _____, _____, and _____.

Multiple-Choice Questions

Circle the best choice to answer or complete the following questions or incomplete statements. For additional practice, use the space provided to explain why one or more of the incorrect options do not work.

6. Assume that research and development result in the discovery of a new technology for electricity generation. This discovery will
   a. increase the supply of electricity.
   b. increase the quantity supplied of electricity.
   c. decrease the supply of electricity.
   d. decrease the quantity supplied of electricity.
   e. have no effect on the supply of electricity.

7. An increase in supply causes which of the following?
   a. the supply curve to shift up
   b. the supply curve to shift to the right
   c. a movement to the right along the curve
   d. the supply curve to shift to the left
   e. a movement to the left along the curve

Helpful Tips

- Be careful when you shift the supply curve. Since quantities are higher as you move to the right along the horizontal axis, shifting a supply curve to the right represents an increase in supply. And since quantities are lower as you move to the left along the horizontal axis, shifting a supply curve to the left is a decrease in supply. Always think of increases and decreases as shifts to the right and left (rather than up or down).

Module Notes

We have been talking about the price at which a good or service is bought *and* sold, as if the two were the same. But shouldn't we make a distinction between the price received by sellers and the price paid by buyers? In principle, yes; but it is helpful at this point to sacrifice a bit of realism in the interest of simplicity—by assuming away the difference between the prices received by sellers and those paid by buyers. In reality, there is often a middleman—someone who brings buyers and sellers together—who buys from suppliers, then sells to consumers at a markup. However, the difference between the buying and selling price is quite small. So it's not a bad approximation to think of the price paid by buyers as being the *same* as the price received by sellers.

A supply curve illustrates the relationship between the price of the good and the quantity supplied at each specific price. In drawing the supply curve, the other determinants of supply are held constant; this constancy is referred to as the other things equal (or *ceteris paribus*) assumption. In the examples throughout the remainder of the course, we typically consider a single change in a situation while holding the other variables constant. Any time you think "But what if…", be careful, you may be violating this assumption!

The supply of a good is affected by changes in each of the following factors: input prices, the price of related goods, technology, expectations, and the number of producers. You will need to remember these factors, recognize them in examples, and know how they affect the supply curve.

MODULE 7   SUPPLY AND DEMAND: EQUILIBRIUM

BEFORE YOU READ THE MODULE

Summary

This module defines equilibrium, shows how to find equilibrium in a supply and demand model, and explains the forces that bring a market into equilibrium. Then, it uses the supply and demand model to determine how changes in a determinant of demand or supply will cause a change in the equilibrium price and quantity. The module presents how to use the supply and demand model to analyze real-world and hypothetical changes.

Module Objectives

Review these objectives before you read the module. Place a "√" on the line when you can do each of the following:

_____ **Objective #1.** Explain how supply and demand curves determine a market's equilibrium price and equilibrium quantity

_____ **Objective #2.** Describe how price moves the market back to an equilibrium in the case of a shortage or surplus

_____ **Objective #3.** Explain how equilibrium price and quantity are affected when there is a change in either supply or demand

_____ **Objective #4.** Explain how equilibrium price and quantity are affected when there is a simultaneous change in both supply and demand

WHILE YOU READ THE MODULE

Key Terms

Define these key terms as you read the module:

Equilibrium:

Equilibrium price:

Equilibrium quantity:

Market-clearing price:

Surplus:

Shortage:

Practice the Model

Sketch a correctly labeled graph showing each of the eight situations described below. Use the following steps to complete each graph.

1) Draw a supply and demand graph and label price on the vertical axis and quantity on the horizontal axis. Label the initial demand curve D_1 and the initial supply curve S_1.
2) Show the initial equilibrium price, labeled P_1 on the vertical axis and the initial equilibrium quantity, labeled Q_1 on the horizontal axis.
3) Draw the new supply and/or demand curve, labeling the new curve(s) D_2 or S_2.
4) Show the new equilibrium price labeled P_2 on the vertical axis and the equilibrium quantity labeled Q_2 on the horizontal axis.

In the first two graphs, some of these steps have been done for you to get you started.

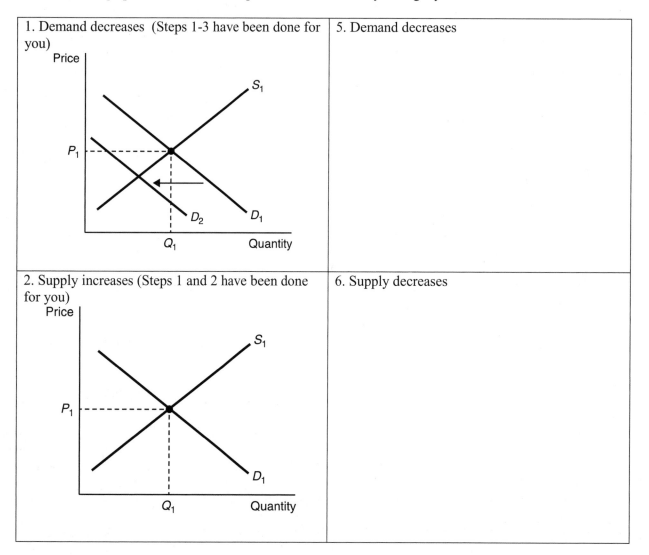

1. Demand decreases (Steps 1-3 have been done for you)

5. Demand decreases

2. Supply increases (Steps 1 and 2 have been done for you)

6. Supply decreases

3. Demand increases and supply increases	7. Demand increases and supply decreases
4. Demand decreases and supply increases	8. Demand decreases and supply decreases

List questions or difficulties from your initial reading of the module:

AFTER YOU READ THE MODULE

Fill-in-the-Blanks

Fill in the blanks to complete the following statements. If you find yourself having difficulties, please refer back to the appropriate section in the text.

- When demand increases, equilibrium price will **1)**_____ and equilibrium quantity

  will **2)**_____. When supply increases, equilibrium price will

  3)_____ and equilibrium quantity will **4)**_____. If there is a

  simultaneous increase in demand and supply, it is certain that equilibrium **5)**_____

  will increase but it is impossible to determine the effect on equilibrium **6)**_____.

Multiple-Choice Questions

Circle the best choice to answer or complete the following questions or incomplete statements. For additional practice, use the space provided to explain why one or more of the incorrect options do not work.

7. On a supply and demand graph, equilibrium price is shown
   a. where supply and demand intersect.
   b. where supply equals demand.
   c. on the horizontal axis below where supply and demand intersect.
   d. on the vertical axis to the left of where supply and demand intersect.
   e. where quantity supplied and quantity demanded are equal.

8. At the current price of peaches, the quantity demanded is less than the quantity supplied. There is a _____ of peaches and price will _____.
   a. shortage, increase
   b. surplus, decrease
   c. shortage, decrease
   d. surplus, increase
   e. shortage, remain the same

Helpful Tips

- Equilibrium is a price and quantity pair. When you are asked to label equilibrium price and quantity, make sure you label the equilibrium price on the vertical axis and the equilibrium quantity on the horizontal axis. For example, Graph 1 below does not correctly label the equilibrium price and quantity on the axes. Graph 2 shows the correct way to identify equilibrium price and quantity.

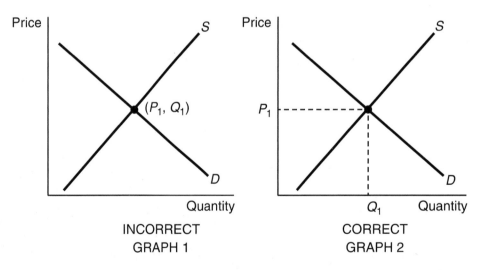

- When supply and demand both shift, without knowing the size of those shifts you will not be able to determine both the new equilibrium price and the new equilibrium quantity: one will be indeterminate. For instance, suppose supply and demand both increase. Both Graph A and Graph B on the following page show this. However, the impact on equilibrium price is different in each graph! Unless we know that one curve shifted by a greater amount, we cannot tell the effect on price; it is indeterminate.

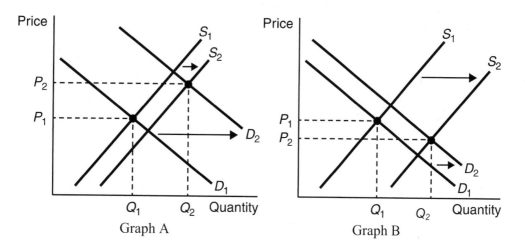

Graph A

Graph B

Module Notes

When the price of a good or service changes, in general, we can say that this reflects a change in either supply or demand. But it is easy to get confused about which one. A helpful clue is the direction of change in quantity. If the quantity sold changes in the *same* direction as the price—for example, if both the price and the quantity rise—this suggests that the demand curve has shifted. If the price and the quantity move in *opposite* directions, the likely cause is a shift of the supply curve.

The main goal of this section is to learn how to use the supply and demand model to answer questions and solve problems. Memorizing definitions, rules, or lists won't get you very far; you need to learn and practice using the supply and demand model. Use the model to help you find answers to questions rather than guessing the answer and trying to make the model fit your preconceived notion.

Often a quick sketch of a demand and supply curve is all that you need to answer questions about the effect of a change in the market on the equilibrium price or equilibrium quantity. Practice drawing a quick representation of the demand and supply curves as you do problems, recognizing that you do not always need a formal graph to find a solution. Use these sketches during your exams!

MODULE 8 SUPPLY AND DEMAND: PRICE CONTROLS

BEFORE YOU READ THE MODULE

Summary

This module looks at government intervention to affect the price in a market. Buyers would like to pay less, and sometimes they can make a strong moral or political case that they should pay lower prices. Sellers would like to receive a higher price, and sometimes they can make a strong moral or political case that they should receive higher prices. Buyers and sellers make strong appeals for governments to intervene in markets. When a government intervenes to regulate prices, we say that it imposes *price controls*. These controls take the form either of *a price ceiling* or a *price floor*. When a government tries to legislate prices, there are predictable side effects, which are presented in this module.

Module Objectives

Review these objectives before you read the module. Place a "√" on the line when you can do each of the following:

_____**Objective #1.** Explain the workings of price controls, one way government intervenes in markets

_____**Objective #2.** Describe how price controls can create problems and make a market inefficient

_____**Objective #3.** Explain why economists are often deeply skeptical of attempts to intervene in markets

_____**Objective #4.** Identify who benefits and who loses from price controls

WHILE YOU READ THE MODULE

Key Terms

Define these key terms as you read the module:

Price controls:

Price ceiling:

Price floor:

Inefficient allocation to consumers:

Wasted resources:

Inefficiently low quality:

Black markets:

Minimum wage:

Inefficient allocation of sales among sellers:

Inefficiently high quality:

Practice the Model

1) In the space below, sketch a correctly labeled graph showing an effective price ceiling on a market. Be sure to correctly label the quantity supplied, quantity demanded, equilibrium price, price ceiling, and any surplus or shortage that exists. Refer to Figure 8.2 in your textbook as a guide.

2) In the space below, sketch a correctly labeled graph showing an effective price floor on a market. Be sure to correctly label the quantity supplied, quantity demanded, equilibrium price, price floor, and any surplus or shortage. Refer to Figure 8.4 as a guide.

List questions or difficulties from your initial reading of the module:

AFTER YOU READ THE MODULE

Fill-in-the-Blanks

Fill in the blanks to complete the following statements. If you find yourself having difficulties, please refer back to the appropriate section in the text.

- One way the government may try to affect markets is to use price controls to set either a minimum or

  maximum legal price in a market. A maximum legal price is called a price **1)**_____

  and a minimum legal price is called a price **2)**_____.

- To be effective, a price ceiling would have to be set **3)**_____ the equilibrium price.

  To be effective, the price floor would have to be set **4)**_____ the equilibrium price.

- When an effective price ceiling is imposed on a market, the result will be a

  5)_____; when an effective price floor is imposed on a market, the result will be a

  6)_____.

Multiple-Choice Questions

Circle the best choice to answer or complete the following questions or incomplete statements. For additional practice, use the space provided to explain why one or more of the incorrect options do not work.

7. If an effective price floor is imposed on a market, the market price can't adjust
   a. upward, resulting in a surplus.
   b. downward, resulting in a surplus.
   c. upward, resulting in a shortage.
   d. downward, resulting in a shortage.
   e. upward, resulting in a new equilibrium.

8. Which of the following is NOT an inefficiency caused by a price ceiling?
   a. inefficient allocation to consumers
   b. inefficient allocation to producers
   c. wasted resources
   d. inefficiently low quantity
   e. black markets

Helpful Tips

- Both price floors and price ceilings result in inefficiencies and both sellers and buyers are hurt by them. For example, buyers are hurt by a price floor because some buyers who were willing and able to pay the equilibrium price may not be willing or able to pay the higher price floor and therefore will no longer purchase the good. Because there are fewer buyers, sellers are also hurt because some sellers who were actually willing and able to sell the good at the lower equilibrium price may be unable to sell that good at the higher price. Similarly, when there is a price ceiling, sellers are hurt because not all of the sellers who were able to sell their good at the equilibrium price can still participate in this market. As a result, buyers who had previously been willing to pay a higher price might find themselves unable to purchase the good at a lower price because of the lower quantity supplied.

Module Notes

A price ceiling below the equilibrium price pushes the price of a good *down.* A price floor above the equilibrium price pushes the price of a good *up.* So it's easy to assume that the effects of a price floor are the opposite of the effects of a price ceiling. In particular, if a price ceiling reduces the quantity of a good bought and sold, doesn't a price floor increase the quantity? No, it doesn't. In fact, both floors and ceilings reduce the quantity bought and sold. Why? When the quantity of a good supplied isn't equal to the quantity demanded, the quantity sold is determined by the "short side" of the market—whichever quantity is less. If sellers don't want to sell as much as buyers want to buy, it's the sellers who determine the actual quantity sold, because buyers can't force unwilling sellers to sell. If buyers don't want to buy as much as sellers want to sell, it's the buyers who determine the actual quantity sold, because sellers can't force unwilling buyers to buy.

A floor is a surface that you stand on and that is solid. Use this vision of a floor to remember that a price floor is the *lowest* price that can be charged for a good. To be effective, a price floor must be set at a price that is greater than the equilibrium price. Otherwise, the floor will not prevent the market from going to equilibrium. An effective price floor results in a surplus of the good, because at high prices, producers want to sell more but consumers want to buy less.

A ceiling is a surface that you hope is solid and stays above your head. Use this visual to remember that a price ceiling is the *highest* price that can be charged for a good. To be effective, a price ceiling must be set at a price that is less than the equilibrium price. Otherwise, the ceiling will not prevent the market from going to equilibrium. An effective price ceiling results in a shortage of the good because at low prices consumers want to buy more but producers don't want to sell as much.

MODULE 9   SUPPLY AND DEMAND: QUANTITY CONTROLS

BEFORE YOU READ THE MODULE

Summary

This module continues the discussion of government intervention in markets by looking at *quantity controls*, or *quotas*. The total amount of the good that can be transacted under the quantity control is called the *quota limit*. Typically, the government limits quantity in a market by issuing *licenses*.

Module Objectives

Review these objectives before you read the module. Place a "√" on the line when you can do each of the following:

_____**Objective #1.**   Explain the workings of quantity controls, another way government intervenes in markets

_____**Objective #2.**   Describe how quantity controls create problems and can make a market inefficient

_____**Objective #3.**   Explain who benefits and who loses from quantity controls

WHILE YOU READ THE MODULE

Key Terms

Define these key terms as you read the module:

Quantity control (Quota):

License:

Demand price:

Supply price:

Wedge:

Quota rent:

Deadweight loss:

Practice the Model

Suppose the equilibrium price in the market for salmon is $4 per pound, the equilibrium quantity is 20 pounds of salmon, and a quota of 10 pounds of salmon is imposed on the market. Draw a correctly labeled graph of the salmon market showing the effect of the quota. Be sure to label the demand price (P_d), the supply price (P_s), and the deadweight loss (DWL).

List questions or difficulties from your initial reading of the module:

AFTER YOU READ THE MODULE

Fill-in-the-Blanks

Fill in the blanks to complete the following statements. If you find yourself having difficulties, please refer back to the appropriate section in the text.

- Whenever the government imposes a limit on the amount that can be sold, it is called a

  1)_____. A government can limit the number of goods supplied in the market by

  requiring a **2)**_____ which grants the right to sell a good; it affects not only the

  amount of the good sold in the market, but also the price.

- When the government imposes a quantity control, it drives a **3)**_____ between the

  price that consumers are willing to pay for the quantity allowed of the good and the price at which

  producers are willing to offer that quantity. The price consumers are willing to pay for the legal

  market quantity is called the **4)**_____ price and the price at which producers are

  willing to offer the legal market quantity is called the **5)**_____ price.

- The price that consumers are willing to pay for a quota is higher than the price at which producers are

  willing to offer it. This difference is known as the quota **6)**_____.

Multiple-Choice Questions

Circle the best choice to answer or complete the following questions or incomplete statements. For additional practice, use the space provided to explain why one or more of the incorrect options do not work.

7. Quantity controls lead to which of the following?
    a. a market surplus
    b. a market shortage
    c. increased efficiency
    d. deadweight loss
    e. inefficiently low quality

8. An effective quantity control will have what effect on the market?
    a. It limits the price that suppliers can charge.
    b. It limits the price that consumers must pay.
    c. It limits the amount of the good or service available.
    d. It increases the quantity of the good sold.
    e. It has no impact on the market.

Helpful Tips

- Price controls and quantity controls are represented differently on a supply and demand graph. A price control is a horizontal line at the controlled price, and a quantity control is a vertical line at the controlled quantity.

Module Notes

In this module, we examine what happens when government intervention directly restricts the quantity of a good or service available in the market. There are similarities between this analysis of quantity controls and our previous analysis of price controls. When price is restricted through a price control, we draw a *horizontal* line on our supply and demand graph, at the level of the price ceiling or floor. When quantity is restricted, we draw a *vertical* line on our supply and demand graph at the maximum quantity permitted under the restriction—the quota limit. Note that we focus on maximum quantities (quotas) and do not talk about *minimum* quantities. In the case of a price control, the restricted price creates a difference between the quantity demanded and the quantity supplied. This leads to shortages or surpluses. In the case of a quantity control, the restriction creates a difference between the supply price and the demand price. This creates a wedge, or quota rent. While the terminology used to analyze quotas may be less familiar, the similarities with price controls can help you understand quantity controls. In each case, government intervention leads to market inefficiencies.

A quota, or quantity control, is a policy implemented by the government to set a maximum amount of the good or service that can be sold in a market. A quota has no effect if it is set at a level greater than the equilibrium quantity; to be effective, a quota must be set at a level lower than the equilibrium quantity.

With an effective quantity restriction, consumers are willing to pay more for each unit of the good, while suppliers are willing to supply the good for less. This difference is referred to as a wedge. This wedge corresponds to the quota rent the license holder of the good receives when the quantity control is imposed in a market.

Draw the Featured Graph: Supply and Demand

Graphing using data

Graph the supply and demand curves using the data in the table. Show equilibrium price and quantity on the axes.

P	Q_d	Q_s
0	8	0
2	6	6
4	4	12

Price
_____
y axis label

Quantity
x axis label

Graphing relationships without numbers

Graph supply and demand curves and show equilibrium price and quantity on the axes.

_____
y-axis label

x-axis label

Graphs like the ones you drew above serve as the starting point when using supply and demand analysis to determine the effects on price and quantity when a determinant of supply or demand changes. Always start your analysis with one of these "starting point" graphs. Then follow these steps:

1) Determine which side of the market is affected – supply or demand – using the lists of factors that affect supply and demand in previous modules. Any single change will affect supply *or* demand – not both.

2) Determine whether supply or demand increases or decreases.

3) Shift the supply or demand curve to the left for a decrease or to the right for an increase. Draw the new equilibrium using the new curve to find your answer. Remember, the equilibrium is the new price (on the vertical axis) and the new quantity (on the horizontal axis) using the new curve. Be sure to clearly label the new price and the new quantity.

Complete the Exercise

Draw a correctly labeled graph showing the effect on equilibrium price and equilibrium quantity in the market for oranges when each of the following (*ceteris paribus*) changes occurs. Use the steps shown in Draw the Featured Graph above.

a. There is a freeze in Florida that kills many of the orange groves.

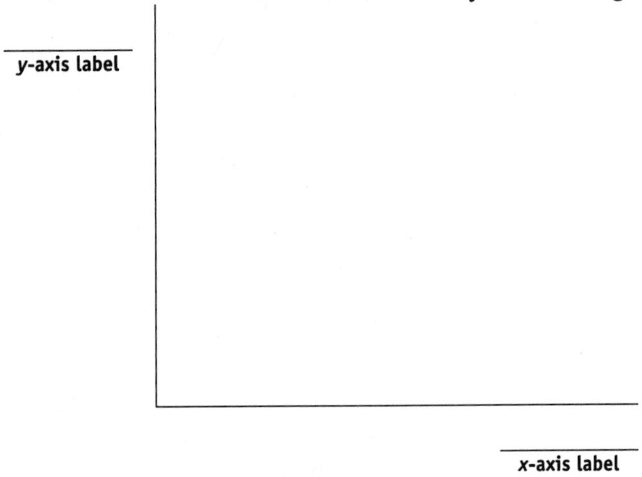

_____
y-axis label

_____
x-axis label

b. The wages of orange workers decrease.

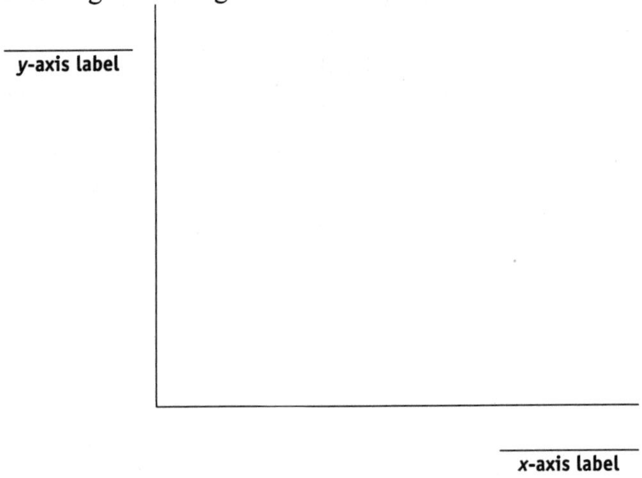

_____
y-axis label

_____
x-axis label

c. Research finds that oranges have additional health benefits.

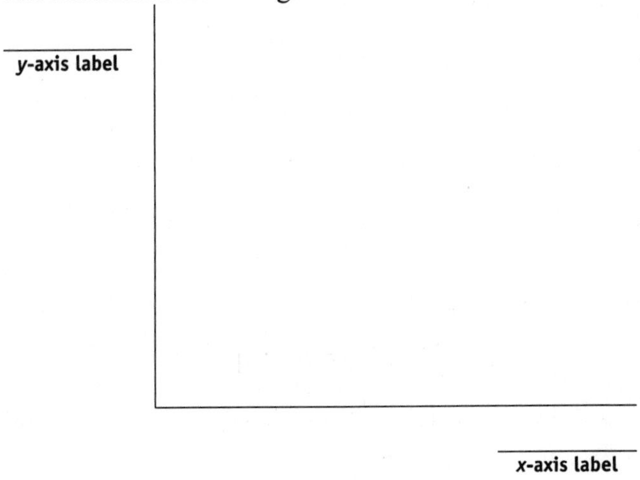

_____
y-axis label

_____
x-axis label

d. The price of tangerines decreases.

y-axis label

x-axis label

Problems

1. You are given the following information about demand in the competitive market for bicycles.

Price per bicycle	Quantity of bicycles demanded per week
$100	0
80	100
60	200
40	500
20	800
0	1,000

a. Draw the demand curve that reflects this demand schedule.

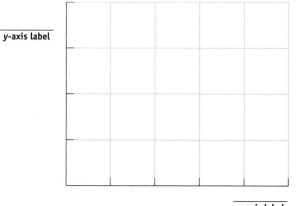

y-axis label

x-axis label

b. Suppose the price is initially $40. If price rises by $20, what happens to quantity demanded?

c. Suppose the price is initially $40. If price falls by $40, what happens to quantity demanded?

2. For each of the following situations in the table below, fill in the missing information. First, determine whether the situation causes a shift or a movement along the demand curve; then, if it causes a shift, determine whether the demand curve shifts to the right or to the left.

Situation	Specified market	Movement or shift	Rightward or leftward
People's income increases	Market for exotic vacations		
People's income decreases	Market for goods sold in secondhand shops		
Price of bicycles increases	Market for bicycles		
Price of tennis balls increases	Market for tennis racquets		
Price of movie tickets decreases	Market for popcorn at movie theatres		
Popularity of music-playing device increases	Market for music-playing device		
Popularity of branded clothing items decreases	Market for brand-name designer clothing		
Winter clothing is expected to go on sale next month	Market for winter clothing		
Increase in urban residents	Market for apartments in urban areas		

3. The following graph represents the supply curve for the production of widgets in Town Center.

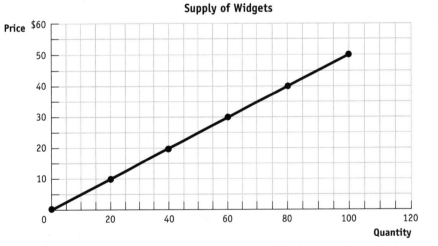

Supply of Widgets

a. At a price of $20, how many widgets are producers willing to supply?

b. At a price of $40, how many widgets are producers willing to supply?

c. Suppose there are ten widget producers in Town Center and the price of widgets is $50. If each producer produces the same number of widgets, how many widgets will each produce?

d. Suppose the price is initially $30 but then falls to $20. What is the change in quantity supplied?

e. Suppose the price is initially $30 but then rises to $50. What is the change in quantity supplied?

f. What price must suppliers receive in order to be willing to supply 80 widgets?

g. What price must suppliers receive in order to be willing to supply 40 widgets?

h. What does the slope of a supply curve imply about the relationship between price and quantity supplied?

4. For each of the following situations in the table below, fill in the missing information: first, determine whether the situation causes a shift or a movement along the supply curve; then, if it causes a shift, determine whether the supply curve shifts to the right or to the left.

Situation	Specified market	Movement or shift	Rightward or leftward
Labor costs for air travel and cruise ships increase	Market for exotic vacations		
Prices of office equipment and phone service rise by 40%	Market for call center services		
Price of bicycles increases	Market for bicycles		
Price of leather boots increases	Market for beef products		
Price of leather boots increases	Market for leather belts		
New technology for music-playing device revealed	Market for music-playing devices		
Price of brand-name designer clothing increases	Market for brand-name designer clothing		
Increase in number of coffee shop owners in the metro area	Market for coffee in the metro area		

5. The demand and supply schedules for Healthy Snacks, Inc., is provided in the table below.

Price	Quantity demanded	Quantity supplied
$0	1,000	0
10	800	125
20	600	275
30	400	400
40	200	550
50	0	675

  a. Sketch the demand and supply curves for Healthy Snacks, Inc. Don't worry about drawing a precise graph. Focus on drawing the underlying relationships from the table. Your graph should be accurate with regard to x-intercepts and y-intercepts and indicate equilibrium.

  b. What are the equilibrium price and quantity in this market? Show these on your graph.

  c. Calculate the excess demand or excess supply at each price in the table below.

Price	Excess demand or supply?	Amount of excess demand or supply
$0		
10		
20		
30		
40		
50		

  d. What is another term for excess demand?

  e. What is another term for excess supply?

6. For each of the following situations, sketch a graph of the initial market demand (D_1), supply (S_1), equilibrium price (P_1) and equilibrium quantity (Q_1). Then sketch any changes in the market demand (D_2) and/or supply (S_2) curves and indicate the new equilibrium price (P_2) and quantity (Q_2).

a. Assume that bicycles and gasoline are substitutes and the price of gasoline increases significantly. What happens in the market for bicycles?

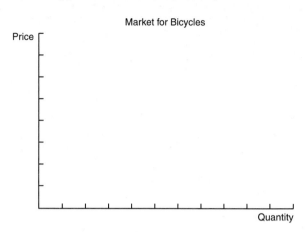

b. The price of gasoline increases by 40 percent. What happens in the market for fuel-inefficient SUVs?

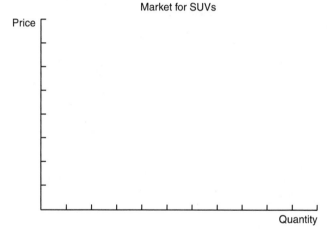

c. New technology for music-playing is developed. What happens in the market for the devices?

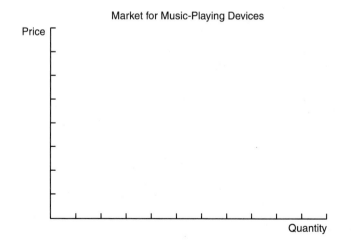

d. The price of labor decreases. What happens in the market for fast-food restaurants?

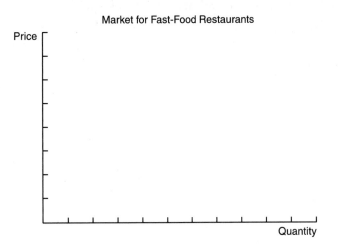

e. Income increases and good X is a normal good. What happens in the market for good X?

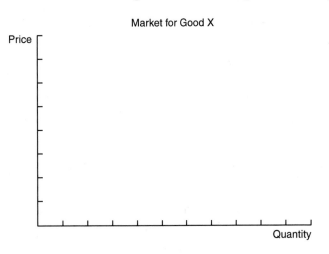

f. Income increases and good X is an inferior good. What happens in the market for good X?

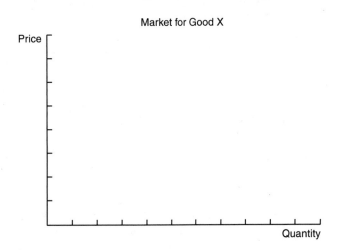

7. Use the graph below to answer the following questions.

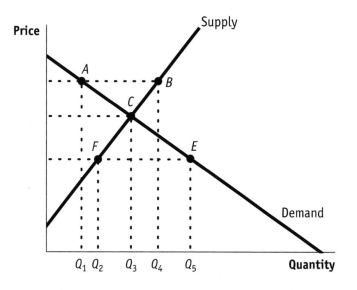

a. Identify the equilibrium price and the equilibrium quantity.

b. Suppose a price floor of P_3 is implemented by the government in this market. Describe what will happen to the price and quantity once this price floor is implemented.

c. Suppose a price floor of P_2 is implemented by the government in this market. Describe what will happen to the price and quantity once this price floor is implemented.

d. What must be true about a price floor in a market for a good or service in order for that price floor to be effective?

e. You are told that an effective price floor has been implemented in this market and that the resulting surplus is greater than $Q_4 - Q_1$. What do you know about the level of this price floor?

8. Use the graph below to answer the following questions.

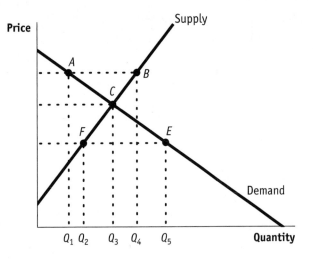

a. Identify the equilibrium price and the equilibrium quantity.

b. Suppose a price ceiling of P_2 is implemented by the government in this market. Describe what will happen to the price and quantity once this price ceiling is implemented.

c. Would both P_2 and P_3 be effective price ceilings? Explain.

d. Suppose a price ceiling of P_3 is imposed on this market. What quantity will be exchanged?

e. You are told that an effective price ceiling has been implemented in this market and that the resultant shortage is smaller than Q_5 - Q_2. What do you know about the level of this price ceiling?

9. Consider the market for housing in Metropolitan City, where all housing units are exactly the same. Currently the equilibrium price of housing is $2,000 a month and local residents consume 1,500 units of housing. The local residents argue that housing is too expensive and an effective price ceiling is implemented. When the price ceiling is implemented by the local government council, only 1,200 units of housing are supplied. Is this an efficient level of housing for Metropolitan City? Explain. To support your answer, provide two sketches: in the first sketch, indicate equilibrium quantity and price; in the second sketch, indicate the price ceiling and the quantity provided by the market. Is the price consumers are willing to pay for the last unit equal to the price suppliers must receive to supply the last unit? Explain.

10. The market for taxi rides in Metropolia this week is described in the following table. Assume that all taxi rides are the same in Metropolia.

Price of taxi rides	Quantity of taxi rides demanded per week	Quantity of taxi rides supplied per week
$1	200	40
2	180	60
3	160	80
4	140	100
5	120	120
6	100	140
7	80	160
8	60	180
9	40	200
10	20	220

a. What is the equilibrium price and quantity of taxi rides in Metropolia per week?

Suppose the government of Metropolia institutes a medallion system that limits the number of taxi rides available in Metropolia per week to 80 taxi rides.

b. At what price will consumers want to purchase 80 taxi rides per week? What is this price called?

c. At what price will suppliers be willing to supply 80 taxi rides per week? What is this price called?

d. What price will a taxi medallion rent for in this market? Explain your answer.

e. Draw a graph of the taxi ride market in Metropolia. On this graph, indicate the quota limit, the demand price, the supply price, and the medallion's rental price.

f. What is the total value of the taxi medallions per week in Metropolia?

Review Questions

Circle your answer to the following questions.

1. Competitive markets are characterized as having
   a. many buyers and a single seller.
   b. many buyers and a few sellers.
   c. many buyers and many sellers.
   d. a few buyers and many sellers.
   e. one buyer and many sellers.

2. Sue goes to the store to purchase a bottle of shampoo. When she gets to the store, she discovers that her brand of shampoo is on sale for $4 a bottle. According to the law of demand, we can expect that
   a. Sue will purchase one bottle of shampoo.
   b. Sue will not purchase the shampoo.
   c. Sue will likely purchase more than one bottle of shampoo.
   d. Sue will substitute for her usual brand of shampoo with an alternative brand.
   e. Sue will sell the shampoo she has at home.

3. Consider the market for mangos. Suppose researchers discover that eating mangos generates large health benefits. Which of the following statements is true? This discovery will
   a. not affect the market for mangos.
   b. cause the demand for mangos to shift to the right.
   c. cause the price of mangos to decrease due to a movement along the demand curve.
   d. cause a movement along the demand curve for mangos.
   e. cause the supply of mangos to decrease.

4. Consider the demand curve for automobiles. An increase in the price of automobiles due to a shift in the supply curve will
   a. cause a movement to the right along the demand curve for automobiles.
   b. result in a decrease in the demand for automobiles.
   c. have no effect on the quantity of automobiles demanded since the change was in supply.
   d. cause the quantity supplied of automobiles to increase.
   e. cause a movement to the left along the demand curve for automobiles.

5. Assume that ham and turkey are substitutes. If the price of ham decreases, then the demand for
   a. turkey will shift to the left.
   b. turkey will shift to the right.
   c. ham will shift to the left.
   d. ham will shift to the right.
   e. ham will not change.

6. Consider two goods: good X and good Y. Holding everything else constant, the price of good Y increases and the demand for good X decreases. Good X and good Y are definitely
   a. complements.
   b. substitutes.
   c. not related to one another.
   d. Cannot be determined
   e. normal goods.

7. Consider a supply curve. When the price of the good increases, this results in a movement along the supply curve resulting in a greater
   a. supply of the good.
   b. quantity supplied.
   c. supply.
   d. demand.
   e. equilibrium.

8. Research and development result in the discovery of a new technology for electricity generation. Holding everything else constant, this discovery will
   a. increase the supply of electricity.
   b. increase the quantity supplied of electricity.
   c. decrease the supply of electricity.
   d. decrease the quantity supplied of electricity.
   e. have no impact on the market for electricity.

9. The sawmill industry expects lumber prices to rise next year due to growing demand for the construction of new homes. Holding everything else constant, this expectation will shift
   a. the supply curve for lumber this year to the left.
   b. the supply curve for lumber this year to the right.
   c. the supply for lumber next year to the left.
   d. the supply for lumber next year to the right.
   e. the demand for lumber this year to the left.

10. In an equilibrium in a competitive market for a good, price has adjusted so that the quantity
    a. demanded is equal to the quantity supplied at that price.
    b. demanded is equal to the quantity supplied at all possible prices.
    c. supplied is greater than the quantity demanded at that price.
    d. demanded is greater than the quantity supplied at that price.
    e. demanded is equal to zero.

11. Consumers in Mayville consider houses and apartments to be substitutes. There is an increase in the price of houses in Mayville at the same time that three new apartment buildings are opened. In the market for apartments in Mayville, the equilibrium
    a. price will rise relative to its level before these two events.
    b. price will fall relative to its level before these two events.
    c. quantity will rise relative to its level before these two events.
    d. quantity will fall relative to its level before these two events.
    e. price will rise, but the equilibrium quantity will be unchanged.

12. An effective price floor will have what effect on the price of the product and the quantity sold?

	Effect on the price of the product	*Effect on the quantity sold*
a.	decreases	increases
b.	increases	increases
c.	decreases	decreases
d.	increases	no impact
e.	increases	decreases

13. A minimum wage that is higher than the market equilibrium wage will have what effect on the wage

	Wage	*Quantity of workers hired*
a.	increase	increase
b.	increase	decrease
c.	decrease	increase
d.	decrease	decrease
e.	increase	stay the same

Use the information in the table below to answer questions 14 and 15.

Price	Quantity demanded	Quantity supplied
$20	200	0
40	150	50
60	100	100
80	50	150
100	0	200

14. Suppose a price floor of $40 is implemented in this market. This results in
   a. an excess demand of 100 units.
   b. an excess supply of 100 units.
   c. no effect in this market, since the price floor is set below the equilibrium price.
   d. no effect in this market, since the price floor is set above the equilibrium price.
   e. an excess demand of 40 units.

15. Suppose a price ceiling of $40 is implemented in this market. This results in
   a. an excess demand of 100 units.
   b. an excess supply of 100 units.
   c. no effect in this market, since the price ceiling is set below the equilibrium price.
   d. a temporary shortage of the good while prices rise.
   e. a reduction in the demand for this good.

16. Black market or illegal activities increase with the imposition of price controls in markets. Black markets
   a. improve the situation of all participants in the price-controlled market.
   b. worsen the situation for those people who obey the rules imposed by the government.
   c. have little or no real impact in price-controlled markets.
   d. create greater respect in society for the need to obey all laws.
   e. do not exist because they are illegal.

17. An effective quantity control
   a. limits the price that suppliers can charge for the good or service in the regulated market.
   b. limits the price that demanders must pay for the good or service in the regulated market.
   c. limits the amount of the good or service available in the regulated market.
   d. increases the quantity of the good in the regulated market to a quantity above equilibrium.
   e. limits the price that suppliers can charge for the good or service in the regulated market without impacting the quantity exchanged.

18. A quota limit imposed on a market
- **a.** restricts the amount of the good available in that market.
- **b.** results in a payment being made by the government to the license holder.
- **c.** places a lower limit on the amount of the good provided in the regulated market.
- **d.** places an upper limit on the price of the good provided in the regulated market.
- **e.** restricts the amount of the good available in the market without having any impact on the price.

19. Which of the following statements is true of a quota?
- **a.** It places a wedge between the quantity demanded and the quantity supplied.
- **b.** It results in efficiency gains because quotas allow fewer goods to be sold, while price controls do not.
- **c.** It results in efficiency gains because quotas only restrict transactions that are not mutually beneficial.
- **d.** A price control results in efficiency gains because price controls allow fewer goods to be sold, while quotas do not.
- **e.** It restricts the sale of goods to those who value a good the least.

20. Quantity controls
- **a.** provide an incentive to engage in illegal activities.
- **b.** result in overproduction of the good in the market with the quota limit.
- **c.** result in a more efficient outcome than the market outcome.
- **d.** enable sellers to sell more of a good regardless of the market price.
- **e.** enable buyers to buy more of a good regardless of the market price.

Section ③ Measurement of Economic Performance

Overview

This section focuses on economic aggregation and what is meant by aggregation when measuring the level of production and prices in an economy. It presents three macroeconomic measures: Gross Domestic Product (GDP), unemployment, and inflation. The definition of GDP and three ways of calculating GDP are discussed in the section. It also discusses the distinction between nominal and real GDP. The module presents the concept of unemployment as well as its definition, calculation, causes, and categories. Finally, it covers the concept of inflation, including the calculation of price indexes as measures of the aggregate price level and how to calculate the inflation rate using a price index.

Featured Model/Graph: The Circular-Flow Diagram

This section presents the circular-flow model of the macroeconomy. This diagram represents the flow of payments through the economy and provides an illustration of the different ways to calculate aggregate production or gross domestic product (GDP).

MODULES IN THIS SECTION

Module 10   The Circular Flow and Gross Domestic Product

Module 11   Interpreting Real Gross Domestic Product

Module 12   The Meaning and Calculation of Unemployment

Module 13   The Causes and Categories of Unemployment

Module 14   Inflation: An Overview

Module 15   The Measurement and Calculation of Inflation

BEFORE YOU TACKLE THE TEST

Draw the Featured Model

Complete the Exercise

Problems

Review Questions

MODULE 10   THE CIRCULAR FLOW AND GROSS DOMESTIC PRODUCT

BEFORE YOU READ THE MODULE

Summary

This module presents the circular-flow diagram and introduces one of the most important macroeconomic measures: gross domestic product (GDP).

Module Objectives

Review these objectives before you read the module. Place a "√" on the line when you can do each of the following:

_____**Objective #1.**   Explain how economists use aggregate measures to track the performance of the economy

_____**Objective #2.**   Interpret the circular-flow diagram of the economy

_____**Objective #3.**   Define and calculate gross domestic product, or GDP

WHILE YOU READ THE MODULE

Key Terms

Define these key terms as you read the module:

National income and product accounts (or national accounts):

Household:

Firm:

Product markets:

Factor markets:

Consumer spending:

Stock:

Bond:

Government transfers:

Disposable income:

Private savings:

Financial markets:

Government borrowing:

Government purchases of goods and services:

Exports:

Imports:

Inventories:

Investment spending:

Final goods and services:

Intermediate goods and services:

Gross domestic product (GDP):

Value-added approach:

Expenditure approach:

Aggregate spending:

Income Approach:

Value added:

Net exports:

Practice the Model

In the diagram on the next page, for each of the arrows representing a flow, cite an example of a type of flow at that place in the model (for instance, "wages" has been labeled for you).

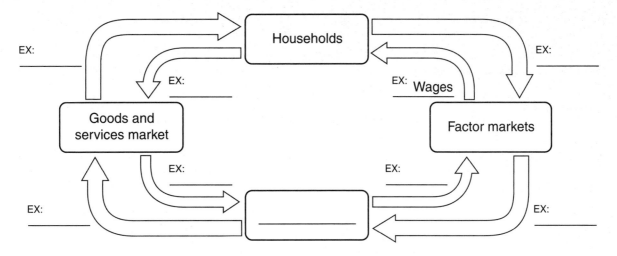

List questions or difficulties from your initial reading of the module.

AFTER YOU READ THE MODULE

Fill-in-the-Blanks

Fill in the blanks to complete the following statements. If you find yourself having difficulties, please refer back to the appropriate section in the text.

- A **1)**_____ diagram of the economy focuses on money flows and illustrates the key

  concepts underlying the national accounts. Note that the flow of money into each market or sector

  must **2)**_____ the flow of money out of each market or sector.

- The sum of consumer spending on goods and services, investment spending, government spending,

  and net exports is known as **3)**_____. It is equal to the total value of all

  4)_____ goods and services produced in an economy during a given time period.

  In the equation GDP = $C + I + G + X - IM$, the variables are **5)**_____,

  _____, _____, _____, and

  _____. GDP can also be measured as the sum of all

  6)_____ earned by factors of production: this is the sum of

  7)_____, _____, _____, and

  _____. The third method of calculating GDP is to sum the

  8)_____ added by firms at each stage of production.

Multiple-Choice Questions

Circle the best choice to answer or complete the following questions or incomplete statements. For additional practice, use the space provided to explain why one or more of the incorrect options do not work.

Use the information in the following table to answer questions 9 – 11. The table represents data about an economy's performance during a year. Assume there are only three firms: American Racquet Co., which produces tennis racquets; American Metal Co., which produces the metals that go into racquet production; and American Ore Co., which mines the ores needed to manufacture the metal. The economy produces 100 racquets that sell for $50 each.

	American Racquet Co.	American Metal Co.	American Ore Co.	Total factor income
Value of sales	$5,000 (X)	$3,000 (Y)	$500 (Z)	
Intermediate goods	3,000 (A)	500 (B)	0	
Wages	1200	1,000	100	2,300 (C)
Interest payments	100	50	20	170 (D)
Rent	500	100	50	650 (E)
Profit	200	1350	330	1,880 (F)
Total expenditures by firm	5,000	3,000	500	
Value added by firm	2,000 (G)	3,000 (H)	500 (I)	

9. GDP for this hypothetical economy is equal to
   a. $5,000.
   b. $8,500.
   c. $5,500.
   d. $1,880.
   e. $3,000.

10. GDP can be measured using different methods. If you were using the factor payments approach, which entries would you combine to get a measure of GDP?
   a. $G + H + I$
   b. $A + B$
   c. $A + B + C + D$
   d. $C + D + E + F$
   e. $A + G + H$

11. GDP can be measured using the value-added method. Using this method, which letters would you add to get GDP?
   a. $A + B + G + H + I$
   b. $G + H + I$
   c. $A + B + G + H + I + C$
   d. $A + C + D + G + H$
   e. $A + B + G$

Helpful Tips

- It's easy to get caught up in a lot of "What if?" questions when thinking about the calculation of GDP. Try to focus on what GDP is trying to measure: the value of final goods and services sold within a country. For instance, what if you have an automobile that is assembled and sold in the United States using tires from Canada by a company headquartered in Germany? Well, careful inspection of this question shows that the answer is quite simple: the final good and service is produced and sold in the United States, so all of the previous inputs have already been accounted for.

- The three different ways of computing GDP are different ways to find the same answer. If you find yourself getting different answers for the value of GDP using each, go back and check your math.

- Investment spending—spending on productive physical capital, construction of structures (residential or commercial), and changes to inventories—is included in GDP, but spending on inputs is not. Why? Recall the distinction between resources that are used up and those that are not used up in production. An input, such as steel, is used up in production. A metal-stamping machine, which is an investment good, is not. It will last for many years and will be used repeatedly to make many cars. Because spending on productive physical capital—investment goods—and construction of structures isn't directly tied to current output, economists consider such spending to be spending on final goods.

- Finally, don't forget that changes in inventories are also counted in the Investment category of GDP. Why? Because, like a machine, additional inventory is an investment in future sales. And when a good is released for sale from inventories, its value is subtracted from the value of inventories and so from GDP. Used goods are not included in GDP because, as with inputs, to include them would be to double-count: counting them once when sold as new and again when sold as used. Financial assets such as stocks and bonds are not included in GDP because they don't represent the production or the sale of final goods and services. Rather, a bond represents a promise to repay with interest, and a stock represents ownership. Finally, foreign-produced goods and services are not included in calculations of GDP either, since they do not represent goods produced domestically.

Module Notes

Here are some important items to note are NOT included in GDP:

Intermediate goods and services   *Financial assets like stocks and bonds*
Inputs   *Foreign-produced goods and services*
Used goods   *Illegal goods and services*

There are three methods for calculating GDP: (1) multiply the price of each final good and service produced in an economy during a given time period by the quantities produced and then add up the values; (2) add up the total expenditures in the domestic economy on final goods and services during a given time period by the sectors of the economy; households, government, firms, and the rest of the world ($C + I + G + X - IM$); and (3) sum the value of factor payments in the domestic economy over the given time period. Each method yields the same value of GDP.

MODULE 11 INTERPRETING REAL GROSS DOMESTIC PRODUCT

BEFORE YOU READ THE MODULE

Summary

This module presents the distinction between nominal GDP and real GDP and discusses how they can be used to measure economic activity.

Module Objectives

Review these objectives before you read the module. Place a "√" on the line when you can do each of the following:

_____**Objective #1.**   Differentiate between real GDP and nominal GDP

_____**Objective #2.**   Explain why real GDP is the appropriate measure of real economic activity

WHILE YOU READ THE MODULE

Key Terms

Define these key terms as you read the module:

Aggregate output:

Real GDP:

Nominal GDP:

Chain-linking:

GDP per capita:

Practice the Model

In 2013, an economy produced only two goods, snarks and bens. It produced 100 snarks which sold for $2 each and 200 bens which sold for $3 each. In 2014, the same economy produced 150 snarks which sold for $3 each and 250 bens which sold for $4 each.

1) Calculate nominal GDP in both years.

2) Calculate the real GDP for both years, using 2013 prices.

3) Calculate the growth rate in real GDP from 2013 to 2014.

List questions or difficulties from your initial reading of the module.

AFTER YOU READ THE MODULE

Fill-in-the-Blanks

Fill in the blanks to complete the following statements. If you find yourself having difficulties, please refer back to the appropriate section in the text.

- GDP can increase over time because the economy is producing more or because the

  1)_____ of the goods and services produced have increased.

  2)_____ GDP calculates the value of aggregate production during a given time

  period, using prices from a base year. In contrast, **3)**_____ GDP is the

  calculation of GDP using current prices. Real GDP measures allow one to compare growth in

  aggregate **4)**_____ in an economy over time.

- To compare GDP across countries, differences in population size are addressed by dividing each

  country's GDP by its population to get GDP **5)**_____, which is the average GDP

  per person.

- Real GDP per capita is a measure of what an economy *can* produce in terms of output per person.

  However, it is not a sufficient goal in itself because it doesn't address how a country uses output to

  improve **6)**_____ of its population.

Multiple-Choice Questions

Circle the best choice to answer or complete the following questions or incomplete statements. For additional practice, use the space provided to explain why one or more of the incorrect options do not work.

7. If prices in an economy are increasing but there is no change in the amount of goods and services being produced, what will happen to real GDP and nominal GDP?

	Change in real GDP	*Change in nominal GDP*
a.	no change	no change
b.	increase	increase
c.	increase	decrease
d.	no change	decrease
e.	no change	increase

Helpful Tips

- Be sure you understand when to use real (versus nominal) GDP. An example can help explain when using real GDP is necessary. According to the Census Bureau, the typical new home cost around $30,000 in 1940. However, in 2013 the typical new home cost over $270,000. So, an income of $10,000 per year would have purchased a lot more housing in 1940 than the same income in 2013.

Module Notes

GDP is intended to measure the value of the true production of goods and services in an economy, that is, what is an economy creating that is valued by society? However, there are a number of things we need to keep in mind about GDP when using it as a measure of a country's standard of living.

Nominal GDP calculates GDP using current prices. Nominal GDP can change over time because the economy is producing more *or* because the prices of the goods and services it produces have increased. By contrast, real GDP calculates the value of aggregate production using prices from a base year, i.e., real GDP uses constant prices. Real GDP allows comparison of the growth in aggregate production in an economy over time without the effects of price increases. In other words, if we did not adjust nominal GDP to account for price changes, we would falsely conclude that an economy was producing more when in fact, only the prices of those goods and services have changed.

The distinction between real and nominal variables is important. Prices are used to measure the relative value of goods and services, but because prices are not constant it is important to measure economic variables that correct for price changes. If our intent is to measure the production of goods and services that are enjoyed by citizens of a country, we must also account for differences in the number of citizens in each country. The enjoyment that 2 friends can get out of $100 worth of goods is different than the enjoyment that 5 friends could get out of $100 worth of goods. To account for this, we adjust real GDP by calculating real GDP per capita. However, even real GDP per capita is not a perfect measure of human welfare. There are many things that society values that are not counted in real GDP per capita (such as leisure time) and things that decrease happiness that may not reduce real GDP per capita (such as disease and pollution). But, real GDP is not intended to be a perfect measure of wellbeing, but rather a measure of a country's potential for certain achievements.

MODULE 12 THE MEANING AND CALCULATION OF UNEMPLOYMENT

BEFORE YOU READ THE MODULE

Summary

This module explains in detail how unemployment is calculated and why the unemployment rate in an economy is significant. The module also explores the relationship between the unemployment rate and economic growth.

Module Objectives

Review these objectives before you read the module. Place a "√" on the line when you can do each of the following:

_____**Objective #1.**   Explain how unemployment is measured

_____**Objective #2.**   Calculate the unemployment rate

_____**Objective #3.**   Summarize the significance of the unemployment rate for the economy

_____**Objective #4.**   Explain the relationship between the unemployment rate and economic growth.

WHILE YOU READ THE MODULE

Key Terms

Define these key terms as you read the module:

Employed:

Unemployed:

Labor force:

Labor force participation rate:

Unemployment rate:

Discouraged workers:

Marginally attached workers:

Underemployed:

Practice the Model

The Unemployment Rate (UR) is calculated as

$$UR = \frac{\#\ Unemployed}{\#\ in\ Labor\ Force} = \frac{\#\ Unemployed}{\#\ Employed + \#\ Unemployed}$$

1) Suppose there were 15 people in an economy who were unemployed and 45 people who were employed. How many people are in the labor force, and what is the unemployment rate?

List questions or difficulties from your initial reading of the module.

AFTER YOU READ THE MODULE

Fill-in-the-Blanks

Fill in the blanks to complete the following statements. If you find yourself having difficulties, please refer back to the appropriate section in the text.

* The **1)**_____ is the sum of the number of employed workers and the number of

  unemployed workers. The unemployed category includes those who are not currently working, but

  who are **2)**_____. The unemployed category excludes workers who are not actively

  looking for work because they do not want to work; it also excludes those who would like to work but

  have given up looking for a job, known as **3)**_____. The

  4)_____ rate is the percent of the labor force that is unemployed. The

  5)_____ rate is the percent of the population that is either employed or

  unemployed.

* The unemployment rate is intended to reflect the true employment situation in an economy, but it is

not perfect. The unemployment rate may **6)**_____ the amount of unemplopyment in an economy because it does not correct for the fact that it takes time for someone looking for work to find a job. The unemployment rate may **7)**_____ the amount of unemployment in an economy because it excludes discouraged workers.

- In general, there is a(n) **8)**_____ relationship between growth in the economy and the rate of unemployment. That is, falling real GDP is associated with a rising rate of unemployment.

Multiple-Choice Questions

Circle the best choice to answer or complete the following questions or incomplete statements. For additional practice, use the space provided to explain why one or more of the incorrect options do not work.

9. In 2013, Theo stopped looking for work after he could not find a job, even though he would take a job if offered one. As a result, the labor force participation rate _____ and the unemployment rate _____.
   a. increased, decreased
   b. remained the same, remained the same
   c. remained the same, decreased
   d. decreased, decreased
   e. decreased, increased

10. Joe works 10 hours per week. Annie works 2 hours per week but would like to work 10 and is looking for another job. Evan works 40 hours per week. Asil is not working but looking for a job. Truman is not working and not looking for a job. If these are the only people in the economy, the unemployment rate for this economy is
    a. 25%.
    b. 20%.
    c. 33%.
    d. 50%.
    e. 10%.

11. When real GDP decreases, _____ goods and services are produced, so _____ workers are needed. Therefore when GDP decreases, the unemployment rate tends to _____.
    a. fewer, more, increase
    b. fewer, fewer, increase
    c. fewer, more, decrease
    d. more, more, decrease
    e. more, fewer, decrease

Helpful Tips

- Not having a job doesn't necessarily mean that a person is unemployed. A common mistake is to count anyone who does not have a job as being unemployed. However, to be counted as unemployed a person must meet all three of the following criteria 1) not working, 2) actively looking for a job, and 3) willing and able to take a job if offered.

- Do not assume that any increase in the unemployment rate is an indication that the employment situation has gotten worse, or any improvement in the unemployment rate is an indication that the employment situation has gotten better. The unemployment rate is meant to capture the fact that there are fewer jobs than there are workers who would like jobs. At times, the unemployment rate can understate the true unemployment situation. In other words, the unemployment rate should reflect that there are more people who would like jobs than there are available. Suppose someone has been looking for a job with no luck for quite some time. They may give up looking for work. However, by doing so, they are no longer counted as unemployed and the unemployment rate can actually decrease, even though the unemployment situation has not actually improved. The unemployment rate can also overstate the true employment situation (in other words, the unemployment rate may be higher than it would be if it captured the true unemployment situation. The unemployment rate is inversely related to changes in output. When more goods and services are produced, more workers are needed, so more jobs are available. When GDP increases, employment increases, but unemployment decreases. Whenever you see a change in output, you should immediately think about what that change in output would mean for the unemployment rate.

Module Notes

The definition of employment is fairly straightforward. A person is defined as employed if he or she has a job, regardless of the number of hours that person works, or the number of hours that person wants to work. However, not having a job is not enough to be considered unemployed. To be considered unemployed, a person must not have a job, be looking for a job, and be willing and able to take a job if offered one. So unemployment is defined as the total number of people who are actively looking for work but aren't currently employed. Many people don't have a job and are not actively seeking one. These people are considered neither employed nor unemployed. They are considered out of the labor force. A country's labor force is the sum of the number of people employed and the number of people unemployed. Be very careful to distinguish between those people who are unemployed and those who are out of the labor force. The key to distinguishing between people in these two groups is to identify whether or not an individual is actively seeking a job (that is, the individual is looking for jobs and is available for work).The unemployment rate is a good indicator of current conditions in the labor market, but it is not a perfect measure. The unemployment rate never falls to zero. Jobs are constantly being created and eliminated because of structural changes in the economy and because the process of locating a job or the job search can take time.

MODULE 13 THE CAUSES AND CATEGORIES OF UNEMPLOYMENT

BEFORE YOU READ THE MODULE

Summary

This module presents the three major kinds of unemployment, which are distinguished by their causes. The module also develops the concept of the natural rate of unemployment.

Module Objectives
Review these objectives before you read the module. Place a "√" on the line when you can do each of the following:

_____**Objective #1.** Explain the three different types of unemployment and their causes

_____**Objective #2.** Identify the factors that determine the natural rate of unemployment

WHILE YOU READ THE MODULE

Key Terms

Define these key terms as you read the module:

Job search:

Frictional unemployment:

Structural unemployment:

Efficiency wages:

Natural rate of unemployment:

Cyclical unemployment:

Practice the Model

Draw a correctly labeled supply and demand graph showing a labor market with an equilibrium wage of $9 per hour. On your graph, show the effect if a minimum wage of $12 is imposed on the market.

List questions or difficulties from your initial reading of the module.

AFTER YOU READ THE MODULE

Fill-in-the-Blanks

Fill in the blanks to complete the following statements. If you find yourself having difficulties, please refer back to the appropriate section in the text.

- 1)_____ unemployment occurs because of the constant process of job creation and

  job destruction and because of the entry of new workers into the job market.

  2)_____ unemployment exists when there are more people seeking jobs in a labor

  market than there are jobs available at the current wage rate. 3)_____

  unemployment is the deviation of the actual rate of unemployment from the natural rate; that is, it is

  the difference between the actual and natural rates of unemployment. As the name suggests, cyclical

  unemployment is unemployment that arises from the 4)_____.

- Wages that employers set above the equilibrium wage rate as an incentive for their workers to deliver

  better performance are called 5)_____ wages.

- The 6)_____ rate of unemployment is the normal unemployment rate around which

  the actual unemployment rate fluctuates.

Multiple-Choice Questions

Circle the best choice to answer or complete the following questions or incomplete statements. For additional practice, use the space provided to explain why one or more of the incorrect options do not work.

7. The natural rate of unemployment is
   a. a country's unemployment rate during a recession.
   b. a country's unemployment rate during an expansion.
   c. the sum of frictional and structural unemployment.
   d. the sum of frictional and cyclical unemployment.
   e. the sum of structural and cyclical unemployment.

8. Which of the following statements is true?
   a. Structural unemployment refers to the unemployment that occurs when there are more employers demanding labor than employees supplying labor.
   b. Structural unemployment refers to a situation in which the market wage rate is lower than the equilibrium wage rate.
   c. Structural unemployment occurs when there is a surplus of labor at the current wage rate.
   d. When there is structural unemployment, frictional unemployment equals zero.
   e. Strcutural unemployment refers to when the unemployment rate is equal to zero.

Helpful Tips

- Not all unemployment is worrisome, In fact some unemployment might be desirable, which is a little counterintuitive. In particular, frictional unemployment may be necessary for a labor market to be efficient. This is the idea that underlies the idea of the natural rate of unemployment: some amount of unemployment is not just necessary, it is healthy. Therefore, the natural rate of unemployment would not be zero.

- Minimum wages, efficiency wages, and unions are all theories about *why* structural unemployment exists, but are not themselves *types* of unemployment (structural, frictional, cyclical). Be sure you know some of these explanations for structural unemployment.

Module Notes

We have presented three types of unemployment: frictional, structural, and cyclical. But if someone is unemployed, does it really matter *why* he or she is unemployed? Yes, if you want to create or evaluate policies to reduce unemployment. The reason a person is unemployed, which is what determines the type of unemployment someone is experiencing, is key to determining how to change his or her employment status.

Another concept presented is the idea that some amount of unemployment is to be expected. The natural rate of unemployment is not constant over time and may be affected by economic policies. The natural rate of unemployment changes with changes in the characteristics of the labor force, labor market institutions, government policies, and productivity.

MODULE 14 INFLATION: AN OVERVIEW

BEFORE YOU READ THE MODULE

Summary

This module presents the economic costs of inflation and deflation, and how inflation and deflation create winners and losers. It also discusses why policymakers want to avoid both inflation and deflation. Finally, the module explains the difference between real and nominal values.

Module Objectives

Review these objectives before you read the module. Place a "√" on the line when you can do each of the following:

_____**Objective #1.** Calculate the rate of inflation

_____**Objective #2.** Specify the economic costs of inflation

_____**Objective #3.** Identify who is helped and who is hurt by inflation

_____**Objective #4.** Explain why policy makers try to maintain a stable rate of inflation

_____**Objective #5.** Differentiate between real and nominal values of income, wages, and interest rates

_____**Objective #6.** Discuss the problems of deflation and disinflation

WHILE YOU READ THE MODULE

Key Terms

Define these key terms as you read the module:

Real wage:

Real income:

Inflation rate:

Shoe-leather costs:

Menu costs:

Unit-of-account costs:

Nominal interest rate:

Real interest rate:

Disinflation:

Practice the Model

The CPI (Consumer Price Index) is one of several measures of the price level. (You will learn more about how the CPI is calculated in Module 15).

Assume the average annual CPI in 2011 was 214.537 and the average annual CPI in 2012 was 218.056. Using the formula to calculate the inflation rate from the textbook module, the rate of inflation was 1.64%:

Inflation rate = (Price level in year 2 – Price level in year 1) × 100 = (218.056 - 214.537)/214.537 × 100
$\quad\quad\quad\quad\quad\quad$ Price level in year 1 $\quad\quad\quad\quad\quad\quad\quad\quad\quad$ = 1.640

1) Use this method to calculate the rate of inflation between 2013 and 2014 if the CPI in 2013 was 201.6 and the CPI in 2014 was 207.342.

List questions or difficulties from your initial reading of the module.

AFTER YOU READ THE MODULE

Fill-in-the-Blanks

Fill in the blanks to complete the following statements. If you find yourself having difficulties, please refer back to the appropriate section in the text.

- If you cut a worker's wage in half, but also cut all prices in half, the worker's real wage, which is calculated as **1)**_____, doesn't change.

- Increased costs of transactions caused by inflation are known as **2)**_____ costs. Changing a listed price has a real cost, called a **3)** _____ cost. The **4)**_____ costs of inflation are the costs arising from the way inflation makes money a less reliable unit of measurement.

- The **5)**_____ interest rate is the interest rate actually paid—for example, the interest rate that someone pays on a student loan. The **6)**_____ interest rate is the nominal interest rate minus the rate of inflation, which is the true amount of interest paid or received. For example, if a loan carries an interest rate of 8%, but there is 5% inflation, the real interest rate is 8% - 5% = 3%.

- Bringing the inflation rate down—a process called **7)**_____—is very difficult and costly once a higher rate of inflation has become well established in the economy.

Multiple-Choice Questions

Circle the best choice to answer or complete the following questions or incomplete statements. For additional practice, use the space provided to explain why one or more of the incorrect options do not work.

8. Theo purchased an asset for $100,000 in cash last year, and there has been 10% inflation in the past year. If he sells that asset this year for $108,000, he will have _____ $_____, which is an illustration of the _____ of inflation.

	Gained or Lost	Amount of Gain or loss	Cost of inflation described
a.	gained	$8,000	benefits to borrowers
b.	gained	$2,000	costs to lenders
c.	lost	$8,000	menu costs
d.	lost	$2,000	unit-of-account costs
e.	lost	$8,000	shoe-leather costs

9. As a result of a doubling of the price level, Jenny had to double all of the prices at her coffee shop and had to change all of her signs to reflect that change, which cost her $800. Therefore, the inflation
    a. had no effect on Jenny, because she was able to double all of her prices.
    b. had a positive effect on Jenny, because she was able to double all of her prices.
    c. had a negative effect on Jenny, because of menu costs.
    d. had a negative effect on Jenny, because of unit-of-account costs.
    e. had a positive effect on Jenny because of shoe-leather costs.

Helpful Tips

*   Be careful not to confuse the terms deflation and disinflation, and to think that either is preferable to inflation. Inflation is an increase in the price level, which has some negative impacts on an economy (menu costs, unit-of-account costs, and shoe-leather costs). It is tempting to assume that the opposite of inflation – deflation, a decrease in the overall price level – has a positive effect on an economy. Deflation is usually the result of a severe recession or depression. On the other hand, disinflation (a slowing of the rate of inflation) is sometimes an objective of policy makers to bring the rate of inflation under control.

*   Don't confuse nominal and real values! An easy way to remember the difference is to think about what the word "nominal" means – "existing in name only." In other words, a nominal value is the value that appears on the surface, and not a real value.

Module Notes

In this module, we introduced key concepts in changes in the price level. Inflation is an increase in the overall price level. Even if all nominal values increase by the same amount, such as an increase in both nominal incomes and prices so that real incomes are not changed, there are still "winnners" and "losers" from inflation. When the inflation rate changes, there are real costs imposed on an economy through shoe-leather costs, menu costs, and unit-of-account costs. Changes in the price level also impact the value of the interest rate. If nominal interest rates are not adjusted to keep up with inflation, real interest rates decrease.

Whenever there is a change in the price level, there are some that benefit from this change. In general, borrowers benefit (and lenders lose) when there is inflation. When prices go down, however, borrowers lose and lenders gain.

MODULE | 15 | THE MEASUREMENT AND CALCULATION OF INFLATION

BEFORE YOU READ THE MODULE

Summary

This module explains how the inflation rate is calculated and how price indexes are used to measure and adjust for inflation and deflation in the economy.

Module Objectives

Review these objectives before you read the module. Place a "√" on the line when you can do each of the following:

_____**Objective #1.** Explain what a price index is and how it is calculated

_____**Objective #2.** Calculate the inflation rate using the values of a price index

_____**Objective #3.** Describe the importance of the consumer price index and other price indexes

WHILE YOU READ THE MODULE

Key Terms

Define these key terms as you read the module:

Aggregate price level:

Market basket:

Price index:

Consumer price index (CPI):

Producer price index (PPI):

GDP deflator:

Practice the Model

The market basket in Theopolis is 4 gallons of milk, 5 bananas, and 10 loaves of bread. Refer to the table below to determine each of the following:
  a) the price index for each period, using the first period as the base
  b) the rates of inflation between the first and second period and the second and third period
  c) the rate of inflation between the first period and the third period
  d) if there was deflation or disinflation between period 2 and period 3. Explain.

	Price of a gallon of milk	Price of a banana	Price of a loaf of bread
Period 1	$1	$2	$3
Period 2	$2	$4	$6
Period 3	$3	$8	$8

List questions or difficulties from your initial reading of the module.

AFTER YOU READ THE MODULE

Fill-in-the-Blanks

Fill in the blanks to complete the following statements. If you find yourself having difficulties, please refer back to the appropriate section in the text.

- Economists measure changes in the **1)**_____ by tracking changes in the cost of

  buying a given market basket of goods. A price index measures the cost of purchasing a given market

  basket of goods in a given year, where that cost is normalized so that the price index is always equal

  to **2)**_____ in the base year. The **3)**_____ measures the cost of a

  basket of goods typically purchased by consumers, while the **4)**_____ measures the

  prices of goods and services purchased by producers.

- The **5)**_____ is the annual percent change in an official price index. The most widely used measure of prices in the United States is the **6)**_____ , often referred

to simply as the CPI. It is calculated by surveying market prices for a **7)**_____ that

is constructed to represent the consumption of a typical family of four living in a typical American

city.

- There are two other price measures that are also widely used to track economy-wide price changes,

  the **8)**_____ , or PPI, which tracks the cost of a typical basket of goods and services

  purchased by producers and the **9)**_____ for a given year, which is equal to 100

  times the ratio of nominal GDP for that year to real GDP for that year expressed in prices of a

  selected base year.

Multiple-Choice Questions

Circle the best choice to answer or complete the following questions or incomplete statements. For additional practice, use the space provided to explain why one or more of the incorrect options do not work.

10. If the inflation rate is negative, it must mean that
   a. there has been deflation.
   b. there has been disinflation.
   c. there has been inflation.
   d. the prices of goods and services have stayed the same for consumers, but not producers.
   e. the real rate of interest cannot be calculated because inflation is negative.

11. Between 2010 and 2011 the rate of inflation was 25%. The CPI in 2010 was 120. Therefore, the CPI
   in 2011 must be
   a. 145.
   b. 160.
   c. 150.
   d. 125.
   e. 95.

Helpful Tips

- The base year doesn't necessarily have to be the first year. In fact, it can be any year that is mutually agreed on. However, the base year will always be equal to 100, and no matter which year you choose as a base year, the rate of inflation will always be the same even if the index for each year has changed. To prove this to yourself, try redoing the Practice the Model section with period 2 as your base year.

- Likewise, you are not restricted to comparing the rate of inflation between any two consecutive years; you can compare the rate of inflation between any two years for which you have a price index. An easy way to remember how to calculate the rate of change for any two periods is "new − old"/"old".

- The rate of inflation is not additive between years. For example, if the rate of inflation between year 1 and 2 is 10% and the rate of inflation between year 2 and 3 is also 10%, the total rate of inflation between year 1 and year three is *not* 20%, but rather 21%. How can this be? Well, inflation is an increase in the prices that currently exist. So if something cost $100 in year 1 and had a 10% price increase, its cost in year 2 would be $110. Then if the price went up by 10% again, then the new price would be $110 + (10% × $110) = $110 + $11 = $121. Price levels therefore increase exponentially. This actually leads to a rather handy rule: the rule of 70. This rule allows us to figure out the doubling time of anything that grows in the same compounding manner. It states that to find the doubling time, divide 70 by the rate of growth. Or, stated mathematically: 70/% rate of increase = doubling time in years. For instance, if the rate of increase is 2%, then prices will double in 70/2 = 35 years. In this way, even very small changes in the price level can lead to very dramatic changes in the price level over time.

Module Notes

In this module, we introduced ways changes in the price level are measured. Economists measure changes in the aggregate price level by tracking changes in the cost of buying a given market basket of goods. A price index measures the cost of purchasing a given market basket of goods in a given year as if prices stayed the same as they were in the base year. To calculate the cost of the market basket of goods, multiply the quantities of each good in the market basket times its price and then sum these products. Then use this information to calculate a price index by dividing the cost of the market basket for a particular time period by the cost of the market basket in the base year and then multiplying by 100. The price index for the base year is always equal to 100 because the prices in the base year are 100% of the prices in that year! An example of a price index is the consumer price index, or the CPI. The producer price index (also known as the wholesale price index), or the PPI, is another price index that measures the cost of a basket of goods typically purchased by producers. The inflation rate between two years can be calculated using this formula:

Inflation rate = [(price index in year 2) - (price index in year 1)/(price index in year 1)] × 100.

Draw the Featured Model: Circular-Flow Diagram

1)

   a. Fill in the labels for the simple circular-flow diagram.

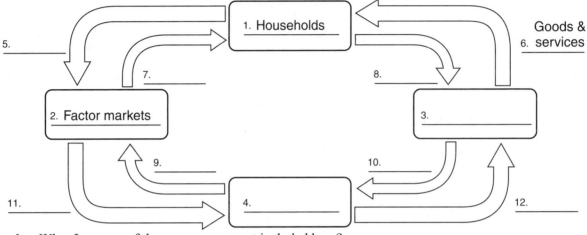

   b. What 3 sectors of the economy are not included here?

2) The diagram below provides a circular-flow diagram for the economy of Littleton.

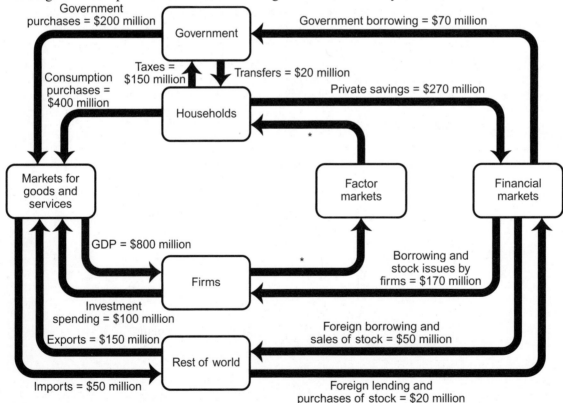

You are also told the following about the economy of Littleton:

Consumer spending (C) = $200 million
Investment spending (I) = $50 million
Spending on exports (X) = $20 million
Wages + profit + interest + rent = $320 million
Government borrowing = $60 million
Taxes = $20 million
Transfers = $10 million

    a. What is the GDP of Littleton? Explain.

    b. What is the value of government spending (G) in Littleton's economy? Explain.

    c. What is the value of imports in Littleton's economy? Explain.

    d. What is the value of private savings in Littleton's economy? Explain.

    e. What is the level of firm borrowing and stock issues in this economy? Explain.

    f. Is the rest of the world a net borrower, a net lender, or neither? Explain.

Complete the Exercise

1. In Montrose, the price index is based upon a market basket consisting of 10 apples, 2 pizzas, and 5 ice cream cones. You are given prices for these three items for 2012, 2013, and 2014 in the following table.

Year	Price of apples	Price of pizzas	Price of ice cream cones
2012	$0.50	$4.00	$1.00
2013	0.52	3.85	1.10
2014	0.49	3.90	1.30

a. Fill in the following table using year 2012 as your base year. The cost of the market basket and the price index value has been done for you for 2012.

Year	Cost of market basket	Price index value
2012	$0.50 \times 10 + $4 \times 2 + $1 \times 5 = $18	($18/$18) \times 100 = 100
2013		
2014		

b. Use the information you computed in part a. to calculate the rate of inflation between 2012 and 2013.

c. Use the information you computed in part a. to calculate the rate of inflation between 2013 and 2014.

d. Fill in the following table using year 2013 as your base year.

Year	Cost of market basket	Price index value
2012		
2013		
2014		

e. Use the information you computed in part d. to calculate the rate of inflation between 2012 and 2013.

f. Use the information you computed in part d. to calculate the rate of inflation between 2013 and 2014.

g. Compare your answers in parts b. and c. to your answers in parts e. and f.

Problems

1. You are given the following information about Macronesia:

During 2014, the government of Macronesia spent $200 million on goods and services as well as $20 million on transfer payments, while collecting $150 million in taxes. During 2014, households paid $150 million in taxes, purchased goods and services worth $400 million, and received $800 million in the form of wages, dividends, interest, and rent. Firms in 2014 had $100 million of investment spending, and they borrowed or had stock issues of $170 million from the financial markets. In 2014, exports to this economy equaled $150 million while imports to this economy equaled $50 million. In the financial markets, there was foreign borrowing of $50 million and foreign lending of $20 million.

a. Sketch a circular-flow diagram of Macronesia's economy showing these flows.

b. What is GDP in 2014 in Macronesia?

c. What is the value of disposable income in Macronesia in 2014?

d. What is the value of household saving in Macronesia in 2014?

e. Is the government running a balanced budget during 2014? Explain your answer.

f. Compute the flow of money into the financial markets and the flow of money out of the financial markets. Are they equal?

g. Compute the flow of money into the market for goods and services and the flow of money out of the market for goods and services. Are they equal?

h. Compute the flow of money into the factor markets and the flow of money out of the factor markets. Are they equal?

2. Decide how each item affects the calculation of GDP for Saxet in 2014. If it affects GDP, indicate which part of GDP = $C + I + G + X - IM$.

a. A new house is constructed in 2014.

b. Annie purchases a home in 2014 that was built in 2011.

c. The government purchases new textbooks in 2014 for schools to use from 2014 until they need to be replaced.

d. $100 million worth of tablets are imported.

e. Janet produces houseplants that are illegal, and sells them on the black market.

f. A candlemaker produces 500 candles during 2014 but only sells 200 candles during 2014; the other 300 candles are added to the candlemaker's inventories.

3. Suppose you are told that Finlandia produces three goods: tennis shoes, basketballs, and lawn mowers. The following table provides information about the prices and output for these three goods for the years 2012, 2013, and 2014.

Years	Price of tennis shoes	Quantities of tennis shoes	Price of basketballs	Quantities of basketballs	Price of lawn mowers	Quantities of lawn mowers
2012	$50	100	$10	200	$100	10
2013	52	108	10	205	100	12
2014	54	115	10	212	110	12

a. Using the previous information, fill in the following table.

Year	Nominal GDP
2012	
2013	
2014	

b. What was the percentage change in nominal GDP from 2012 to 2013?

c. What was the percentage change in nominal GDP from 2013 to 2014?

d. Using 2012 as the base year, fill in the following table.

Year	Real GDP
2012	
2013	
2014	

e. What was the percentage change in real GDP from 2012 to 2013?

f. What was the percentage change in real GDP from 2013 to 2014?

g. Using 2012 as the base year, fill in the following table.

Year	GDP deflator
2012	
2013	
2014	

4. You are given the following information about the small economy of Hyattville:

Hyattville's economy is composed of three firms: Hyattville Forest, Inc., that harvests trees that are used by Hyattville Lumber Products, Inc., to manufacture various lumber products that are used by Hyattville Houses, Inc., to produce houses. Assume lumber is the only raw material used to produce the houses in Hyattville.

	Hyattville Forest, Inc.	Hyattville Lumber Products, Inc.	Hyattville Houses, Inc.	Total Factor Income
Value of sales	$15,000	(a)	$100,000	
Intermediate goods	(b)	$15,000	40,000	
Wages	6,000	15,000	35,000	(g)
Interest payments	1,000	3,000	6,000	(h)
Rent	3,000	(d)	3,000	(i)
Profit	5,000	4,000	(f)	(j)
Total expenditures by firm	15,000	40,000	100,000	
Value added per firm	(c)	(e)	60,000	

a. Fill in the missing entries [(a)–(j)] in the above table.

b. Explain how you would use the value-added approach to calculate the value of GDP using the data above.

c. Explain how you would use the factor income approach to calculate the value of GDP using the data above.

d. Explain how you would use the aggregate spending on domestically produced final goods and services approach to calculate the value of GDP using the data above.

5. The population of Stephensville is 20,000. There are 4,000 full-time workers and 3,000 part-time workers. There are also 3,000 people looking for work. Of these 3,000 people, there are 2,000 who are currently working part-time but would like to have full-time work and 1,000 who are not working at all. There are 2,500 people who have given up trying to find a job but would take one if offered, and 7,500 people who are too young or too old to work.

    a. What is the size of the labor force in Stephensville?

    b. What is the employment rate in Stephensville?

    c. What is the unemployment rate in Stephensville?

    d. What is the labor force participation rate?

    e. What would be the impact of the discouraged workers re-entering the labor force?

    f. Suppose you are told that 100 people find jobs for every $10,000 increase in the level of aggregate output in Stephensville. If you wanted the unemployment rate to equal 8%, what would the change in output need to be? Assume no changes in the number of young and old in the population or in the number of discouraged workers.

6. Suppose that there are 10,000 adults in Finlandia and that 5,000 of these adults are employed, 2,000 are unemployed, 500 are discouraged workers, and the rest are not currently working and/or not seeking employment.

    a. What is the labor force equal to in Finlandia?

    b. What is the unemployment rate in Finlandia?

    c. What would the unemployment rate equal in Finlandia if discouraged workers were counted as unemployed workers?

    d. Currently, the Bureau of Labor Statistics does not count discouraged workers as unemployed workers. How does this decision affect the calculated value of the unemployment rate?

7. Jay's employment contract includes an annual automatic increase in salary tied to the rate of inflation. Jose got a performance-based increase in salary of 5%. Beth is retired and receives half of her monthly income in the form of a fixed pension each month, as well as a national retirement insurance payment which is indexed to the inflation rate.

   a. Suppose the rate of inflation is 8% this year. What is the impact this inflation has on the real purchasing power of each person's income? (*Note*: it might be useful to begin with the assumption that before the increases described above, they each had an income of $1,000 per month.) Explain.

   b. Suppose the rate of inflation is 2% this year. Describe the effect of this inflation rate on Jay, Jose, and Beth.

Review Questions

Circle your answer to the following questions.

Use the information in the following table to answer questions 1 – 3:

	Price in 2013	Price in 2014
Carrots	$0.75	$0.50
Squash	1.00	2.00
Beets	1.00	1.50

Suppose 2013 is the base year and the market basket for purposes of constructing a price index consists of 20 carrots, 15 squash, and 40 beets.

1. What is the value of the price index in 2013?
   a. 60
   b. 100
   c. .65
   d. 160
   e. 35

2. What is the value of the price index in 2013, using 2014 as the base year?
   a. 142.85
   b. 42.85%
   c. 100
   d. 40
   e. 140

3. What is the rate of inflation between 2013 and 2014 in this economy?
   a. 20.75%
   b. 42.85%
   c. 103.15%
   d. 3%
   e. There is no inflation because not all prices increased.

4. In Macroland the GDP deflator for 2009 is 105, with 2008 the base year. Real GDP in 2009 equals $210 billion. Nominal GDP in 2009 equals ___ billion and nominal GDP in 2008 equals ___ billion.

	Nominal GDP 2009	*Nominal GDP 2008*
a.	$220.5	$200
b.	$220.5	$210
c.	$200	$210
d.	$200	$220.5
e.	$210	$220.5

5. The factor income received in an economy is $12 million dollars and the total amount of value added in an economy is $12 million dollars. Therefore, $C + I + G + X - IM$ must equal
   a. $0.
   b. $12 million.
   c. $24 million.
   d. $36 million.
   e. The answer cannot be determined using the above information.

6. $C + I + G + X - IM$ is the value of
   a. all goods and services produced within an economy at any stage in the production process.
   b. all final goods and services produced in an economy during a given time period.
   c. intermediate goods and services produced in an economy.
   d. all consumer goods sold in an economy.
   e. all goods purchased by firms in an economy.

7. Which of the following is *not* included in the calculation of GDP?
   a. Joey's Electronics manufactures CD players that individuals install.
   b. Susy's Leather Goods manufactures leather pieces that are sold to manufacturers who use them to produce handbags and wallets.
   c. Harry's Ice Cream Shoppe sells ice cream cones at the beach.
   d. Monica's Hair Salon sells haircuts and manicures to the residents of Macroland.
   e. Beth purchases maternity clothing from a store.

8. The natural rate of unemployment is
   a. a country's unemployment rate during a recession.
   b. a country's unemployment rate during an expansion.
   c. the sum of frictional and structural unemployment.
   d. the sum of frictional and cyclical unemployment.
   e. always equal to zero.

9. Which of the following statements is true?
   a. Structural unemployment refers to the unemployment that occurs when there are more employers demanding labor than there are employees supplying labor.
   b. Structural unemployment refers to a situation in which the market wage rate is lower than the equilibrium wage rate.
   c. Structural unemployment occurs when there is a surplus of labor at the current wage rate.
   d. When there is structural unemployment, frictional unemployment equals zero.
   e. When there is no structural unemployment, the natural rate of unemployment is zero.

10. The natural rate of unemployment is
    a. equal to zero, but only if there are no discouraged workers.
    b. structural unemployment minus underemployment.
    c. always lower than the reported unemployment rate.
    d. always equal to zero.
    e. frictional unemployment plus structural unemployment.

11. Mary expects the inflation rate to be 5%, and she is willing to pay a real interest rate of 3%. Joe expects the inflation rate to be 5%, and he is willing to lend money if he receives a real interest rate of 3%. If the actual inflation rate is 6% and the loan contract specifies a nominal interest rate of 8%, then
    a. Joe is glad he lent out funds even though his real interest rate has fallen.
    b. Joe is sorry he lent out funds since his real interest rate is now 9%.
    c. Mary is glad she borrowed the funds because her real interest rate has fallen.
    d. Mary is sorry she borrowed funds since her real interest rate is now 9%.
    e. Mary is sorry she borrowed funds since her real interest rate is now 8%.

12. Disinflation in an economy which has grown to expect inflation is
    a. easy to achieve and does not affect actual output.
    b. difficult to accomplish and results in an increase in the natural rate of unemployment.
    c. possible only if policymakers are willing to accept higher rates of unemployment and a lower level of aggregate output.
    d. the same as deflation occurring in that economy.
    e. going to have no effect on the economy because it was unexpected.

13. In a period of unexpected deflation,
    a. borrowers find that it is easier for them to make their loan payments, since prices are falling.
    b. lenders benefit, since there are more people eager to borrow money during a period of deflation.
    c. lenders benefit, since they are repaid dollars with greater real value than they anticipated when signing the loan contract.
    d. neither borrowers nor lenders benefit, because the deflation was unexpected.
    e. there will be a benefit to lenders, but there will be no effect on borrowers.

14. Which of the following statements is true?
    a. The two principal goals of macroeconomic policy are price stability and low frictional unemployment.
    b. The primary goals of macroeconomic policy are price stability and zero unemployment.
    c. The primary goals of macroeconomic policy are price stability and low unemployment.
    d. In order to achieve the two primary goals of macroeconomic policy of price stability and low unemployment, it is necessary for policymakers to reduce the level of frictional unemployment.
    e. The primary goal of macroeconomic policy is price stability even if that creates high levels of unemployment.

15. Which of these is necessary for a person to be considered unemployed?
    a. One must have worked fewer hours than desired.
    b. One must not have a job, whether or not you are looking for work.
    c. One must have a full-time job that does not use all of your skills.
    d. One must be looking for a job, regardless of how many hours you currently work.
    e. One must not have a job and be looking for a job.

16. Job search refers to the time workers spend looking for employment. Job search results in
   a. cyclical unemployment.
   b. structural unemployment.
   c. frictional unemployment.
   d. both structural and frictional unemployment.
   e. a natural rate of unemployment equal to zero.

17. The extra time and effort to make transactions due to inflation imposes
   a. shoe-leather costs.
   b. menu costs.
   c. unit-of-account costs.
   d. deflation costs.
   e. disinflation costs.

18. In 2013, the economy of Ansela had a real GDP of $20,000 per capita and in 2014, the economy of Ansela had a real GDP of $22,000 per capita. Which of the statements is definitely true?
   a. Ansela experienced economic growth.
   b. Ansela has entered a recession.
   c. Ansela has had an economic expansion.
   d. Ansela experienced deflation.
   e. Ansela had an increase in unemployment.

19. The price index for year 2 is 120. The cost of a basket of goods in year 2 was 150. Year 1 is the base year. Therefore, the price of a basket of goods in year 1 was _____ and the rate of inflation between the two years was _____.

	Price of basket	Rate of inflation
a.	170	20%
b.	130	10%
c.	180	20%
d.	20	5%
e.	270	70%

20. The price index in 2013 was 120 and the price index in 2014 was 110. Therefore, there was
   a. inflation.
   b. deflation.
   c. disinflation.
   d. reinflation.
   e. hyperinflation.

Section ④ National Income and Price Determination

Overview

This section develops the aggregate supply and demand model (*AD–AS* model) of the macroeconomy. It introduces *multiplier analysis* and looks at aggregate demand and its two most important components, consumer spending and investment spending. The section also introduces aggregate supply and explores how the relationship between the two curves—aggregate supply and aggregate demand—determines the equilibrium levels of aggregate output and aggregate prices in the economy. Here and in following sections, this model is used to evaluate the state of the economy and determine appropriate economic policies.

Featured Model/Graph: The Aggregate Demand and Supply Model

This section presents the *AD-AS* model and shows how it is used to understand the behavior of the economy. The *AD–AS* model is the basic model we use to understand macroeconomic fluctuations.

MODULES IN THIS SECTION

Module 16   **Income and Expenditure**

Module 17   **Aggregate Demand: Introduction and Determinants**

Module 18   **Aggregate Supply: Introduction and Determinants**

Module 19   **Equilibrium in the Aggregate Demand-Aggregate Supply Model**

Module 20   **Economic Policy and the Aggregate Demand-Aggregate Supply Model**

Module 21   **Fiscal Policy and Multiplier Effects**

BEFORE YOU TACKLE THE TEST

Draw the Featured Model

Complete the Exercise

Problems

Review Questions

MODULE 16 INCOME AND EXPENDITURE

BEFORE YOU READ THE MODULE

Summary

This module introduces multiplier analysis and explains how an initial change in spending will multiply and contribute to business cycles.

Module Objectives

Review these objectives before you read the module. Place a "√" on the line when you can do each of the following:

_____**Objective #1.** Describe the multiplier process by which initial changes in spending lead to further changes in spending

_____**Objective #2.** Use the consumption function to show how current disposable income affects consumer spending

_____**Objective #3.** Explain how expected future income and aggregate wealth affect consumer spending

_____**Objective #4.** Identify the determinants of investment spending

_____**Objective #5.** Explain why investment spending is considered a leading indicator of the future state of the economy

WHILE YOU READ THE MODULE

Key Terms

Define these key terms as you read the module:

Marginal propensity to consume (*MPC*):

Marginal propensity to save (*MPS*):

Autonomous change in aggregate spending:

Spending multiplier:

Consumption function:

Autonomous consumer spending:

Aggregate consumption function:

Planned investment spending:

Inventory investment:

Unplanned inventory investment:

Actual investment spending:

Practice the Model

Suppose a consumer's autonomous spending is $1,000 per month and the marginal propensity to consume is .75. Use Figure 16.2 in your textbook as your guide to draw a correctly labeled graph of the consumer's consumption function. How much will the consumer spend if his or her income is $500? Label this point *A* on your consumption function. How much will the consumer spend if his or her income is $800? Label this point *B* on your consumption function.

List questions or difficulties from your initial reading of the module.

AFTER YOU READ THE MODULE

Fill-in-the-Blanks

Fill in the blanks to complete the following statements. If you find yourself having difficulties, please refer back to the appropriate section in the text.

- The marginal propensity to consume (*MPC*) is the additional consumer spending resulting from a $1

  change in disposable **1)**_____. The additional saving that results from the same $1

  change in income is called the **2)**_____. An initial rise or fall in aggregate

  spending at a given level of GDP is known as a(n) **3)**_____ change in aggregate

  spending, and will cause a series of income and spending increases.

- The final change in aggregate spending that results from an autonomous change in aggregate

  spending is **4)**_____ (greater/less) than the initial change due to this "chain

  reaction," which is known as the **5)**_____effect.

- Stocks of goods held to satisfy future sales are known as **6)**_____. When a

  business sells less than it anticipated, it does not reduce the amount of stock it has in inventory,

  known as **7)**_____.

Multiple-Choice Questions

Circle the best choice to answer or complete the following questions or incomplete statements. For additional practice, use the space provided to explain why one or more of the incorrect options do not work.

8. The *MPC* is equal to which of the following?
   a. *MPS* + 1
   b. *MPS* - 1
   c. 1 - *MPS*
   d. 1 × *MPS*
   e. 1/*MPS*

9. Assume households typically save 20% of any disposable income. A $200 million increase in aggregate spending will increase GDP by how much?
   a. $200 million
   b. $40 million
   c. $1,000 million
   d. $250 million
   e. $240 million

Helpful Tips

- Use the spending multiplier to find the final impact on *AD* that an increase (or decrease) in government spending will have. Don't get caught up in the math of the multiple rounds of impact that an increase in investment or in autonomous changes in aggregate spending will trigger. Instead, focus on what is happening in the economy and use the following equation:

$$Increase \ in \ Y = \frac{1}{1 - MPC} x (Increase \ in \ AAS \ or \ Invesment)$$

Module Notes

Part of managing a firm is to plan for the future. This includes making decisions about when and how much to spend on capital investments, such as new equipment. The idea of planned investment spending is fairly intuitive. But how can a firm experience an "unplanned" investment in capital? Unplanned investment spending refers to unintended changes in a firm's inventories. A firm will determine the desired level of its inventories (e.g. the amount of output held in its warehouse). But because of miscalculations or changes in the economy, the firm may find that it has more or less than the desired level of output in inventories.

If, for example, demand for the firm's output is lower than expected, inventories will build up in the warehouse. The additional inventories represent unplanned inventory investment. The firm has unintentionally invested in its own output (when no one else would buy it from the firm). On the other hand, if firms sell more than expected, then they will not be able to keep the desired inventories in the warehouse. Their output flies off the shelves! In this case, the firm has engaged in less investment spending than it intended because it is reducing its level of inventories. Unplanned inventory investment signals firms to produce more or less. If inventories pile up, firms decrease production. If inventories decline, firms increase production.

A thorough understanding of the aggregate consumption function and the variables that shift it is essential. Make sure you review the aggregate consumption function and understand the relationship between consumer spending and autonomous consumer spending, the marginal propensity to consume, and disposable income. The consumption function will shift upward with increases in wealth or expected future disposable income.

An understanding of investment spending and its components is a critical aspect of this module. Make sure you can distinguish between planned investment spending and unplanned inventory investment.

This module develops the concept of the multiplier, which is central to understanding the sections that follow. Review the definition of the multiplier and its calculation, and then practice using this concept in questions provided in the text and the study guide.

MODULE $\boxed{17}$ AGGREGATE DEMAND: INTRODUCTION AND DETERMINANTS

BEFORE YOU READ THE MODULE

Summary

This module begins the development of the aggregate demand and supply model by presenting the aggregate demand curve.

Module Objectives

Review these objectives before you read the module. Place a "√" on the line when you can do each of the following:

_____**Objective #1.**   Use the aggregate demand curve to illustrate the relationship between the aggregate price level and the quantity of aggregate output demanded in the economy

_____**Objective #2.**   Explain how the wealth effect and the interest rate effect give the aggregate demand curve a negative slope

_____**Objective #3.**   Identify the factors that can shift the aggregate demand curve

WHILE YOU READ THE MODULE

Key Terms

Define these key terms as you read the module:

Aggregate demand curve:

Wealth effect of a change in the aggregate price level:

Interest rate effect of a change in the aggregate price level:

Fiscal policy:

Monetary policy:

Practice the Model

1) As a result of a decrease in the price level, households' assets have greater purchasing power (they can afford to buy more). Draw a correctly labeled graph to show the effect of a decrease in the price level on the Aggregate Demand Curve. Label the initial point on the *AD* curve 1 and label the corresponding real GDP on the horizontal axis Y_1. Label the new point on the *AD* curve 2 and label the corresponding real GDP on the horizontal axis Y_2.

2) As a result of a change in expectations, consumers and firms are now more optimistic. Show the effect of this change on a correctly labeled graph of the Aggregate Demand Curve. Label any initial position 1 and any new position 2 and use an arrow to show the direction of the change. Be sure to completely and correctly label your graph, including the vertical axis and horizontal axis.

List questions or difficulties from your initial reading of the module.

AFTER YOU READ THE MODULE

Fill-in-the-Blanks

Fill in the blanks to complete the following statements. If you find yourself having difficulties, please refer back to the appropriate section in the text.

- The aggregate demand curve has a negative slope, indicating that higher aggregate price levels are

  associated with a lower level of aggregate **1)**_____. When the price level increases,

  households feel less wealthy, which is called the **2)**_____ effect. This effect is one

  of the reasons that the aggregate demand curve is downward-sloping. The aggregate demand curve also slopes downward because an increase in the price level causes households' money demand to increase, which places an upward pressure on the interest rate. This is called the

3)_____ effect. Shifts in the aggregate demand curve can occur for many reasons. An increase in aggregate demand can occur when consumers are more optimistic, which is also called a change in 4)_____. Changes in the 5)_____ can also shift the aggregate demand curve because there is less incentive to increase investment if there is already a lot of existing capital. Both 6)_____ policy (the use of government purchases to impact the economy) and 7)_____ policy (the use of the money supply to impact the economy) can shift aggregate demand as well. Finally, 8)_____ can shift the aggregate demand curve when households' assets increase or decrease.

Multiple-Choice Questions

Circle the best choice to answer or complete the following questions or incomplete statements. For additional practice, use the space provided to explain why one or more of the incorrect options do not work.

9. Which of the following is a possible reason that the *AD* curve slopes downward?
    a. An increase in government spending causes the quantity of GDP to increase.
    b. A decrease in price level will mean that consumers keep more money in banks, which lowers the interest rate and will cause the quantity of GDP to increase.
    c. A decrease in investment spending causes the quantity of GDP to decrease.
    d. A decrease in net exports will cause the quantity of GDP to decrease.
    e. A decrease in nominal wages will cause the quantity of GDP to decrease.

10. If the government decreases taxes, what is the most likely effect on the aggregate demand curve?
    a. The *AD* curve will shift to the left.
    b. There will be a movement to the left along the *AD* curve.
    c. The *AD* curve will shift to the right.
    d. There will be a movement to the right along the *AD* curve.
    e. The *AD* curve will not be affected.

Helpful Tips

- The terms *aggregate output* and *Real GDP* are often used interchangeably.

- Think about shifts in *AD* as to the left or to the right and not as "up" or "down." As you move to the right along the horizontal axis, the numbers increase; as you move to the left, numbers decrease. This is true for demand and will be true in the next module for supply. Emphasize the direction of curve shifts by using arrows on your graphs showing the direction of the shift.

- One of the easiest ways to lose points on the AP® exam is to mislabel your axes. When you are using the *AD-AS* model, make sure you label your vertical axis as PL or Aggregate price level, and your horizontal axis as Real Output or Real GDP. Do <u>not</u> label them as P and Q! This is not a market, but instead is a model of the macro-economy and must be labeled accordingly.

- The aggregate demand curve looks a lot like a market demand curve, but there are important differences. It slopes downward like a market demand curve, but for different reasons. It also shifts like a demand curve, but also for different reasons. Be careful not to confuse these very similar appearing concepts.

Module Notes

We explained that one reason the *AD* curve is downward-sloping is due to the wealth effect of a change in the aggregate price level: a higher aggregate price level reduces the purchasing power of households' assets and leads to a fall in consumer spending, *C*. But we also explained that changes in wealth lead to a shift of the *AD* curve. Aren't those two explanations contradictory? Which one is it—does a change in wealth move the economy along the *AD* curve or does it shift the *AD* curve?

The answer is both: it depends on the *source* of the change in wealth. A movement along the *AD* curve occurs when a change in the aggregate price level changes the purchasing power of consumers' existing wealth (the real value of their assets). This is the *wealth effect of a change in the aggregate price level*—a change in the aggregate price level is the source of the change in wealth. For example, a fall in the aggregate price level increases the purchasing power of consumers' assets and leads to a movement down the *AD* curve.

In contrast, a change in wealth *independent of a change in the aggregate price level* shifts the *AD* curve. For example, a rise in the stock market or a rise in real estate values leads to an increase in the real value of consumers' assets at any given aggregate price level. In this case, the source of the change in wealth is a change in the values of assets without any change in the aggregate price level—that is, a change in asset values holding the prices of all final goods and services constant.

It is important to understand why the *AD* curve is downward-sloping. Note that the inverse relationship between the aggregate price level and aggregate output are explained by the wealth and interest rate effects.

MODULE ⟦18⟧ AGGREGATE SUPPLY: INTRODUCTION AND DETERMINANTS

BEFORE YOU READ THE MODULE

Summary

This module continues developing the *AD-AS* model by presenting the aggregate supply (*AS*) curve.

Module Objectives

Review these objectives before you read the module. Place a "√" on the line when you can do each of the following:

_____ **Objective #1.** Use the aggregate supply curve to illustrate the relationship between the aggregate price level and the quantity of aggregate output supplied in the economy

_____ **Objective #2.** Identify the factors that can shift the aggregate supply curve

_____ **Objective #3.** Explain why the aggregate supply curve is different in the short run from the long run

WHILE YOU READ THE MODULE

Key Terms

Define these key terms as you read the module:

Aggregate supply curve:

Nominal wage:

Sticky wages:

Short-run aggregate supply curve:

Long-run aggregate supply curve:

Potential output:

Practice the Model

1) Draw a correctly labeled *AD-AS* graph that illustrates the effect of an increase in the price level on the *AS* curve. Label the initial point on the *AS* curve 1 and the new point on the *AS* curve 2.

2) Draw a correctly labeled *AD-AS* graph that illustrates the effect of producers' expectations that the price level will increase in the future on the *AS* curve. Label the initial *AS* curve AS_1 and the new *AS* curve AS_2.

List questions or difficulties from your initial reading of the module.

AFTER YOU READ THE MODULE

Fill-in-the-Blanks

Fill in the blanks to complete the following statements. If you find yourself having difficulties, please refer back to the appropriate section in the text.

- The aggregate supply curve shows the relationship between the aggregate price level and

  1)_____ GDP. The short-run aggregate supply curve has a positive slope

  because nominal wages are **2)**_____.

- Actual inflation will cause a **3)** (shift of/movement along) _____ the aggregate supply

  curve, while expectations of inflation will cause a **4)** (shift of/movement along) _____

  the aggregate supply curve. Another determinant of the aggregate supply curve, which shifts the *AS* curve when wages or the prices of commodities change, is **5)**_____, which

changes *AS* because it changes the cost of production for all producers. Furthermore, changes in

6)_____ can also shift the *AS* curve because if more can be produced with the

same amount of inputs, the per unit cost for each output decreases. Finally, changes in government

policies, such as taxation, may also cause a **7)** (shift of/movement along) _____

the *AS* curve.

- The long-run supply curve is **8)**_____ at the economy's **9)**_____

  output level because changes in the aggregate price level do not affect **10)**_____

  in the long run. Potential output is the level of real GDP the economy would produce if all prices and

  wages were fully **11)**_____. In the long run, the economy returns to potential

  output through shifts in the **12)**_____ curve.

Multiple-Choice Questions

Circle the best choice to answer or complete the following questions or incomplete statements. For additional practice, use the space provided to explain why one or more of the incorrect options do not work.

13. How does an increase in workers' nominal wages effect the long-run aggregate supply curve and the short-run aggregate supply curve?

	Effect on LRAS	*Effect on SRAS*
a.	no effect	increase
b.	no effect	decrease
c.	increase	increase
d.	decrease	decrease
e.	no effect	no effect

14. The economy experiences an increase in the price level. As a result, there will be
    a. a movement along the *SRAS* curve.
    b. a shift of the *LRAS* curve.
    c. a shift of the *SRAS* curve.
    d. a decrease in the *SRAS* curve.
    e. a decrease in the *AD* curve.

Helpful Tips

- Keep in mind that just like *AD* is not quite like demand, *AS* is not quite like supply. Short-run aggregate supply slopes upward, and shifts, for very different reasons than a market supply curve.

- Remember that the *SRAS* curve, rather than the *LRAS* curve, changes in the short run. *SRAS* shifts as prices adjust, whereas *LRAS* does not respond to price changes. This is because nominal wages (and other input prices) don't adjust very quickly. However, over time, as those wages fully adjust, the ultimate amount of output supplied will instead depend more on the stock of the factors of production than changes in the price level, which is why the *LRAS* curve is not affected.

- It can be difficult, or at least time consuming, to write down increase and decrease many times. Using an abbreviation for increase (↑) and an abbreviation for decrease (↓) when describing changes in *AD*, *SRAS*, or *LRAS* are useful. For example, you can use ↑ *SRAS* to shorten "an increase in short-run aggregate supply." However, be careful when translating such abbreviations from your notes to a graph. An increase in *SRAS* is a shift to the right, and NOT a shift "up" of the *SRAS* curve.

Module Notes

The *long-run aggregate supply curve* depicts the economy's potential output: the level of aggregate output that the economy would produce if all prices, including nominal wages, were fully flexible. Because the economy always tends to return to potential output in the long run, actual aggregate output *fluctuates around* potential output. As a result, the economy's rate of growth over long periods of time— say, decades—is very close to the rate of growth of potential output. And potential output growth is determined by long-run economic growth. So that means that the "long run" of long-run economic growth and the "long run" of the long-run aggregate supply curve coincide.

It is important to distinguish between a movement along versus a shift of the *AD* or *SRAS* curve. A change in the aggregate price level causes a movement along either curve. A change in commodity prices, nominal wages, or productivity shifts the *SRAS* curve; a change in expectations, wealth, physical capital, fiscal or monetary policy shifts the *AD* curve.

Make sure to distinguish between short-run and long-run *AS*. In the short run, wages are sticky; this stickiness results in a short-run *AS* curve (*SRAS*) that is upward-sloping. In the long run, wages are fully flexible, leading the economy to always produce its long-run equilibrium at the potential output level of real GDP. This is the output level the economy produces when all wages and prices are fully flexible.

The *LRAS* curve is vertical, and its position represents the economy's potential output when all resources are fully employed. It is important to understand why the *LRAS* curve is vertical as well as the relevance of its position on the horizontal axis. Over time, if an economy experiences economic growth, the *LRAS* curve shifts to the right, indicating that the economy's potential output has increased.

MODULE 19 EQUILIBRIUM IN THE AGGREGATE DEMAND – AGGREGATE SUPPLY MODEL

BEFORE YOU READ THE MODULE

Summary

This module puts the aggregate supply curve and the aggregate demand curve together so we can use them to understand the behavior of the economy. The *AD–AS* model is the basic model we use to understand macroeconomic fluctuations; this model will be expanded throughout future sections.

Module Objectives

Review these objectives before you read the module. Place a "√" on the line when you can do each of the following:

_____ **Objective #1.** Explain the difference between short-run and long-run macroeconomic equilibrium

_____ **Objective #2.** Describe the causes and effects of demand shocks and supply shocks

_____ **Objective #3.** Determine if an economy is experiencing a recessionary gap or an inflationary gap and explain how to calculate the size of an output gap

WHILE YOU READ THE MODULE

Key Terms

Define these key terms as you read the module:

AD–AS model:

Short-run macroeconomic equilibrium:

Short-run equilibrium aggregate price level:

Short-run equilibrium aggregate output:

Demand shock:

Supply shock:

Stagflation:

Long-run macroeconomic equilibrium:

Recessionary gap:

Inflationary gap:

Output gap:

Self-correcting:

Practice the Model

1) Draw a correctly labeled *AD-AS* graph showing an economy in long-run equilibrium. Show what happens if there is a decrease in aggregate demand. Label the initial output and price level as Y_1 and PL_1, and the new output and price level as Y_2 and PL_2. Label the full employment output as Y_f.

2) Draw a correctly labeled *AD-AS* graph showing an economy in long-run equilibrium. Show what happens if there is an increase in aggregate demand. Label the initial output and price level as Y_1 and PL_1, and the new output and price level as Y_2 and PL_2. Label the full employment output as Y_f.

List questions or difficulties from your initial reading of the module.

AFTER YOU READ THE MODULE

Fill-in-the-Blanks

Fill in the blanks to complete the following statements. If you find yourself having difficulties, please refer back to the appropriate section in the text.

- The short-run macroeconomic equilibrium is found where the aggregate demand curve intersects the

  1)_____ curve. An event that shifts the aggregate demand (or aggregate supply)

  curve is called a demand (or supply) **2)**_____.

- When a curve shifts to the left (or decreases), this is referred to as a

  3) (positive/negative) _____ shock; when a curve shifts to the right (or

  increases) this is called a **4)** (positive/negative) _____ shock. With a supply

  shock, the effect on aggregate price level and aggregate output are in **5)**_____

  directions, but with a demand shock, the effect on aggregate price level and aggregate output will be

  in **6)**_____ direction.

- When there is an increase in the aggregate price level accompanied by a decrease in aggregate output,

  this is called **7)**_____.

- When representing a long-run macroeconomic equilibrium using the *AD-AS* model, the short-run

  macroeconomic equilibrium will occur at a point that is also on the **8)**_____

  curve. If short-run equilibrium occurs at an aggregate output level that is higher than potential output,

  which is to the right of this curve, the economy is experiencing a(n) **9)**_____

  gap. If the short-run equilibrium output is below potential output, which is to the left of the *LRAS*

  curve, there is a(n) **10)**_____ gap.

Multiple-Choice Questions

Circle the best choice to answer or complete the following questions or incomplete statements. For additional practice, use the space provided to explain why one or more of the incorrect options do not work.

11. The full potential output of an economy is $100 million. The current output in the economy is $140 million. Which of the following statements correctly describes this situation?
    a. The economy is experiencing a recessionary gap of $40 million.
    b. This is not possible because an economy cannot produce more than potential output.
    c. The economy is experiencing an inflationary gap of $40 million.
    d. The economy is experiencing an inflationary gap of $100 million.
    e. The economy is experiencing an inflationary gap of $140 million.

12. An economy is in long-run equilibrium and then experiences a supply shock. Which of the following statements must be true?
    a. The aggregate price level must increase.
    b. The aggregate price level must decrease.
    c. The new output level will be different than the full output level.
    d. The long-run aggregate supply curve must shift right.
    e. Aggregate demand must also shift in the short run.

Helpful Tips

- The idea of producing a level of output that is *above* potential output may be difficult to comprehend. How can you produce more than is possible?! For starters, potential output represents the aggregate output that is produced when all prices have had a chance to adjust. As an analogy, consider getting enough sleep. You can temporarily work more, and give up sleep to do so. However, there is a limit to how long you can keep that up. Eventually, the costs of not getting enough sleep will catch up to you, and you will need to decrease your work (and go back to a normal amount of sleep).

Module Notes

In the *AD-AS* model, we refer to both short-run macroeconomic equilibrium and long-run macroeconomic equilibrium. But how can there be two different equilibrium points? Short-run macroeconomic equilibrium occurs when the quantity of aggregate output demanded equals the quantity of aggregate output supplied in the short run. If this occurs at a level of aggregate output other than potential output, over time wage adjustments in the labor market will return aggregate output back to potential output. Short-run macroeconomic equilibrium happens before nominal wages adjust and before the *SRAS* curve shifts. An economy reaches long-run macroeconomic equilibrium after nominal wages fully adjust and the *SRAS* curve shifts so that equilibrium aggregate output is equal to potential output. If short-run equilibrium aggregate output is below potential output, unemployment will put downward pressure on nominal wages; if short-run equilibrium aggregate output is above potential output, high employment will put upward pressure on nominal wages. While nominal wages are sticky in the short run, in the long run nominal wages adjust, shifting *SRAS* so that short-run macroeconomic equilibrium coincides with long-run macroeconomic equilibrium.

Be sure you understand the difference between short-run and long-run macroeconomic equilibria and the relationship between them. In long-run macroeconomic equilibrium, aggregate output equals potential output and the economy's *AD* equals both its short-run and long-run *AS*. In the short run, macroeconomic equilibrium aggregate output need not equal potential output, but the economy's *AD* must intersect the *SRAS*.

MODULE 20 ECONOMIC POLICY AND THE AGGREGATE DEMAND-AGGREGATE SUPPLY MODEL

BEFORE YOU READ THE MODULE

Summary

This module describes how stabilization policy can be used to improve the economy's performance.

Module Objectives

Review these objectives before you read the module. Place a "√" on the line when you can do each of the following:

_____**Objective #1.** Discuss how the *AD–AS* model is used to formulate macroeconomic policy

_____**Objective #2.** Explain the rationale for stabilization policy

_____**Objective #3.** Describe the importance of fiscal policy as a tool for managing economic fluctuations

_____**Objective #4.** Identify the policies that constitute expansionary fiscal policy and those that constitute contractionary fiscal policy

WHILE YOU READ THE MODULE

Key Terms

Define these key terms as you read the module:

Stabilization policy:

Social insurance:

Expansionary fiscal policy:

Contractionary fiscal policy:

Practice the Model

1) Use a correctly labeled *AD-AS* graph to show an economy that has a recessionary gap. Label the current output Y_1, the potential output Y_f, the current price level PL_1, the current *AD* curve as AD_1 and the current *SRAS* curve as $SRAS_1$.

2) On the graph you drew for **1)**, show the effect of expansionary fiscal policy. Label the new output Y_2 and the new price level PL_2. Label any new curve with the subscript "2" and indicate the direction of the change.

List questions or difficulties from your initial reading of the module.

AFTER YOU READ THE MODULE

Fill-in-the-Blanks

Fill in the blanks to complete the following statements. If you find yourself having difficulties, please refer back to the appropriate section in the text.

- Government policy to reduce the severity of recessions and rein in excessively strong expansions is

    called **1)**_____ policy. When there is a recessionary gap, the government can use

    2)_____ fiscal policy to move equilibrium real GDP toward potential output. Three

    ways that fiscal policy can impact an expansionary or inflationary gap are by changing

    3)_____, _____, or _____.

- To eliminate an inflationary gap, the government can use **4)**_____ fiscal policy by

    decreasing **5)**_____ and /or raising **6)**_____. To eliminate a

    recessionary gap, the government can use **7)**_____ policy by decreasing

    8)_____ or increasing **9)**_____.

- Economists caution against an extremely active stabilization policy, arguing that a government that tries too hard to stabilize the economy can end up making the economy less stable, especially because of time **10)**_____.

Multiple-Choice Questions

Circle the best choice to answer or complete the following questions or incomplete statements. For additional practice, use the space provided to explain why one or more of the incorrect options do not work.

11. If an economy is currently producing at a point where current output is less than potential output, then the economy has a(n) _____ gap, and can use _____ fiscal policy to combat it.

	Type of gap	*Policy to combat the gap*
a.	recessionary	contractionary
b.	expansionary	recessionary
c.	recessionary	expansionary
d.	expansionary	contractionary
e.	expansionary	expansionary

12. If an economy is currently producing at a point at which current output is the same as potential output and expansionary fiscal policy is used, this will
    a. create a recessionary gap.
    b. have no effect on the economy.
    c. create an inflationary gap.
    d. shift the *LRAS* curve left.
    e. create a new lower potential output.

Helpful Tips

- You may see potential output called different things. For instance, potential output may also be referred to with terms such as full employment output, or long-run output. They all refer to the same thing: the amount of output that an economy can produce given that the stock of the inputs of production is constant and the prices of those inputs are fully flexible. It is also worth noting that the concept of potential output can be illustrated in different ways using different graphs. On the *AD-AS* graph, potential output is the amount of output where a vertical *LRAS* curve intersects the horizontal axis. On the production possibilities model, potential output is represented by a choice of production that is on the production possibilities curve (rather than a point on the interior of the production possibilities curve).

- Remember that, all else equal, increases in government spending increase *AD*, while increases in taxes decrease aggregate demand.

Module Notes

From the beginning of our study of macroeconomics, we have recognized that increased aggregate output in the economy is a key macroeconomic goal. Why would we ever want to pursue a contractionary fiscal policy and reduce real output? When equilibrium aggregate output is above potential output, it creates inflationary pressures in the economy, and, as we have seen in previous chapters, inflation has costs to the economy. The rising employment required to increase aggregate output above potential output leads to an increase in nominal wages that will eventually shift the *SRAS* curve leftward. This, in turn, brings the economy back to potential output with a higher aggregate price level. So, the ultimate goal of contractionary fiscal policy is not to reduce aggregate output. Aggregate output will eventually decrease back to potential output in any case. The goal of contractionary fiscal policy is to bring the economy back to potential output without a higher aggregate price level. The policy choice is not higher or lower aggregate output in the long run but rather between potential output with inflation or potential output without inflation.

Inflationary gaps can be addressed with contractionary fiscal policy, which involves either an increase in taxes, or a decrease in government spending or transfer payments. Recessionary gaps can be addressed with expansionary fiscal policy, which involves either a decrease in taxes, or an increase in government spending or transfer payments. Even though the goal of expansionary and contractionary fiscal policy is to reduce the impact of large swings in aggregate demand, economists generally do not recommend attempting to "fine tune" the economy, as this can actually backfire and itself cause inflationary or recessionary gaps. Rather, stabilization policy is meant to reduce the impact of inflationary and recessionary gaps, not eliminate them entirely.

MODULE 21 | FISCAL POLICY AND MULTIPLIER EFFECTS

BEFORE YOU READ THE MODULE

Summary

This module applies the multiplier process to the use of fiscal policy to stabilize the economy.

Module Objectives

Review these objectives before you read the module. Place a "√" on the line when you can do each of the following:

_____**Objective #1.** Explain why fiscal policy has a multiplier effect

_____**Objective #2.** Describe how automatic stabilizers influence the multiplier effect

WHILE YOU READ THE MODULE

Key Terms

Define these key terms as you read the module:

Tax multiplier:

Balanced budget multiplier:

Lump-sum taxes:

Automatic stabilizers:

Discretionary fiscal policy:

Practice the Model

Assume an economy is currently producing $400 million in real GDP, but full employment real GDP is $600 million. The economy has a marginal propensity to consume of .75.

1) Calculate the effect of an increase in government spending of $20 million.

2) Determine real GDP after the multiplier effect.

3) Use a correctly labeled *AD-AS* graph to show the impact of the increase in government spending on equilibrium real GDP and price level. Label the initial equilibrium with the price level PL_1 and the output $400 million. Label the full employment output $600 million. Label the new equilibrium after the increase in government spending with a price level of PL_2 and the new real GDP that you found in part 2) as the new equilibrium output.

List questions or difficulties from your initial reading of the module.

AFTER YOU READ THE MODULE

Fill-in-the-Blanks

Fill in the blanks to complete the following statements. If you find yourself having difficulties, please refer back to the appropriate section in the text.

- Any increase in government spending will lead to a larger increase in total spending due to the

    1)_____ effect.   The eventual size of this "chain reaction" will depend on the

    additional consumer spending that happens at each stage of the reaction which is measured by the

    2)_____ or *MPC*. For example, if the *MPC* is .80, the final effect of an

    autonomous increase in aggregate spending will be the amount of the increase in aggregate spending

    multiplied by 3)_____ (the value of the multiplier).

- The effect of changes in taxes and transfers would be **4)**_____ than the effect of changes in government spending because households will **5)**_____ part of the initial change in these. If a government increases government spending, and that increase is paid for by increasing taxes by the same amount, then the final effect on real GDP will be whatever the increase in government spending is, because the balanced budget multiplier is always equal to **6)**_____.

- A **7)**_____ tax is a tax that is owed by households, regardless of what their income is. Government spending and taxation rules that cause fiscal policy to be automatically expansionary when the economy contracts and automatically contractionary when the economy expands, without requiring any deliberate action by policy makers, are called **8)**_____. When fiscal policy isn't automatic, it is known as **9)**_____ fiscal policy.

Multiple-Choice Questions

Circle the best choice to answer or complete the following questions or incomplete statements. For additional practice, use the space provided to explain why one or more of the incorrect options do not work.

10. What would be the final impact on aggregate spending of a decrease in government spending of $100 million, along with a decrease in taxes of $100 million, if the marginal propensity to consume is 0.5?
    a. +$100 million
    b. -$100 million
    c. +$50 million
    d. No change
    e. -$50 million

11. Real GDP in Maxistan is currently $500 million. The government of Maxistan increases government spending by $200 million and increases taxes by $100 million. If the *MPC* in Maxistan is 0.6, real GDP in Maxistan will be:
    a. $850 million.
    b. $350 million.
    c. $20 million.
    d. $80 million.
    e. $800 million.

Helpful Tips

- An increase in government spending and a decrease in taxes both will increase aggregate demand. However, an increase (or decrease) in government spending will always have a larger impact than an increase (or decrease) in taxes. For instance, if taxes are cut by $100 million, this would have less of an impact on real GDP than an increase in government spending in the same amount. This is because the tax multiplier is always smaller than the government spending multiplier.

Module Notes

Suppose that a government decides to spend $50 billion building bridges and roads. The government's purchases of goods and services will directly increase total spending by $50 billion. But there will also be an indirect effect because the government's purchases will start a chain reaction throughout the economy. When you buy something, the money you spend doesn't disappear. For example, it goes into a cash register and becomes income for the seller. The seller will then spend some part of that new income. That spending becomes someone else's income, and so on. The initial spending has a multiplier effect.

How does this multiplier process affect fiscal policy? If any change in spending has a multiplier effect on income, that effect must be considered when determining the amount that G, T, or transfers are changed. If the multiplier process is not considered, then changes in G, T, or transfers will be too large and move the economy past potential output (creating a different problem).

Make sure you are comfortable with the calculations associated with implementing the appropriate fiscal policy in hypothetical situations. Remember that the spending multiplier equals $1/(1 - MPC)$. Start any multiplier problem by finding your multiplier! Then use the equation:

Autonomous change in aggregate spending × multiplier = final change in real GDP

You can then add that change to whatever real GDP was prior to the change to determine what GDP will be as a result of the change (current GDP + final change in real GDP = real GDP after change). For instance, suppose you know the marginal propensity to consume is 0.75 and there is a $100 million autonomous change in government spending. First, find the multiplier

$$1/(1-0.75) = 4$$

Then find the final change in real GDP from the $100 million increase in government spending:

$$\$100 \text{ million} \times 4 = \$400 \text{ million}$$

Two multipliers are presented and used in this module: the multiplier for a change in government spending and the multiplier for a change in taxes. The multiplier for a change in government spending equals $1/(1 - MPC)$, while the multiplier for a change in taxes is smaller $[- MPC/(1 - MPC)]$. For example, if the MPC equals 0.8, then the multiplier for a change in government spending is equal to 5, while the multiplier for a change in taxes is equal to -4. Make sure you work some problems using these multipliers and that you understand why they do not have equivalent values. Also, spend time thinking about why the multiplier for government spending is positive while the multiplier for a change in taxes is negative. Understand the distinction between fiscal policy that is discretionary versus fiscal policy that reflects the impact of automatic stabilizers.

Draw the Featured Model: Aggregate Demand-Aggregate Supply Model

1) Draw an *AD-AS* graph showing long-run macroeconomic equilibrium. Label *AD*, *SRAS*, *LRAS*, potential output (*Yp*), equilibrium aggregate price level (*PL₁*) and output.

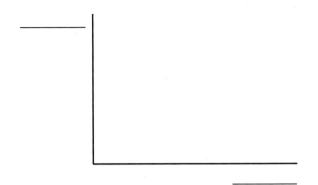

2) Draw a correctly labeled *AD-AS* graph showing a short-run equilibrium when the economy is operating in a recessionary gap. Label *AD*, *SRAS*, *LRAS*, potential output (*Yp*), equilibrium aggregate price level (*PL₁*), and output (*Y₁*).

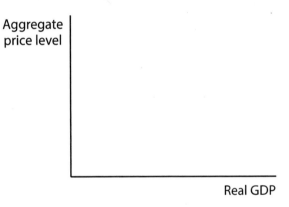

3) Draw a correctly labeled *AD–AS* graph showing a short-run equilibrium when the economy is operating in an inflationary gap. Label *AD*, *SRAS*, *LRAS*, potential output (*Yp*), equilibrium aggregate price level (*PL₁*), and output (*Y₁*).

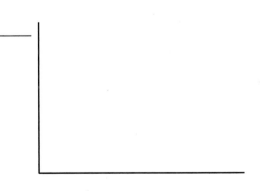

Complete the Exercise

1. Consider an economy that is initially in long-run equilibrium as drawn in the following graph.

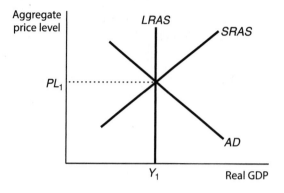

a. For each of the following events, draw an *AD-AS* graph to show the effect of each of the following (*ceteris paribus*) changes. Explain what happens to the aggregate output and price level in each case.

(1) The economy's central bank decreases the money supply.

(i) Aggregate output will_____   (ii) and price level will _____.

_____

(2) Productivity decreases in the economy.   _____

(i) Aggregate output will_____   (ii) and price level will _____.

_____

_____

(3) Consumer confidence in the economy increases.

(i) Aggregate output will____   **(ii)** and price level will _____.

———————

———————

(4) Commodity prices fall dramatically.

(i) Aggregate output will _____   **(ii)** and price level will _____.

———————

———————

b. For each of the cases, in part **a.**, determine whether the economy faces a short-run recessionary gap or an inflationary gap.

Case	Recessionary or Inflationary?
1	_____
2	_____
3	_____
4	_____

c. For each of the cases in part **a.**, what would the impact of a program of expansionary fiscal policy be?

Case	Recessionary or Inflationary or no effect?
1	_____
2	_____
3	_____
4	_____

d. For each of the cases in part **a.**, what would happen in the long run to the aggregate price level and the output level without active stabilization policy?

Case	*Long-run effect on aggregate price level*	*Long-run effect on output*
1	_____	_____
2	_____	_____
3	_____	_____
4	_____	_____

2. For each of the following scenarios, calculate the final increase or decrease in real GDP that is caused by the tax and spending policies described. For all instances, assume that the *MPC* = 0.75. Show all work.

a. Government spending increases by $100 million. There is no change in taxes.

b. Government spending decreases by $20 million. There is no change in taxes.

c. Taxes increase by $100 million. There is no change in government spending.

d. Taxes decrease by $20 million. There is no change in government spending.

e. Taxes increase by $100 million and government spending decreases by $100 million.

f. Taxes increase by $100 million and government spending increases by $100 million.

Problems

1. Mainland is a small, closed economy with no government sector, where the aggregate price level and interest rate are fixed. When disposable income in Mainland is $600, consumption spending is $600. When disposable income is $1,600, consumption spending is $1,350.

a. What equation describes the relationship between consumer spending and disposable income? Use this equation to describe the relationship between consumer spending and disposable income using the values given above. (Your answer should include three equations: the equation that describes the relationship between consumer spending and disposable income in general terms, and two equations that "plug in" the values of disposable income and consumption spending given).

b. Graph the consumption function using the data that is given in the preceding scenario, and use it to calculate the *MPC*.

c. Graph the consumption function for Mainland. On your graph, show the two points representing the consumption and disposable income pairs given in the question, the value of the *MPC* that you found in part **b.**, and the autonomous consumer spending you found in part **b.**

2. You are given the following information about Macroland, a small, closed economy where Y is real GDP, T is taxes, C is consumption spending, and I is planned investment spending. Assume that government spending is currently equal to $0, taxes are constant at $50, and the aggregate price level is originally fixed at $100.

Year	Y	T	C	I
1	$100	$50	$40	$50
2	150	50	80	50
3	300	50	200	50

a. GDP = $C + G + I + X - M$. What are we saying about the calculation of Macroland's GDP if it is a "closed economy"?

b. Fill in the following table using the information given above.

Year	Disposable income
1	
2	
3	

c. What is the *MPC* for this economy?

d. What is the *MPS* for this economy?

e. What is the value of the spending multiplier for this economy?

f. What is the consumption function for this economy?

g. Given the above information, what is the equilibrium output level for this economy?

3. Use a graph of the *AD-AS* model to illustrate long-run economic growth in an economy. Explain how your graph illustrates economic growth. Assume *AD* does *not* change over time.

4. Macroland is a small, closed economy that is currently operating at the long-run equilibrium level of output. It is therefore producing Y_p where Y_p is potential output. Its aggregate price level is PL_1.

   a. Draw a graph of long-run equilibrium for Macroland depicting the *AD*, *SRAS* and *LRAS* curves. Label both axes and identify Y_p and PL_1 on your graph.

b. Suppose that Macroland experiences a negative demand shock. Draw a new graph depicting the short-run changes in the original equilibrium that will occur because of this demand shock. On your graph, identify the new short-run equilibrium level of output Y_2 and the new short-run equilibrium aggregate price level PL_2. Label any shifts in AD or AS clearly.

c. Given the change in part **b.**, draw a third graph illustrating the long-run adjustment to the negative demand shock. Label any shifting curves clearly and identify the new long-run equilibrium level of aggregate output Y_3 and the new long-run aggregate price level PL_3.

d. Given the change in part **b.**, suppose the government wishes to engage in activist fiscal policy in order to restore the economy to its initial equilibrium. Provide two fiscal policies that would accomplish this.

5. For each of the following, describe the effect on the AD, $SRAS$, and $LRAS$ curves, identify if the effect causes a shift of or movement along the curve, and identify the direction of the shift/movement.

   a. An increase in the money supply causes interest rates to fall.

   b. The price of commodities increases by 10% this year.

   c. The price of oil falls.

   d. Labor unions successfully negotiate an increase in nominal wages for their workers.

e. The supply of unsold houses in an economy increases by 20%.

f. There is an increase in labor productivity due to increases in human capital.

g. The government increases spending in order to finance a war.

6. For each of the following situations, identify whether it is an example of expansionary discretionary fiscal policy, contractionary discretionary fiscal policy, or an automatic stabilizer.

   a. During 2011, tax revenue for Macrovia falls as the economy enters a recession.

   b. During 2011, in light of projected deficiencies in *AD*, Macrovia's legislature authorizes an expenditure of $200 million in order to build a new hydroelectric dam.

   c. In 2013, fearing a too rapidly expanding economy, Macrovia adopts a budget that calls for 10% spending cuts in all government departments for the following fiscal year.

   d. In 2012, unemployment benefits rise 5% in response to rising unemployment in Macrovia.

7. The following graph depicts the economy of Macroland's short-run aggregate supply curve (*SRAS*), its long-run aggregate supply curve (*LRAS*), and its aggregate demand curve (*AD*). Macroland is currently producing at point *E*.

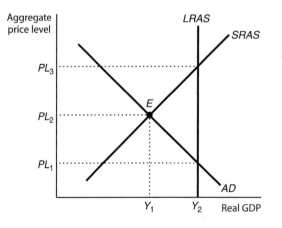

   a. Is potential GDP for Macroland equal to Y_1 or Y_2? Describe Macroland's current production relative to its potential production.

b. Does Macroland have a recessionary gap or an inflationary gap? Explain your answer.

c. Is the current rate of unemployment in Macroland equal to, less than, or greater than the natural rate of unemployment? Explain.

d. Holding everything else constant, which of the following policy initiatives might help Macroland produce at its potential output? Explain how each would increase or decrease the gap you described in **b.**

   i. The government initiates policies that encourage private investment spending.

   ii. The government increases taxes on consumers and corporations.

   iii. The government authorizes new spending programs.

e. What is the current price level in Macroland? If Macroland engages in expansionary fiscal policy so that *AD* shifts and actual output equals potential output, what will happen to the price level?

8. Funlandia's economists estimate its potential output is $100 in year 1 and grows 5% per year. Assume Funlandia is a closed economy.

a. Fill in the following table for Funlandia, given the above information.

Year	Potential output
Year 1	$100
Year 2	
Year 3	
Year 4	

Suppose Funlandia's economists provide you with the following data (all numbers are in dollars).

Year	Potential output	Actual output	T	YD	C	I	G
Year 1	100		10	90	55	30	15
Year 2		104	10			30	17
Year 3		115	10			30	22.5
Year 4			10	108	64	30	24

b. What is the consumption function for this economy?

c. Fill in the missing values for the table using the information you have been given or that you computed in parts **a.** and **b.**

d. Fill in the following table for Funlandia.

Year	Recessionary gap	Inflationary gap	Actual output equals potential output
Year 1	No	No	Yes
Year 2			
Year 3			
Year 4			

e. Suppose Funlandia maintains a policy of using discretionary fiscal policy to ensure that actual output equals potential output. Summarize the recommended discretionary fiscal policy necessary to achieve this goal in the following table.

Year	Discretionary fiscal policy
Year 1	
Year 2	
Year 3	
Year 4	

9. The *AD-AS* model is said to have a self-correcting mechanism. Explain what this means and how this self-correcting mechanism works.

10. Explain why automatic stabilizers reduce the size of the multiplier. Provide several examples of automatic stabilizers and their effect on the economy during economic fluctuations.

Review Questions

Circle your answer to the following questions.

1. A shift in the consumer spending function is caused by changes in
   a. current disposable income and expected future disposable income.
   b. current disposable income and aggregate wealth.
   c. aggregate wealth and the marginal propensity to consume.
   d. the marginal propensity to consume and expected future disposable income.
   e. expected future disposable income and aggregate wealth.

2. Gabriella's disposable income increases by $100 and she saves $20 of it. How much does Gabriella spend and what is her *MPC* and *MPS*?

	Gabriella spends	*MPC*	*MPS*
a.	$120 if she gets a $100 increase in income	0.2	0.8
b.	$80 if she gets a $120 increase in income	0.8	0.2
c.	$400 if she gets a $500 increase in income	0.8	0.2
d.	$100 if she gets a $500 increase in income	0.2	0.8
e.	$100 if she gets a $400 increase in income	0.8	0.2

3. Suppose when Sue's disposable income is $10,000 she spends $8,000 and when her disposable income is $20,000 she spends $14,000. Sue's autonomous consumer spending is equal to _____ and her *MPS* is equal to _____.

	Autonomous Spending	*MPS*
a.	$0	0.2
b.	$2,000	0.2
c.	$0	0.4
d.	$2,000	0.4
e.	$10,000	0.8

4. Planned investment spending depends on the
   a. past level of real GDP.
   b. marginal propensity to consume.
   c. unplanned investment spending.
   d. interest rate.
   e. future production capacity.

5. When interest rates rise, this
   a. does not affect the profitability of investments financed through retained earnings.
   b. makes any given investment project more profitable.
   c. does not affect the opportunity cost of an investment financed through retained earnings.
   d. leads to a lower level of planned investment spending, holding everything else constant.
   e. does not affect planned investment spending.

6. Nominal wages
   a. are never determined by contracts that were signed at some previous point in time.
   b. are slow to decrease in times of high unemployment, since employers may be reluctant to alter wages as a response to economic conditions.
   c. are fully flexible in the short run.
   d. are adjusted for inflation.
   e. are not flexible in the long run.

7. Which of the following statements is true? In the short run, holding everything else constant,
    a. as production costs increase, profit per unit decreases, and this causes suppliers to increase their production.
    b. as production costs increase, profit per unit decreases, and this causes suppliers to reduce their production.
    c. as production costs decrease, profit per unit increases, and this causes suppliers to reduce their production.
    d. the *AS* curve is unaffected by changes in production costs.
    e. the *AS* curve can fully adjust to all changes in the cost of production.

8. Which of the following will make the *AS* curve shift to the left?
    a. a decrease in the aggregate price level
    b. a decrease in commodity prices
    c. an increase in nominal wages
    d. a positive supply shock
    e. a decrease in unemployment

9. Suppose the economy is in short-run equilibrium and the level of aggregate output is less than potential output. Then it must be true that
    a. unemployment in this economy is relatively low.
    b. over time the short-run *AS* curve will shift to the left.
    c. over time nominal wages will fall.
    d. the economy is also in long-run equilibrium.
    e. there has been technological progress.

10. Which of the following statements is true?
    a. In a recessionary gap, aggregate output exceeds potential output.
    b. In an inflationary gap, aggregate output exceeds potential output.
    c. A recessionary gap is a long-run phenomenon that requires government action to eliminate.
    d. Recessionary gaps and inflationary gaps, if they exist, will be eliminated in the short run by the natural workings of the economy.
    e. A recessionary gap will cause the long-run aggregate supply curve to increase.

11. An increase in the interest rate, holding everything else constant,
    a. reduces investment spending since the cost of borrowing is now higher.
    b. increases consumer spending since households respond to higher interest rates by buying more.
    c. leads to an increase in the level of aggregate demand for final goods and services.
    d. increases planned investment.
    e. shifts the aggregate demand curve to the right.

12. Which of the following policies will shift the *AD* curve to the right?
    a. The government increases its level of taxation in the economy.
    b. The government decreases the money supply in the economy.
    c. The government decreases its level of taxation in the economy.
    d. The government decreases its level of spending in the economy.
    e. The government decreases government spending but decreases taxes by an equivalent amount.

13. Suppose an economy is currently in short-run equilibrium where the level of real GDP is less than potential output. Which of the following statements is true?
    a. In the long run, nominal wages will fall and the *SRAS* curve will shift to the left, restoring the economy to potential output.
    b. In the long run, nominal wages will fall and the *SRAS* curve will shift to the right, restoring the economy to potential output.
    c. In the long run, nominal wages will fall and the *AD* curve will shift to the left, restoring the economy to potential output.
    d. In the long run, nominal wages will fall and the *AD* curve will shift to the right, restoring the economy to potential output.
    e. In the long run, the long-run aggregate supply curve will shift to the right, restoring the economy to potential output.

14. Suppose a government increases government spending by $300 million and the *MPC* = 0.75. If the government wanted to completely offset the effect of this increase in spending, by how much would it have to increase taxes?
    a. $1,200 million
    b. $300 million
    c. $400 million
    d. $100 million
    e. $375 million

15. Suppose an economy is initially in long-run equilibrium. Then, holding everything else constant, there is an increase in people's wealth in this economy. If the government wishes to maintain the same aggregate price level and aggregate level of real GDP as it had initially, it should increase
    a. government spending.
    b. the money supply.
    c. the level of investment spending.
    d. the level of taxes.
    e. the long-run aggregate supply curve.

16. Contractionary fiscal policy
    a. is most helpful for restoring an economy to the potential output level of production when there is a recessionary gap.
    b. shifts the *AD* curve to the right, restoring the equilibrium level of output to the potential output level for the economy.
    c. often causes inflation or an increase in the aggregate price level.
    d. if effective, shifts *AD* to the left, resulting in a reduction in the aggregate output and the aggregate price level for a given short-run aggregate supply curve (*SRAS*).
    e. uses the money supply to influence aggregate demand.

17. Which of the following statements is true?
    a. An economy can eliminate an inflationary gap by increasing government spending.
    b. Expansionary fiscal policy refers to an increase in taxes.
    c. When potential output is greater than actual aggregate output, the economy faces an inflationary gap.
    d. When *SRAS* intersects *AD* to the right of the long-run aggregate supply (*LRAS*) curve, the economy faces a recessionary gap.
    e. Increasing taxes and decreasing government spending by an equivalent amount will have no effect on *AD*.

18. Monetary and fiscal policy
   a. affect the economy in predictable ways and with relatively short time lags.
   b. involve significant time lags with regard to their implementation and effect on the economy.
   c. take so long to implement in the economy that they prove to be useless policies.
   d. when implemented always worsen economic fluctuations because of the lags involved in their implementation.
   e. can only be used to fix inflationary gaps.

19. All else equal, which statement below is true of the relationship between the tax multiplier and the spending multiplier?
   a. The spending multiplier is always less than the tax multiplier.
   b. The tax multiplier is always less than the spending multiplier.
   c. The tax multiplier is always twice as much as the spending multiplier.
   d. The spending multiplier is always twice as much as the tax multiplier.
   e. The tax multiplier is always equal to the spending multiplier.

20. The economy of Grizzly has a recessionary gap of $500 million. The marginal propensity to consume in Grizzly is 0.75. In response, the government increases government spending by $125 million and increases taxes by $50 million. What is the final impact of the increase in government spending and the increase in taxes on aggregate demand, and will the recessionary gap be closed?

	Final impact of increase in government spending on AD	*Will recessionary gap be closed?*
a.	Increase *AD* by $125 million	Yes
b.	Increase *AD* by $112.5 million	No
c.	Increase *AD* by $600 million	No
d.	Increase *AD* by $600 million	Yes
e.	Increase *AD* by $500 million	No

Section ⑤ The Financial Sector

Overview

This section presents the financial sector of the economy and explains how it facilitates economic activity. It discusses the various types of financial assets, savings, and investment, and looks at the operation of the financial system. It also discusses the institutions that make up the financial system, including banking and the Federal Reserve System, and the role of these institutions in economic policy. Finally, it explores the money market and the loanable funds market.

Featured Model/Graph: Money Market/Loanable Funds Market

This section presents two closely related markets - the money market and the market for loanable funds. Understanding these two markets, their similarities and their differences, is essential for understanding monetary policy.

MODULES IN THIS SECTION

Module 22   **Saving, Investment, and the Financial System**

Module 23   **The Definition and Measurement of Money**

Module 24   **The Time Value of Money**

Module 25   **Banking and Money Creation**

Module 26   **The Federal Reserve System: History and Structure**

Module 27   **The Federal Reserve System: Monetary Policy**

Module 28   **The Money Market**

Module 29   **The Market for Loanable Funds**

BEFORE YOU TACKLE THE TEST

Draw the Featured Model

Complete the Exercise

Problems

Review Questions

MODULE 22 · SAVING, INVESTMENT, AND THE FINANCIAL SYSTEM

BEFORE YOU READ THE MODULE

Summary

This module explains how investment spending is financed through the relationship between savings and investment spending for the economy as a whole.

Module Objectives

Review these objectives before you read the module. Place a "√" on the line when you can do each of the following:

_____**Objective #1.** Describe the relationship between savings and investment spending

_____**Objective #2.** Explain how financial intermediaries help investors achieve diversification

_____**Objective #3.** Identify the purposes of the four principal types of financial assets: stocks, bonds, loans, and bank deposits

WHILE YOU READ THE MODULE

Key Terms

Define these key terms as you read the module:

Interest rate:

Savings–investment spending identity:

Budget surplus:

Budget deficit:

Budget balance:

National savings:

Capital inflow:

Wealth:

Financial asset:

Physical asset:

Liability:

Transaction costs:

Financial risk:

Diversification:

Liquid:

Illiquid:

Loan:

Default:

Loan-backed security:

Financial intermediary:

Mutual fund:

Pension fund:

Life insurance company:

Bank deposit:

Bank:

Practice the Model

The text explains the Savings = Identity equation (see equations 22-1 through 22-5) in a situation without government. Government can be added to the model by including government spending and taxes. Domestic savings now has two parts: saving by households and saving by the government:

$$\text{Savings} = (\text{Income - Consumption - Taxes}) + (\text{Taxes - Government Spending})$$

Use this equation to answer the following:

1)   What is the impact on savings if there is a budget deficit (taxes are less than government spending)?

2)   What is the impact on savings if there is a budget surplus (taxes are greater than government spending)?

List questions or difficulties from your initial reading of the module.

AFTER YOU READ THE MODULE

Fill-in-the-Blanks

Fill in the blanks to complete the following statements. If you find yourself having difficulties, please refer back to the appropriate section in the text.

- It is an accounting fact that investment spending will always be equal to **1)**_____.

  Governments, as well as individuals, can save. The government saves when its tax revenues exceed

  its spending; this difference is called a budget **2)**_____. If government spending

  exceeds tax revenue, it is called a budget **3)**_____. The term "budget balance"

  refers to either situation (a budget surplus or a budget deficit). The sum of private savings and the

  budget balance is called **4)**_____.

- The savings of people who live in any one country can be used to finance investment spending that

  takes place in other countries. The amount of foreign savings that come into a country, minus the

  amount of domestic savings that goes to other countries, are known as **5)**_____ in-

  flows.

- The three tasks of a financial system are to reduce **6)**_____and _____,

  and to provide **7)**_____. An institution that transforms funds from many

  individuals into financial assets is called a(n) **8)**_____.

Multiple-Choice Questions

Circle the best choice to answer or complete the following questions or incomplete statements. For additional practice, use the space provided to explain why one or more of the incorrect options do not work.

9. GDP in the nation of Erd is $400 million, taxes are $50 million, and consumption spending is $200 million. If total investment is $75 million, what is the amount of government spending? (Assume Erd is a closed economy.)
   a. The answer cannot be determined without knowing more information.
   b. $125 million
   c. -$125 million
   d. $150 million
   e. $25 million

10. GDP in the nation of Mek is $500 million, consumption spending is $300 million, taxes are $75 million, and government spending is $160 million. If Mek is an open economy and investment is $90 million, what must the capital flow equal?
  a. $160 million, a net capital outflow
  b. -$40 million, a net capital outflow
  c. $40 million, a net capital inflow
  d. $50 million, a net capital inflow
  e. $160 million, a net capital inflow

11. A bank deposit is a(n) _____ to a bank and a(n) _____ to the person who made the deposit.
  a. liability, liability
  b. bond, liability
  c. liability, bond
  d. asset, liability
  e. liability, asset

Helpful Tips

- The idea of private savings is fairly intuitive; we are used to the idea of households saving a portion of their income. But it is important to remember that savings comes from other sources as well – the budget balance and capital inflows.

- The budget balance and a balanced budget sound the same, but they are not! A balanced budget means specifically that taxes and government spending are equal to each other. The budget balance, on the other hand, has three possibilities: a balanced budget ($T = G$), a budget deficit ($G > T$), or a budget surplus ($G < T$).

Module Notes

When macroeconomists use the term *investment spending,* they almost always mean "spending on new physical capital." This can be confusing, because in ordinary life we often say that someone who buys stocks or purchases an existing building is "investing." The important point to keep in mind is that only spending that adds to the economy's stock of physical capital is "investment spending." In contrast, the act of purchasing an asset such as a share of stock, a bond, or existing real estate is "making an investment."

It's important to understand clearly the three different kinds of capital: physical capital, human capital, and financial capital. Physical capital consists of manufactured resources such as buildings and machines. Human capital is the improvement in the labor force generated by education and knowledge. Financial capital is funds from savings that are available for investment spending. So, a country that has a positive capital inflow is experiencing a flow of funds into the country from abroad that can be used for spending on physical capital.

It is important to understand that savings and investment spending are always equal whether the economy is open or closed. This is an accounting fact and is referred to as the savings-investment spending identity.

It is good to have a basic idea of the definition of and differences between the types of financial assets. However, don't spend lots of time memorizing specific definitions and detailed distinctions. Strive to understand the categories of assets in the context of the macroeconomic models we are developing.

MODULE 23 THE DEFINITION AND MEASUREMENT OF MONEY

BEFORE YOU READ THE MODULE

Summary

This module defines money and explains what distinguishes money from other forms of wealth.

Module Objectives

Review these objectives before you read the module. Place a "√" on the line when you can do each of the following:

_____**Objective #1.** Identify the functions of money

_____**Objective #2.** Explain the various roles money plays and the many forms it takes in the economy

_____**Objective #3.** Describe how the amount of money in the economy is measured

WHILE YOU READ THE MODULE

Key Terms

Define these key terms as you read the module:

Money:

Currency in circulation:

Checkable bank deposits:

Money supply:

Medium of exchange:

Store of value:

Unit of account:

Commodity money:

Commodity-backed money:

Fiat money:

Monetary aggregate:

Near-moneys:

Practice the Model

The nation of Ted uses the dollar as its currency. The dollar is not a commodity-backed currency. The following table describes Ted's assets.

Currency in circulation	$40 million
Checkable deposits	$80 million
Savings account deposits	$70 million
Money market funds	$30 million
Gold bricks	$100 million

1) For each of the assets listed above, indicate whether or not it is counted in the money supply. If it is included in the money supply, indicate whether it is part of M1 or M2.

2) Calculate the value of M1 and M2.

List questions or difficulties from your initial reading of the module.

AFTER YOU READ THE MODULE

Fill-in-the-Blanks

Fill in the blanks to complete the following statements. If you find yourself having difficulties, please refer back to the appropriate section in the text.

- Any asset that is liquid (i.e. can easily be used to purchase goods and services) is considered

  1)_____. When money is used as the commonly accepted way of measuring the

  value of goods, money is serving as a 2)_____. When money is used to purchase

  goods and services, money is serving as a 3)_____.

- When a particular form of money loses its purchasing power over time, the money no longer serves as

  a 4)_____. When the value of money derives entirely from its official status as a

  means of exchange, it is known as 5)_____ money. If money is backed by an asset

  with intrinsic value, it is called 6)_____ money. The monetary aggregates measure

  the value of the money supply as defined from most liquid to least liquid. The most liquid measure

  form of the money supply is 7)_____. The slightly less liquid measure of the

  money supply is 8)_____, Other types of even less liquid assets are known as

  9)_____.

Multiple-Choice Questions

Circle the best choice to answer or complete the following questions or incomplete statements. For additional practice, use the space provided to explain why one or more of the incorrect options do not work.

10. Commodity money is
    a. backed by faith in the government.
    b. used to buy agricultural products.
    c. backed by gold or silver.
    d. also a good.
    e. earned by selling goods and services.

11. Eric goes to buy a $10 box of dog treats at the store. When he arrives at the store, his $10 can no longer buy a box of dog treats. Eric's money has failed to serve as a

   a. commodity money.
   b. unit of account.
   c. medium of exchange.
   d. money supply.
   e. store of value.

Helpful Tips

- Don't forget that M1 is included in M2. For instance, suppose an economy has $40 million in M1 and $80 million in M2. If people move $5 million from checkable deposits to savings accounts, M1 decreases but M2 does not because M2 includes M1.

Module Notes

Why aren't financial assets like stocks and bonds part of the money supply? The answer ultimately has to do with liquidity. Remember that the definition of liquidity is anything that can easily be used to purchase goods or services. M1 consists, roughly speaking, of assets you can use to buy groceries: currency, traveler's checks, and checkable deposits. These are very liquid assets. M2 is broader, because it includes things like savings accounts that can easily and quickly be converted into M1. Savings accounts are slightly less liquid than checking accounts; for example, many savings accounts require you to wait 10 days after a deposit to withdraw some or all of those funds. Likewise, certificates of deposit have some time limits on when they can be converted into currency. By contrast, converting a stock or a bond into cash requires selling the stock or bond—something that usually takes some time and also involves paying a broker's fee. That makes these assets much less liquid than bank deposits.

It is important to understand the distinction between assets and liabilities. Make sure you clearly understand what an asset and a liability are and then recognize that any financial instrument represents both an asset and a liability. For example, a mortgage represents a liability for the borrower and an asset for the lender; similarly, a checking account deposit represents a liability for the bank providing the check service and an asset to the individual depositing the funds.

MODULE 24   THE TIME VALUE OF MONEY

BEFORE YOU READ THE MODULE

Summary

This module explains how time is an issue in economic decision-making.

Module Objectives

Review these objectives before you read the module. Place a "√" on the line when you can do each of the following:

_____**Objective #1.**   Explain why a dollar today is worth more than a dollar a year from now

_____**Objective #2.**   Use the concept of present value to make better decisions about costs and benefits that come in the future

WHILE YOU READ THE MODULE

Key Terms

Define these key terms as you read the module:

Future value:

Present value:

Net present value:

Practice the Model

1) Assume you have just won an essay competition, and you are offered two options for your prize money, either $500 one year from now or $450 today. If the interest rate is 5%, which prize do you accept? Explain.

2) What amount of prize money offered today would be the same as being paid $500 in two years?

List questions or difficulties from your initial reading of the module.

AFTER YOU READ THE MODULE

Fill-in-the-Blanks

Fill in the blanks to complete the following statements. If you find yourself having difficulties, please refer back to the appropriate section in the text.

- Which is worth more, having a dollar today or having a dollar one year from now? Having a dollar

  1)_____ is worth more. The amount you would be willing to accept today, in

  exchange for $1 paid one year from today, is known as **2)**_____. The present value

  of $1 paid one year from today when the interest rate is "r" is equal to **3)**_____.

  The present value of current and future benefits minus the present value of current and future costs is

  called **4)**_____.

Multiple-Choice Questions

Circle the best choice to answer or complete the following questions or incomplete statements. For additional practice, use the space provided to explain why one or more of the incorrect options do not work.

5. The net present value of _____in one year is $800 if the interest rate is 20%.
   a. $960
   b. $1,000
   c. $820
   d. $780
   e. $1,200

6. What is the value in one year of an asset worth $400 today if the interest rate is 25%?
   a. $425
   b. $500
   c. $475
   d. $375
   e. $525

Helpful Tips

- Make sure to use present value and future value calculations whenever payments occur over time. Any payment received in the future is not worth as much as if it were received today and any payment received today is worth more than if it were received in the future. Another way to look at it, if you are receiving interest, the future value is greater, and if you are paying interest, the present value is greater.

Module Notes

Understanding present value requires understanding two important points. First, a dollar today is worth more than a dollar in the future. If you receive a dollar today, you can either spend the dollar immediately (and enjoy the benefits of what you buy with it) OR you can save the dollar (and earn interest on it until you decide to spend it in the future). In either case, spending now or saving for later, you gain more from having the dollar right away. Second, the interest rate determines the tradeoff between receiving a dollar today and receiving it tomorrow. The interest rate is what borrowers are willing to pay to have a dollar to spend immediately and what lenders must receive in order to give up their dollar until a future date. Approach present value with this in mind and you will be better able to apply the concept to decision making when costs and/or benefits come in the future than if you try to memorize a formula without understanding its underlying principles.

MODULE 25 | BANKING AND MONEY CREATION

BEFORE YOU READ THE MODULE

Summary

This module presents the monetary role of banks.

Module Objectives

Review these objectives before you read the module. Place a "√" on the line when you can do each of the following:

_____**Objective #1.** Describe the role of banks in the economy

_____**Objective #2.** Identify the reasons for and types of banking regulation

_____**Objective #3.** Explain how banks create money

WHILE YOU READ THE MODULE

Key Terms

Define these key terms as you read the module:

Bank reserves:

T-account:

Reserve ratio:

Required reserve ratio:

Bank run:

Deposit insurance:

Reserve requirements:

Discount window:

Excess reserves:

Monetary base:

Money multiplier:

Practice the Model

Suppose an economy has $1,000 currency in circulation and no checkable deposits or other near monies.

1) What is the money supply in this economy, and why does M1 = M2 in this case?

2) Assume that all $1,000 of currency is deposited into the only bank in this economy. Before any loans are made using the deposit, what is the money supply in this economy? Does M1 still equal M2? Has the money supply changed? Show the T-account for the bank as a result of this deposit.

3) Assume the reserve requirement for this economy is 10%. How much can the bank loan from this initial deposit?

4) Suppose the bank loans the amount you found in **3)** to an individual. What are M1, M2, and the money supply at this point if that individual keeps that loan as cash? Show the bank's T-account after the loan is made.

5) Suppose instead that the individual deposits that loan into a bank, banks keep no excess reserves, and no one keeps loans as cash. What is the maximum amount that the money supply can increase based on a reserve requirement of 10% and an initial deposit of $1,000?

List questions or difficulties from your initial reading of the module.

AFTER YOU READ THE MODULE

Fill-in-the-Blanks

Fill in the blanks to complete the following statements. If you find yourself having difficulties, please refer back to the appropriate section in the text.

- Currency in bank vaults and bank deposits held at the Federal Reserve are called

  1)_____. The fraction of bank deposits that a bank holds as reserves is its

  2)_____. When many of a bank's depositors try to withdraw their funds due to

  fears of a bank failure, it is known as a **3)**_____. Banking regulation to prevent

  bank failures has three main features: **4)**_____, _____, and

  _____. FDIC deposit insurance guarantees the first **5)**_____

  dollars of each bank account. Reserve requirements are set by the **6)**_____, which

  also makes loans to banks through its **7)**_____ window. Banks create money by

  lending out their **8)**_____ reserves.

Multiple-Choice Questions

Circle the best choice to answer or complete the following questions or incomplete statements. For additional practice, use the space provided to explain why one or more of the incorrect options do not work.

9. Which of the following is counted as part of M2?
   a. required reserves
   b. excess reserves
   c. checkable deposits
   d. treasury bonds
   e. gold

10. Suppose the reserve requirement is 20% and there is a $100,000 initial deposit into a bank. The money supply will increase by how much after the multiple expansion of deposits?
    a. $20,000
    b. $200,000
    c. more than $2,000,000
    d. $50,000
    e. less than $500,000

Helpful Tips

- Reserves kept in vaults are not money. The key to why this is so is to remember that money is something that can easily be converted into a liquid asset. Since money kept as reserve cannot be spent, it doesn't perform that function of money and so is not counted in the money supply. This is why lending creates money.

- Creating money is not the same as creating/printing currency. In a fiat money system, currency is just one of the forms that money can take. This is why banks create money, and the United States Treasury (which prints it) does not.

Module Notes

The idea that banks can "create" money can be difficult to understand unless you understand the definition of money and how it is measured. When we say that banks create money, we don't mean that they create it in the same way they did before the Civil War – by printing certificates that could be redeemed for silver coins on demand. We mean that banks are able to expand the money supply through lending.

Today, dollar bills are printed by the Treasury Department and issued into the economy by regional Federal Reserve banks. Banks no longer create currency. But recall that the supply of money in the economy consists of more than currency. The M1 definition of money includes currency in circulation, traveler's checks, and checkable bank deposits. It is through loans, which change the amount of checkable deposits, that banks create money. Because we have a fractional reserve banking system (banks are required to keep only a fraction of their deposits as cash in their vaults or on deposit at the Fed), when banks receive a new deposit, they can increase their loans. When they make a loan, they increase the amount of checkable deposits, thereby increasing the money supply.

It is important to understand the definitions of and the distinction between the monetary base, the money supply, and reserves. The money supply is the value of financial assets in the economy that are considered money: this would include cash in the hands of the public, checkable bank deposits, and traveler's checks. Bank reserves are composed of the currency banks hold in their vaults plus their deposits at the Federal Reserve. The monetary base is the sum of currency in circulation and bank reserves. The monetary base is smaller than the money supply.

MODULE 26 THE FEDERAL RESERVE SYSTEM: HISTORY AND STRUCTURE

BEFORE YOU READ THE MODULE

Summary

This module introduces the Federal Reserve System, the U.S. central bank. It explains how central banks oversee and regulate the banking system, and control the monetary base.

Module Objectives

Review these objectives before you read the module. Place a "√" on the line when you can do each of the following:

_____**Objective #1.**   Discuss the history of the Federal Reserve System

_____**Objective #2.**   Describe the structure of the Federal Reserve System

_____**Objective #3.**   Explain how the Federal Reserve has responded to major financial crises

WHILE YOU READ THE MODULE

Key Terms

Define these key terms as you read the module:

Central bank:

Commercial bank:

Investment bank:

Savings and loan (thrift):

Practice the Model

Suppose a bank has 4 deposits in the amounts of $2,000, $4,000, $6,000, and $5,000 and loans in the amount of $10,000. Deposits are shown as liabilities in the bank's T-account and loans are shown as assets. If the reserve ratio is 20%, the bank's T-account would look like this:

Assets	Liabilities
Required reserves: $3,400 (20% of $17,000) Loans: $10,000 Excess reserves: $3,600	$2,000 Deposit 1 $4,000 Deposit 2 $6,000 Deposit 3 $5,000 Deposit 4
Total:$17,000	Total: $17,000

1) Suppose deposit #1 is withdrawn. Show the bank's T-account after the withdrawal.

2) Would the bank be able to provide cash to depositor #3 for withdrawal?

List questions or difficulties from your initial reading of the module.

AFTER YOU READ THE MODULE

Fill-in-the-Blanks

Fill in the blanks to complete the following statements. If you find yourself having difficulties, please refer back to the appropriate section in the text.

- The **1)**_____ is the central bank of the United States. It is overseen by the

  2)_____, which is part of the federal government, and its services are provided by

  the **3)**_____ regional reserve banks. There are **4)**_____

  governors appointed to the Board of Governors for **5)**_____ year terms. The New

  York Federal Reserve bank carries out the most important function of monetary policy, conducting

  6)_____.

- The Glass- Steagall Act of 1933 separated banks into two categories; **7)**_____ and

  8)_____ banks.

9. Which of the following events led to the creation of the Federal Reserve System?
   a. The Great Depression
   b. The 2008 Great Recession
   c. The Glass-Steagall Act of 1933
   d. The Panic of 1907
   e. The 1980 Elimination of Regulation Q

10. Which of the following is responsible for making monetary policy decisions?
   a. The Federal Reserve Bank of Washington
   b. The Federal Reserve Bank of New York
   c. The Treasury
   d. Congress and the President of the United States
   e. The Federal Open Market Committee

Helpful Tips

- Make sure you understand the difference between fiscal policy and monetary policy, and the decision makers for each. Monetary policy is conducted by a central bank, while fiscal policy is conducted by the government (e.g. Congress and the President).

Module Notes

The central bank of the United States is more than a single bank – it is a multi-part system. When the Fed was created in 1913, its creation was influenced by the politics and geography of the country at that time (for example, look at the locations of the 12 regional Federal Reserve banks). The Federal Reserve System has both public and private elements as well as regional banks spread across the country. The important parts of the Federal Reserve System are summarized below.

The Board of Governors is a government agency located in Washington, D.C., that oversees the Federal Reserve System. The Board has 7 members, appointed by the President and approved by the Senate for 14-year terms. Because Governors can be appointed to complete the terms of a Governor who did not complete his or her 14-year term (and can then serve their own 14-year term), some Governors serve more than 14 years. The Chairman of the Board of Governors is appointed every 4 years.

The 12 Federal Reserve banks are privately owned. They are owned by the member commercial banks in their district. They are overseen by Boards of Directors, which appoint their presidents. Federal Reserve banks are non profit --their operating budgets come from fees charged to the commercial banks they serve. If regional Federal Reserve Bank revenues exceed their expenses, the difference is given to the Treasury. Fed banks are not government agencies and are not funded by taxes.

The Federal Open Market Committee (FOMC) makes decisions about monetary policy. The FOMC has 12 voting members at any given time. It is made up of the 7 members of the Board of Governors, the president of the New York Federal Reserve Bank, and the other 11 regional Federal Reserve Bank presidents. Only 4 of the other 11 regional Federal Reserve Bank presidents vote at any given time. Voting seats are rotated among the 11 other regional Federal Reserve Bank presidents.

MODULE ⟨27⟩   THE FEDERAL RESERVE SYSTEM: MONETARY POLICY

BEFORE YOU READ THE MODULE

Summary

This module presents the functions of the Federal Reserve System and how it serves them.

Module Objectives

Review these objectives before you read the module. Place a "√" on the line when you can do each of the following:

_____ **Objective #1.** Describe the functions of the Federal Reserve System

_____ **Objective #2.** Explain the primary tools the Federal Reserve uses to influence the economy

WHILE YOU READ THE MODULE

Key Terms

Define these key terms as you read the module:

Federal funds market:

Federal funds rate:

Discount rate:

Open-market operation:

Practice the Model

Use the information about a bank provided in the table to answer the following questions.

Deposits	$1,000,000
Required reserve ratio	10%
Bank's current reserves	$100,000
Loans issued by the bank	$400,000
Treasury bonds owned by the bank	$500,000

1) Show the T-account for this bank. Use Figure 27.2 in your textbook as your guide.

2) Can the bank make any loans? Explain.

3) Suppose the Federal Reserve purchases the $500,000 in Treasury bonds from the bank. Show how the bank's T-account would change.

4) Does the bank have to keep 10% of the $500,000 payment for the bonds as reserves? Explain.

List questions or difficulties from your initial reading of the module.

AFTER YOU READ THE MODULE

Fill-in-the-Blanks

Fill in the blanks to complete the following statements. If you find yourself having difficulties, please refer back to the appropriate section in the text.

- The four functions of The Fed are **1)**_____, **2)**_____,

  3)_____, and most importantly **4)**_____.

- The Fed has three main tools it uses to conduct monetary policy: **5)**_____,

  _____, and _____. Of these, **6)**_____ are

  the primary tool of monetary policy.

- When banks need to borrow additional reserves from other banks, they do so through the

  7)_____ market. When banks need to borrow reserves from the Fed, they may do

  so by paying the **8)**_____ rate. **9)**_____ operations occur when

  the Fed buys or sells U.S. Treasury bills through a transaction with commercial banks.

Multiple-Choice Questions

Circle the best choice to answer or complete the following questions or incomplete statements. For additional practice, use the space provided to explain why one or more of the incorrect options do not work.

10. If the Fed purchases securities on the open market, this will _____ the money supply and _____ change the Fed's balance sheet.
   a. increase; will not
   b. increase; will
   c. decrease; will not
   d. decrease; will
   e. not change; will

11. The money supply will decrease if the Fed does which of the following?
   a. increases taxes
   b. sells securities
   c. increases the discount rate
   d. increases the federal funds rate
   e. prints more currency

Helpful Tips

- Open market operations are the most common action the Fed uses to conduct monetary policy. When a question asks about performing open market operations to conduct monetary policy, make sure your answer is an open market operation – buying or selling bonds. For instance, while it is true that the Fed could use the discount rate to alter the money supply, changing the discount rate is not an "open market operation."

Module Notes

The term "open market operations" refers to buying and selling United States Treasury securities (Treasury bills, notes, and bonds). The Federal Reserve Bank of New York plays an important role in monetary policy because it conducts the purchases and sales of securities for the Fed. The Open Market Desk at the NY Fed buys and sells securities through auctions (i.e. on the "open market"). First, Treasury securities are bought and sold to finance the federal government debt and to conduct monetary policy. Most Treasury securities sold through Federal Reserve auctions are bought by primary dealers - financial institutions that buy and sell large quantities of government securities and have established business relationships with the New York Fed. Currently, there are approximately 19 primary dealers. Others can purchase Treasury bills, notes, and bonds from banks or brokers in the secondary market.

In addition to selling securities to finance the federal debt, the New York Fed's Open Market Desk buys and sells Treasury bills, notes, and bonds to carry out the monetary policy designated by the FOMC.

Remember that when the Fed purchases Treasury bills, it injects reserves into the banking system, increasing the money supply. On the other hand, when the Fed sells Treasury bills, it removes reserves from the banking system, decreasing the money supply.

MODULE 28   THE MONEY MARKET

BEFORE YOU READ THE MODULE

Summary

This module examines the money market and how it is used to determine *the interest rate and the quantity of money* in the economy.

Module Objectives

Review these objectives before you read the module. Place a "√" on the line when you can do each of the following:

_____**Objective #1.**   Illustrate the relationship between the demand for money and the interest rate with a graph

_____**Objective #2.**   Explain why the liquidity preference model determines the interest rate in the short run

WHILE YOU READ THE MODULE

Key Terms

Define these key terms as you read the module:

Short-term interest rates:

Long-term interest rates:

Money demand curve:

Liquidity preference model of the interest rate:

Money supply curve:

Practice the Model

1) Draw a correctly labeled money market graph showing the liquidity preference model of interest rate determination. Label your money supply curve *MS*, your money demand curve *MD*, the equilibrium interest rate r_1, and the equilibrium quantity of money M_1. Use Figure 28.1 in your textbook as your guide.

2) On your graph, show the effect of an increase in the money supply on the interest rate. Label your new money supply curve MS_2 and new equilibrium interest rate r_2.

List questions or difficulties from your initial reading of the module.

AFTER YOU READ THE MODULE

Fill-in-the-Blanks

Fill in the blanks to complete the following statements. If you find yourself having difficulties, please refer back to the appropriate section in the text.

- The opportunity cost of holding money is equal to the **1)**_____ rate. The

  relationship between the interest rate and the quantity of money demanded by the public is illustrated

  by the **2)**_____ curve. When the interest rate increases, the opportunity cost of

  holding money increases, and therefore people will **3)**_____ their money holding.

  When the interest rate decreases, people **4)**_____ their holdings of money which

  results in a movement **5)**_____ the demand curve. The money demand curve will

  shift as a result of changes in **6)**_____, _____, _____,

  or _____. The money supply curve is **7)**_____ and its location

  is determined by **8)**_____.

- This model of interest rates is known as the liquidity preference model, but there is another model of

  interest rates known as the **9)**_____.

Multiple-Choice Questions

Circle the best choice to answer or complete the following questions or incomplete statements. For additional practice, use the space provided to explain why one or more of the incorrect options do not work.

10. If the Federal Reserve sells treasury bonds, the money supply will ___ and the interest rate will ___.

	Effect on money supply	*Effect on interest rate*
a.	increase	increase
b.	decrease	no change
c.	increase	decrease
d.	decrease	decrease
e.	decrease	increase

11. Suppose that there is a technological advance that makes it easier for people to withdraw money from the bank. As a result of this change, the money _____ will _____, and the equilibrium interest rate will _____.

	Curve that will shift	*Increase or decrease*	*Effect on interest rate*
a.	supply curve	increase	decrease
b.	supply curve	decrease	increase
c.	demand curve	decrease	decrease
d.	demand curve	increase	increase
e.	interest rate curve	increase	decrease

Helpful Tips

- There are two different models of how interest rates are determined. One you learned in this module, the money market. In the next module, you will learn the second one (the market for loanable funds). Make sure that when you graph either of these markets that someone looking at your graph can tell immediately what market you are trying to represent. Key features that will help distinguish your graph as the *money market* are:
  a. a vertical Money Supply curve, clearly labeled
  b. quantity of money on the horizontal axis
  c. *r* or interest rate on the vertical axis
  d. a downward-sloping money demand curve, clearly labeled

Module Notes

There are many different interest rates in the economy. For example, there are mortgage interest rates, automobile loan interest rates, credit card interest rates, and the prime interest rate. The different interest rates tend to move in the same general direction, moving together like a "web" of interest rates. It is important that you are able to distinguish between two important interest rates in our macroeconomic models, the federal funds rate and the discount rate. The federal funds rate is the interest rate banks charge each other for overnight loans. It is set in the federal funds market, but is targeted by the Fed. Other interest rates tend to follow the federal funds rate, rising when it rises and falling when it falls.

The other interest rate in our macroeconomic models is the discount rate. The discount rate is the interest rate the Fed charges banks to borrow. The discount rate is set directly by the Fed. Interest rates reflect the supply and demand for money in the money market. The Fed sets a *target* interest rate that it works to achieve by increasing or decreasing the money supply.

MODULE 29 THE MARKET FOR LOANABLE FUNDS

BEFORE YOU READ THE MODULE

Summary

This module explains how savers and borrowers are brought together in the loanable funds market. It also compares and contrasts the two models of interest rate determination, the loanable funds market and liquidity preference model (money market).

Module Objectives

Review these objectives before you read the module. Place a "√" on the line when you can do each of the following:

_____**Objective #1.** Describe how the loanable funds market matches savers and investors

_____**Objective #2.** Identify the determinants of supply and demand in the loanable funds market

_____**Objective #3.** Explain how the two models of interest rates can be reconciled

WHILE YOU READ THE MODULE

Key Terms

Define these key terms as you read the module:

Loanable funds market:

Rate of return:

Crowding out:

Fisher effect:

Practice the Model

1) Draw a correctly labeled graph of the loanable funds market. Label the equilibrium interest rate r_1 and the quantity of loanable funds Q_{LF1}. Use Figure 29.3 in your textbook as your guide.

2) Suppose the government borrows money to finance additional government spending. Which curve will be affected by the increased government borrowing and which direction will the curve shift? Show the effect on your graph above, and label the new equilibrium quantity Q_{LF2} and the new equilibrium interest rate r_2.

List questions or difficulties from your initial reading of the module.

AFTER YOU READ THE MODULE

Fill-in-the-Blanks

Fill in the blanks to complete the following statements. If you find yourself having difficulties, please refer back to the appropriate section in the text.

- A market that brings together those who want to lend money (savers) and those who want to borrow

  (firms with investment spending projects) is called the **1)**_____ market. The

  demand curve represents the willingness of investors to **2)**_____ and the supply

  curve represents the willingness of savers to **3)**_____. The demand for loanable

  funds depends on the interest rate and the **4)**_____ businesses earn on projects.

  The demand for loanable funds will shift in response to a change in **5)**_____ or

  _____. The negative effect of government budget deficits on investment spending

  is called **6)**_____. The supply of loanable funds will shift in response to changes in

  7)_____ or **8)**_____. The most important factor affecting interest

  rates over time is expectations about the future rate of **9)**_____.

Multiple-Choice Questions

Circle the best choice to answer or complete the following questions or incomplete statements. For additional practice, use the space provided to explain why one or more of the incorrect options do not work.

10. Suppose the equilibrium interest rate is initially 5% with no expected inflation. If expected inflation increases to 6%, then according to the Fisher effect, the nominal interest rate will be_____and the real interest rate will be _____.

	New nominal interest rate	*New real interest rate*
a.	5%	11%
b.	11%	5%
c.	0%	1%
d.	1%	6%
e.	6%	1%

11. If the cost of a project is $400,000 and the revenue from that project is $600,000, the rate of return for the project is
    a. 150%.
    b. 50%.
    c. 33%.
    d. 167%.
    e. 250%.

Helpful Tips

- The market for loanable funds looks a lot like the markets we saw in section 2. However, be very careful to label the market for loanable funds using the correct axes and curve labels. If you do not, the person reading your answers will think you are sketching a market for a good or service instead of the market for loanable funds.

- It might seem confusing that there are two different ways in which the interest rate is determined, the money market and the market for loanable funds. So how do you know which model to use if you are asked to explain how monetary policy will affect the macroeconomy? You must understand both models and be prepared to discuss either one. Pay particular attention to the labels on the axes and curves and the slope of the supply curve in each graph.

Module Notes

To discuss monetary policy and interest rates, we have used both the liquidity preference model (the money market) and the loanable funds model. In this module, we have shown how these two models are related. Since the Federal Reserve determines the supply of money in the economy, the equilibrium quantity of money is not affected by the interest rate – therefore, the money supply curve is vertical in the money market.

As the interest rate rises, the quantity of loanable funds supplied increases – the incentive to save is higher when interest rates are higher. Therefore, the supply curve for loanable funds has a positive slope. You may be asked specifically to use one or the other of these models to explain your answer to questions dealing with monetary policy.

When you are not asked specifically to use one model or the other, remember that the money market determines the interest rate in the short run and the loanable funds market determines the interest rate in the long run. Use the money market to discuss short-run changes and the loanable funds market to discuss changes in the long run. However, in some cases it is possible to explain a situation using either model. In these cases, just be certain that your explanation is consistent and correct for the model you choose.

Draw the Featured Models: Money Market/Loanable Funds Market

1) Label the type of market shown in the following graphs.

   a. This is the graph of the _____ market.

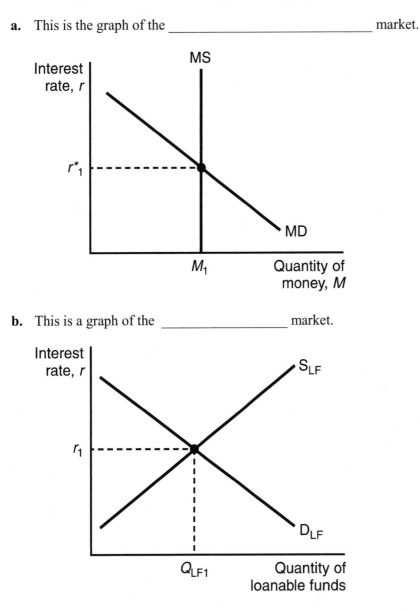

   b. This is a graph of the _____ market.

   c. Draw a correctly labeled graph of the money market and show the equilibrium interest rate as r_1 and the equilibrium quantity M_1.

d. Draw a corectly labeled graph of the loanable funds market and show the equilibrium interest rate as r_1 and the equilibrium quantity Q_{LF1}.

2) a. Suppose the Fed increases the money supply. Show the effect of an increase in the money supply on the money market in the space below. Be sure to clearly label the effect of this change on the interest rate. On the lines to the right, list actions that the Fed could take to cause this change.

_____

_____

b. Supose that the Fed decreased the money supply instead. Show the effect of a decrease in the money supply on the money market in the space below. Be sure to clearly label the effect of this change on the interest rate. On the lines to the right, list actions that the Fed could take to cause this change.

_____

_____

3) a. Show the effect of an increase in capital inflows on the market for loanable funds. Be sure to clearly label the effect of this change on the interest rate.

b. Show the effect of an increase in government borrowing to finance government spending on the loanable funds market. Be sure to clearly label the effect of this change on the interest rate.

Complete the Exercise

1. Use the *AD-AS* model to answer this question.

The economy of Macroland is initially in long-run equilibrium. Then the FOMC of Macroland decides to reduce interest rates through an open-market operation.

a. Draw a graph representing the initial situation in Macroland. In your graph, be sure to include the short-run aggregate supply curve (*SRAS*), the long-run aggregate supply curve (*LRAS*), and the aggregate demand curve (*AD*). On your graph, mark the equilibrium aggregate price level and the aggregate output level as well as potential output.

b. Draw a graph of the money market depicting Macroland's initial situation before the FOMC engages in monetary policy as well as the effect of the FOMC's monetary policy actions. Be sure to indicate the initial equilibrium as well as the equilibrium after the monetary policy.

c. How does this monetary policy action affect the aggregate economy in the short run? Explain your answer in your own words while also including a graph of the *AD-AS* model to illustrate your answer.

d. How does this monetary policy action affect the aggregate economy in the long run?

Problems

1. You have won the lottery and can receive your winnings as a single payment of $2 million in cash now or you can receive a payment of $500,000 a year for 5 years starting now. The interest rate is constant at 10% per year. Which payment plan do you prefer? Explain.

2. Suppose Fantasia has a single bank that initially has $10,000 of deposits, reserves of $2,000, and loans of $8,000. To simplify our example, we will assume that bank capital equals zero. Furthermore, Fantasia's central bank has a required reserve of 10% of deposits. All monetary transactions are made by check: no one in Fantasia uses currency.

   a. Construct a T-account depicting the initial situation in Fantasia. In your T-account, make sure you differentiate between required and excess reserves and that your T-account's assets equal its liabilities.

   b. Explain how you calculated the level of excess reserves in Fantasia.

   c. Suppose the bank in Fantasia lends these excess reserves (the amount of excess reserves you calculated in part **b.**) until it reaches the point where its excess reserves equal zero. How does this change the T-account?

   d. Did the money supply in Fantasia change when the bank loaned out the excess reserves? Explain your answer.

   e. What is the value of the money multiplier in Fantasia? Using the money multiplier, compute the maximum change in deposits that can occur based on the value of the excess reserves you found in part **b.**

3. You are provided the following T-accounts for both the central bank of Economia and the only commercial bank in Economia. In Economia, all financial transactions occur within the banking system; no one holds currency. The required reserve ratio imposed by the central bank is 20% of deposits. Suppose the central bank in Economia purchases $2,000 of Treasury bills from the commercial bank.

Central Bank of Economia

Assets		Liabilities	
Treasury bills	$20,000	Monetary Base	$20,000
Total assets	$20,000	Total liabilities	$20,000

Commercial Bank of Economia

Assets		Liabilities	
Required reserves	$20,000	Deposits	$100,000
Loans	$70,000	Capital	$20,000
Treasury bills	$30,000		
Total assets	$120,000	Total liabilities and capital	$120,000

a. Provide a T-account for both the central bank and the commercial bank showing the immediate effect of this transaction. Be sure to differentiate between required and excess reserves for the commercial bank.

b. Provide a T-account for the commercial bank once the commercial bank lends out its excess reserves and all adjustments have been made through the money multiplier process.

c. What happens to the money supply when the central bank purchases $2,000 of Treasury bills from the commercial bank?

d. Relate the change in the money supply to the money multiplier.

e. What was the monetary base initially?

f. What is the monetary base after all adjustments to the central bank's monetary policy have taken effect?

4. Use the following information about Theopolis to answer this question.

Currency in bank vaults	$120 million
Currency held by the public	$100 million
Checkable deposits	$2,800 million
Traveler's checks	$10 million
Bank deposits at the central bank	$300 million

    a. What are bank reserves equal to in Theopolis?

    b. Suppose banks hold no excess reserves in Theopolis. What is the required reserve ratio given the information in this table?

    c. What will happen to checkable deposits in Theopolis if the central bank purchases $10 million in securities? Assume that the public does not change its holding of currency. Explain and provide a numerical answer.

    d. If the public does not change its currency holdings, what will happen to the money supply in Theopolis, relative to its initial level, if the central bank of Theopolis sells $5 million in Treasury bills in the open market? Explain your answer.

5. Use the following graph of the money market to answer these questions. Assume this market is initially in equilibrium with the quantity of money equal to M_1 and the interest rate equal to r_1.

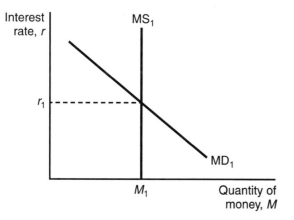

    a. Suppose the FOMC engages in an open-market purchase of Treasury bills. Holding everything else constant, what happens to the equilibrium quantity of money and the equilibrium interest rate? Sketch a graph illustrating these changes.

b. Suppose the FOMC engages in an open-market sale of Treasury bills. Holding everything else constant, what happens to the equilibrium quantity of money and the equilibrium interest rate? Sketch a graph illustrating these changes.

c. Suppose the aggregate price level increases. Holding everything else constant, what happens to the equilibrium quantity of money and the equilibrium interest rate? Sketch a graph illustrating the change and explain.

6. The economy of Macroland is initially in long-run equilibrium. Then the central bank of Macroland decides to purchase Treasury bills on the open market.

a. Draw a correctly labeled graph representing the initial situation in Macroland. In your graph, be sure to include the short-run aggregate supply curve (*SRAS*), the long-run aggregate supply curve (*LRAS*), and the aggregate demand curve (*AD*). On your graph, mark the equilibrium aggregate price level (PL_1) and the aggregate output level (Y_1), as well as potential output (*Yf*).

b. Draw a graph of the money market depicting Macroland's initial situation before the purchase of Treasury bills as well as the effect of the purchase. Be sure to indicate the initial equilibrium as well as the final equilibrium.

c. How does the purchase of Treasury bills affect aggregate output in the short run? Explain.

d. Show the impact of the change in the interest rate you found in part **b.** on your *AD-AS* graph. Mark the new equilibrium price level PL_2 and the new equilibrium output Y_2.

e. As a result of the change you showed in part **d.**, what is the impact on the market for loanable funds? Explain.

f. As a result of the changes you showed in parts **a.- c.**, how does the purchase of Treasury bills affect aggregate output in the long run? Explain and show on your *AD-AS* graph.

7. Suppose the nominal interest rate is 5% and the current rate of inflation is 0%.

a. Draw a correctly labeled graph of the market for loanable funds showing the nominal interest rate on the vertical axis and the quantity of loanable funds on the horizontal axis.

b. Suppose there is an increase in government spending that is financed through borrowing. Explain what effect this would have on:

i. the aggregate price level

ii. the real interest rate

c. As a result of the changes you indicated in **b.**, suppose the rate of inflation is 3%. Show the effect of the change you described in part **b.** on the equilibrium real interest rate. Be sure to label the new equilibrium interest rate with the number representing the new real interest rate.

d. What is the real interest rate as a result of these changes? Explain.

8. Suppose that when the FOMC reduces the interest rate by 1 percentage point, it increases the level of investment spending by $500 million in Macroland. If the marginal propensity to save equals 0.25, what will be the total rise in real GDP, assuming the aggregate price level is held constant? Explain.

9. For each of the following situations, determine the appropriate central bank monetary response.

a. The central bank adopts an interest rate target of 5%. Currently the interest rate in the economy is at 8%.

b. The central bank adopts an inflation target of 3%. Currently the inflation rate is 4%.

c. The central bank adopts an inflation target of 4%. Current inflation is 4%. However, this quarter the central bank expects data to reveal that the economy is entering a recession and has a projected negative output gap.

d. Current unemployment is greater than the natural rate of unemployment.

10. For each of the following situations, state the effect on the equilibrium interest rate and the equilibrium quantity of loanable funds. In your answer, make reference to how the demand and supply curves in the loanable funds market are affected. Hold everything else constant.

a. Capital inflows into a country increase.

b. The government reduces the government deficit.

c. There is an increase in the expected inflation rate. Comment on the real interest rate as well as the nominal interest rate in your answer to this question.

d. Private savings increase.

e. Perceived business opportunities decrease.

Review Questions

Circle your answer to the following questions.

1. Which of the following groups supply loanable funds?
   a. foreign borrowers
   b. domestic borrowers
   c. governments with budget deficits
   d. domestic investors
   e. foreign savers

2. Which of the following is not a source of funds for investment in the loanable funds market?
   a. domestic household savings
   b. foreign household savings
   c. the Federal Reserve System
   d. domestic government saving
   e. foreign government saving

3. Which of the following groups demands loanable funds?
   a. the Federal Reserve
   b. domestic savers
   c. foreign savers
   d. domestic investors
   e. governments with a budget surplus

4. When government spending is greater than taxes,
   a. government savings is positive.
   b. there is a budget surplus.
   c. there is a positive surplus.
   d. there is a budget deficit.
   e. net government saving is zero.

5. Suppose a country exports goods and services worth $50 million, while it imports goods and services worth $60 million. This country
   a. has a positive capital inflow.
   b. lends funds to foreigners.
   c. has a negative capital inflow.
   d. has a positive capital outflow.
   e. has $10 million that it can supply to foreign loanable funds markets.

Use the following T-account to answer questions 6 through 8.

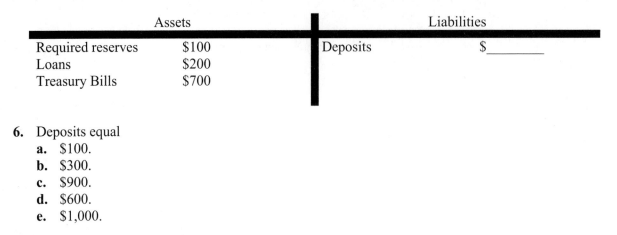

Assets		Liabilities	
Required reserves	$100	Deposits	$_____
Loans	$200		
Treasury Bills	$700		

6. Deposits equal
    a. $100.
    b. $300.
    c. $900.
    d. $600.
    e. $1,000.

7. Given this T-account and assuming the bank holds no excess reserves, what is the required reserve ratio?
    a. 10%
    b. $100
    c. 70%
    d. 30%
    e. 1%

8. Refer to the T-account above. Suppose this is the only bank in the banking system. Furthermore, suppose all money is held in this bank and the bank holds no excess reserves. If the Fed makes an open-market sale of $50 worth of T-bills to this bank, what will happen to the money supply after all adjustments are made?
    a. The money supply will increase by $50.
    b. The money supply will decrease by $50.
    c. The money supply will increase by $500.
    d. The money supply will decrease by $500.
    e. The money supply will decrease by $5,000.

9. The monetary base consists of
    a. currency in circulation plus bank deposits.
    b. bank deposits plus bank reserves.
    c. bank deposits, bank reserves, and currency in circulation.
    d. currency in circulation plus bank reserves.
    e. currency in circulation only.

10. In a simple banking system, where banks hold no excess reserves and all funds are kept as bank deposits, the money multiplier is equal to
    a. 1 divided by the required reserve ratio.
    b. the amount of reserves multiplied by the reciprocal of the required reserve ratio.
    c. zero.
    d. 1.
    e. the required reserve ratio.

11. The three primary policy tools available to the Federal Reserve include
    a. reserve requirements, the ability to tax banks, and the discount rate.
    b. reserve requirements, income taxes, and open-market operations.
    c. reserve requirements, the discount rate, and open-market operations.
    d. reserve requirements, the ability to tax banks, and open-market operations.
    e. the ability to tax banks, the discount rate, and open-market operations.

12. When banks borrow from one another, the rate of interest they pay for this loan is called the
    a. discount rate.
    b. federal funds rate.
    c. inflation rate.
    d. monetary rate.
    e. mutual fund rate.

13. Suppose a central bank has determined that it must increase the money supply by $100 million to reach its target interest rate of 5%. If the required reserve ratio is 20%, the bank must purchase securities worth
    a. $4 million.
    b. $5 million.
    c. $20 million.
    d. $100 million.
    e. $120 million.

14. The opportunity cost of holding money
    a. is always greater than the short-term interest rate.
    b. is the difference between the interest rate on assets that are not money and the interest rate on assets that are money.
    c. is the long-term interest rate.
    d. is always zero since it costs you nothing to hold money.
    e. is the reserve requirement.

15. Which of the following statements is true about the real quantity of money?
    a. It is the nominal amount of money multiplied by the aggregate price level.
    b. It measures the purchasing power of the nominal quantity of money.
    c. It is proportional to the nominal quantity of money for any given interest rate.
    d. It is fixed in the short run and the long run.
    e. It is equal to the nominal quantity of money multiplied by the velocity of money.

16. The Federal Open Market Committee sets a target interest rate and achieves it through
    a. open-market purchases, if the federal funds rate is initially less than the target rate.
    b. open-market sales, if the federal funds rate is initially less than the target rate.
    c. legislative action by Congress that decrees the level of the discount rate and thus the federal funds rate.
    d. stimulating the demand for money, if the initial interest rate is less than the target rate.
    e. setting an interest rate at which banks must loan to the public.

17. The liquidity preference model of interest rate determination states that
    a. interest rates are determined solely by the Federal Open Market Committee.
    b. interest rates are determined by the supply of and demand for money.
    c. people always prefer liquidity and do not consider the opportunity cost of holding money when they decide how much money they wish to hold at any given point in time.
    d. interest rates are determined in the market for non-monetary assets and not the market for money.
    e. the higher the interest rate, the higher the quantity of money demanded.

18. The money supply curve in the liquidity preference model is drawn as a vertical line because
    a. there is only one level of money supply that will enable an economy to produce at the full employment level of output and the appropriate aggregate price level.
    b. by law, Congress sets the level of the money supply in the economy.
    c. the Fed can control the level of the money supply through its open-market operations.
    d. the money supply curve is unimportant in determining the equilibrium level of interest rates in the liquidity preference model.
    e. People have no use for money when there are checkable deposits.

19. The money supply curve shifts to the left. Which open-market operation would cause this shift?
    a. purchasing Treasury bills
    b. selling Treasury bills
    c. lowering the Federal Funds rate
    d. raising the discount rate
    e. lowering the reserve requirement

20. Which of the following will cause the money demand curve to shift to the right?
    a. an increase in the interest rate
    b. a decrease in the interest rate
    c. allowing banks to pay lower rates of interest on checking accounts
    d. an increase in price level
    e. open-market operations by the Fed

21. Which of the following will occur if the Fed buys bonds?

	Effect on MS	*Effect on AD*
a.	Increase	Decrease
b.	Increase	Increase
c.	Increase	No change
d.	No change	Decrease
e.	Decrease	Increase

22. Suppose in the short run the level of aggregate output in an economy decreases at the same time the aggregate price level decreases. This is most likely due to a
    a. leftward shift in the short-run aggregate supply curve, holding everything else constant.
    b. rightward shift in the short-run aggregate supply curve, holding everything else constant.
    c. leftward shift in the aggregate demand curve, holding everything else constant.
    d. rightward shift in the aggregate demand curve, holding everything else constant.
    e. leftward shift in the long-run aggregate supply curve, holding everything else constant.

23. Inflation targeting means that
  a. the central bank adheres to maintaining a very strict interest rate target.
  b. the central bank announces the inflation rate that it is trying to achieve and then uses monetary policy to achieve this inflation rate.
  c. there may be a range of acceptable inflation rates or a specific inflation rate that the central bank hopes to achieve through monetary policy.
  d. the central bank has a goal of zero inflation.
  e. the central bank does not intervene to affect inflation.

24. The loanable funds market
  a. provides a market where borrowers can make beneficial loans, but savers must be willing to take the interest rate set by the Fed.
  b. interest rate is the nominal interest rate.
  c. interest rate is the return a lender receives for allowing borrowers the use of a dollar for one year.
  d. has a vertical supply curve.
  e. has no demand curve.

25. When the government runs a deficit, this shifts the
  a. supply of loanable funds curve to the right.
  b. supply of loanable funds curve to the left.
  c. demand for loanable funds curve to the right.
  d. demand for loanable funds curve to the left.
  e. supply of loanable funds to the right and the demand for loanable funds to the right.

26. In the loanable funds market, which of the following statements is true?
  a. Savers are best represented by the demand for loanable funds curve.
  b. Borrowers are best represented by the demand for loanable funds curve.
  c. The equilibrium interest rate equates the quantity of money supplied to the quantity of loanable funds demanded.
  d. The equilibrium interest rate equates the quantity of loanable funds demanded to the nominal interest rate.
  e. Government spending has no impact on the market for loanable funds.

Section ⑥ Inflation, Unemployment, and Stabilization Policies

Overview

This section uses the models introduced in Sections 4 and 5 to further develop an understanding of two kinds of stabilization policies - fiscal policy and monetary policy – and their long-run effects on the economy. In addition, the Phillips curve is used to investigate the role of expectations in the economy. The section ends with a brief summary of the history of macroeconomic thought and the development of the modern consensus view of stabilization policy.

Featured Model/Graph: The Phillips Curve

This section presents the Phillips Curve which shows the relationship between the inflation rate and the unemployment rate.

MODULES IN THIS SECTION

Module 30   **Long-Run Implications of Fiscal Policy: Deficits and the Public Debt**

Module 31   **Monetary Policy and the Interest Rate**

Module 32   **Money, Output, and Prices in the Long Run**

Module 33   **Types of Inflation, Disinflation, and Deflation**

Module 34   **Inflation and Unemployment: The Phillips Curve**

Module 35   **History and Alternative Views of Macroeconomics**

Module 36   **Consensus and Conflict in Modern Macroeconomics**

BEFORE YOU TACKLE THE TEST

Draw the Featured Model

Complete the Exercise

Problems

Review Questions

MODULE 30 LONG-RUN IMPLICATIONS OF FISCAL POLICY: DEFICITS AND THE PUBLIC DEBT

BEFORE YOU READ THE MODULE

Summary

This module presents some of the long-term effects of fiscal policy, including the budget balance, deficits, and the debt.

Module Objectives

Review these objectives before you read the module. Place a "√" on the line when you can do each of the following:

_____**Objective #1.** Explain why governments calculate the cyclically adjusted budget balance

_____**Objective #2.** Identify problems posed by a large public debt

_____**Objective #3.** Discuss why implicit liabilities of the government are also a cause for concern

WHILE YOU READ THE MODULE

Key Terms

Define these key terms as you read the module:

Cyclically adjusted budget balance:

Government debt:

Fiscal year:

Public debt:

Debt–GDP ratio:

Implicit liabilities:

Practice the Model

Recall that a cyclically adjusted budget balance assumes that GDP is in long-run equilibrium. Using an *AD—AS* model, show the relationship between current real GDP and potential output under the assumptions of a cyclically adjusted budget balance. Label current real GDP Y_1 and potential output Y_f.

List questions or difficulties from your initial reading of the module.

AFTER YOU READ THE MODULE

Fill-in-the-Blanks

Fill in the blanks to complete the following statements. If you find yourself having difficulties, please refer back to the appropriate section in the text.

- The amount of government saving, also known as the budget balance, is defined by the equation

  1)_____. When an economy is in recession and unemployment increases, the

  2)_____ component of the budget balance will increase and the

  3)_____ component of the budget balance will decrease, which causes the entire

  budget balance to increase even if there is no change in discretionary government spending. An

  increase in the **4)**_____ component of the budget balance will cause the budget

  balance to increase.

- When the government spends more than it receives in tax revenue in a given year, it results in a

  budget **5)**_____. In these situations, the government must borrow money and

  over time that borrowing increases the national **6)**_____. An estimate of what

  the budget balance would be if real GDP were exactly equal to potential output (i.e. if there were no

  business cycle) is known as the **7)**_____ budget balance. Even if there is no change in discretionary government spending (represented by G in the budget balance equation) during a recession, the budget balance will decrease as tax revenue decreases and transfer payments increase, which will likely **8)**_____ the national debt; while during economic expansions the increase in the budget balance will likely **9)**_____ the national debt.

- The **10)**_____ ratio is used to assess the ability of governments to pay their debt. But the financial situation of a country can be worse than it appears because of

  11)_____, which are spending promises made by governments that are effectively a debt, despite the fact that they are not included in the usual debt statistics.

Multiple-Choice Questions

Circle the best choice to answer or complete the following questions or incomplete statements. For additional practice, use the space provided to explain why one or more of the incorrect options do not work.

12. The cyclically adjusted budget balance is the budget balance that exists when there is
    a. a recessionary gap.
    b. an inflationary gap.
    c. a depression.
    d. neither an inflationary gap nor a recessionary gap.
    e. hyperinflation.

Refer to Scenario 30-1 for questions 13 and 14.

Scenario 30-1
Suppose a country's government currently collects $100 million in tax revenues, $75 million in government spending, and $25 million in transfer payments.

13. What is the country's current budget balance?
    a. $0
    b. $200 million
    c. $50 million
    d. $100 million
    e. $175 million

14. Assume that as the result of a recession, tax revenues decrease to $75 million and transfer payments increase to $50 million. How can the government change its spending to maintain a budget balance of zero and how will the change affect the level of GDP? Would it improve or worsen the recession?

	Change in G	*GDP*	*Effect on recession*
a.	decrease to $50 million	increase	improve
b.	increase to $75 million	increase	improve
c.	decrease to $25 million	decrease	worsen
d.	increase to $75 million	decrease	worsen
e.	decrease to $0	decrease	worsen

Helpful Tips

- Many people think of deficits and debt as "bad." However, recall the distinction between positive and normative analysis discussed in Section 1. Normative analysis describes what "should" be, while positive analysis describes how things are. Be careful to focus on a positive analysis of the budget balance and deficits.

- One common mistake—it happens all the time in newspaper reports—is to confuse *deficits* with *debt.* A *deficit* is the difference between the amount of money a government spends and the amount it receives in taxes over a *given period*—usually a year. Deficit numbers always come with a statement about the time period to which they apply, as in "the U.S. budget deficit *in fiscal 2008* was $410 billion." A *debt* is the sum of money a government owes at a particular point in time. Debt numbers usually come with a specific date, as in "U.S. public debt *at the end of fiscal 2008* was $5.8 trillion." A deficit occurs in a single time period, whereas the debt is the sum of deficits that have accumulated over time. Deficits and debt are linked, because government debt grows when governments run deficits, but they aren't the same.

- Make sure you understand what the cyclically adjusted budget balance is and how it relates to the budget balance and to potential GDP. The cyclically adjusted budget balance is an estimate of what the budget balance would be if real GDP were exactly equal to potential GDP. This measure takes into account the extra tax revenue the government would receive and the smaller level of transfer payments the government would make if the recessionary gap were eliminated or the tax revenue the government would lose and the extra transfer payments the government would make if the inflationary gap were eliminated. The cyclically adjusted budget balance fluctuates less than the actual budget deficit because years with a large budget deficit are typically associated with large recessionary gaps.

Module Notes

In Module 20, we learned how fiscal policy can be used to correct recessions or bring down inflation. However, the policies that can be used to do this – raising and lowering taxes and raising and lowering government spending – do not just have short-run effects. In this module, we learned how changes in government spending and taxes can create budget deficits, and how those deficits accumulate over time to create debt. We also learned that debts are problematic because they place a strain on future budgets, when governments have to repay debt with additional interest. The budget balance, then, is a measure of fiscal policy that is sometimes used as a quick way of examining whether fiscal policy is expansionary or contractionary.

MODULE | 31 | MONETARY POLICY AND THE INTEREST RATE

BEFORE YOU READ THE MODULE

Summary

This module shows how to use the money market and the loanable funds market to explain how the Federal Reserve can use monetary policy to stabilize the economy in the short run.

Module Objectives

Review these objectives before you read the module. Place a "√" on the line when you can do each of the following:

_____**Objective #1.**   Describe how the Federal Reserve implements monetary policy, moving the interest rate to affect aggregate output

_____**Objective #2.**   Explain why monetary policy is the main tool for stabilizing the economy

WHILE YOU READ THE MODULE

Key Terms

Define these key terms as you read the module:

Target federal funds rate:

Expansionary monetary policy:

Contractionary monetary policy:

Taylor rule for monetary policy:

Inflation targeting:

Practice the Model

Assume the unemployment rate in the economy is currently below the natural rate of unemployment and the economy is experiencing inflation (graphically, this means the intersection of the *AD* and *SRAS* curve is to the right of the *LRAS* curve). To combat inflation, the central bank decides to sells bonds. How does selling bonds combat inflation? Selling bonds takes money out of the economy when bonds are paid for which decreases the money supply. A decrease in the money supply increases the interest rate and higher interest rates decrease the investment component of aggregate demand. Decreased aggregate demand leads to a decrease in real GDP and the price level. We can express this chain of events concisely using commonly accepted abbreviations and arrows as follows:

Sell bonds $\rightarrow \downarrow MS \rightarrow \uparrow i \rightarrow \downarrow I \rightarrow \downarrow AD \rightarrow \downarrow$rGDP & $\downarrow PL$

Now assume instead that the economy is experiencing a recession, which means the unemployment rate is above the natural rate of unemployment. Graphically, the intersection of the *AD* and *SRAS* curves is to the left of the *LRAS* curve.

1) Fill in the blanks to describe the chain of events that will occur if the central bank takes action to combat the recession.

_____ bonds $\rightarrow$ ____ MS $\rightarrow$ ___ i $\rightarrow$ ____ I $\rightarrow$ ____ AD & ____ rGDP & ____ PL

2) Draw a correctly labeled graph of the money market and show the effect of the central bank action on the interest rate. Refer to Figure 31.1 and Figure 31.3 in your textbook for help constructing your graphs..

3) Draw a correctly labeled graph representing the economy before the action by the central bank and then use it to illustrate the effect of the central bank's action on real GDP and the price level. Assume the central bank action returns the economy to long-run equilibrium.

List questions or difficulties from your initial reading of the module.

AFTER YOU READ THE MODULE

Fill-in-the-Blanks

Fill in the blanks to complete the following statements. If you find yourself having difficulties, please refer back to the appropriate section in the text.

- At each FOMC meeting, the Federal Reserve sets the target **1)**_____ rate. The

  target is enforced by the Open Market Desk of the Federal Reserve Bank of **2)**_____.

  If the rate needs to be lowered, the Open Market Desk will **3)**_____ Treasury

  bills to **4)**_____ the money supply so that the rate will fall. This is called

  5)_____ monetary policy.

- If the Fed pursues contractionary monetary policy, it **6)**_____ bonds or treasury

  bills, which will **7)**_____ the money supply so that the interest rate will

  8)_____. The new interest rate will result in **9)**_____

  investment spending which will **10)**_____ real GDP.

Multiple-Choice Questions

Circle the best choice to answer or complete the following questions or incomplete statements. For additional practice, use the space provided to explain why one or more of the incorrect options do not work.

11. If GDP is below full employment output, the central bank is most likely to
    a. buy bonds.
    b. sell bonds.
    c. increase government spending.
    d. decrease government spending.
    e. increase the discount rate.

12. According to the Taylor rule, as inflation increases, the target federal funds rate should _____ and as the unemployment rate increases, target federal funds rate should _____.
    a. increase, increase
    b. decrease, increase
    c. decrease, decrease
    d. increase, decrease
    e. increase, not change

Helpful Tips

- There are many different interest rates in the economy. The interest rate that the Fed targets with monetary policy is the Fed Funds Rate. The federal funds rate is the interest rate that banks charge each other for overnight loans. While it is true that all interest rates tend to move together, the focus of monetary policy is the federal funds rate. A common error is to confuse the federal funds rate and the discount rate. The discount rate, which is also set by the Fed, is the amount charged to banks when they borrow from the Fed. There are many other interest rates in the economy, but when the FOMC announces a change in the interest rate, it means the federal funds rate.

- Be careful you do not confuse the types of monetary policy (expansionary and contractionary) with the actions associated with those policies (buying and selling bonds). Expansionary and contractionary are different types of monetary policy. Buying and selling bonds are the actions taken to pursue those different policies. If you are asked what *actions* a central bank would need to pursue, you must refer to buying or selling bonds. The Fed will *buy* bonds if an expansionary policy is appropriate and *sell* bonds if a contractionary policy is appropriate.

- It is easy to make a mistake thinking through the chain of events resulting from monetary policy actions. To keep straight why buying bonds (or selling bonds) leads to changes in GDP, work through and write down each step in the chain of events rather than jumping to the conclusion. For instance, if you are told that the central bank wants to increase the money supply, and you are asked to identify the effect on the economy, make it a habit to start with the action (buy or sell bonds) and write down each step in the chain of events. For example:

$$\text{buy bonds} \rightarrow \uparrow MS \rightarrow \downarrow i \rightarrow \uparrow I \rightarrow \uparrow AD \rightarrow \uparrow \text{rGDP} \,\&\, \uparrow PL.$$

Module Notes

While we often say that the Fed sets the interest rate in the economy, it is more precise to say that the Fed uses its control of the money supply to achieve a target interest rate in the money market. The Fed sets a target interest rate and uses market forces in the money market to achieve it. The money market works the same way the markets did when we introduced them back in Section 1. The interest rate is the "price" of money and is determined by the intersection of the supply and demand curves for money. The important difference in the money market is that the Fed adjusts the supply of money to achieve its target interest rate. The Fed conducts monetary policy through this indirect control of the interest rate.

Most economists agree that monetary policy in some form has an important role in correcting severe recessions. However, there is disagreement about whether monetary policy should be at the discretion of the Fed, or follow a set of rules that dictate what monetary policy should be in different circumstances (such as the Taylor rule).

MODULE 32   MONEY, OUTPUT, AND PRICES IN THE LONG RUN

BEFORE YOU READ THE MODULE

Summary

This module analyzes how a counter-productive action by a central bank can actually destabilize the economy in the short run.

Module Objectives

Review these objectives before you read the module. Place a "√" on the line when you can do each of the following:

_____**Objective #1.**   Identify the effects of an inappropriate monetary policy

_____**Objective #2.**   Explain the concept of monetary neutrality and its relationship to the long-term economic effects of monetary policy

WHILE YOU READ THE MODULE

Key Term

Define the key term as you read the module:

Monetary neutrality:

Practice the Model

1) Suppose the economy is initially in long-run equilibrium. Show the current state of the economy using the *AD-AS* model and label current GDP Y_0, full employment output Y_f, and the current price level PL_0.

2) Now suppose the central bank mistakenly believes that the economy is in a recession and engages in expansionary monetary policy. Show the effect of expansionary monetary policy on the *AD-AS* graph you constructed for question **1)** (Hint: determine which curve shifts and in which direction). Label the new level of real GDP Y_1 and the new price level PL_1 and indicate the direction of change in real GDP and the price level on your graph.

3) As a result of an increase in the price level, the economy will experience an increase in nominal wages and the prices of other inputs. Recall that change in the cost of inputs shifts the *SRAS* curve. Show the effect of the change in the price level on the *AD-AS* graph you constructed for questions **1)** and **2)**. Assume that the increase in input prices brings the economy back to long-run equilibrium. Label the new output Y_2 and the new price level PL_2.

4) What impact did the expansionary monetary policy have on real GDP and the price level in the long run?

List questions or difficulties from your initial reading of the module.

AFTER YOU READ THE MODULE

Fill-in-the-Blanks

Fill in the blanks to complete the following statements. If you find yourself having difficulties, please refer back to the appropriate section in the text.

- Monetary policy can further destabilize an economy if the Fed pursues **1)**_____

  policies during a recession or **2)**_____ policies when there is inflation.

- Attempts to move the economy to a point above potential output in the long run will not work

  because the economy will adjust through a shift in the aggregate supply curve caused by a change in

  3)_____.

- In the long run, the only effect of an increase in the money supply is to raise the aggregate price level

  by an equal percentage. This describes the concept known as money **4)**_____.

Multiple-Choice Questions

Circle the best choice to answer or complete the following questions or incomplete statements. For additional practice, use the space provided to explain why one or more of the incorrect options do not work.

5. If expansionary monetary policy increases aggregate demand, the resulting inflation will cause the demand for money to _____, which will cause the interest rate to _____.
   a. increase, decrease
   b. increase, increase
   c. decrease, decrease
   d. stay the same, decrease
   e. decrease, stay the same

6. If the Fed increases the money supply, what will happen to the price level in the long run?
   a. It will increase but only if the economy had been in long-run equilibrium before the increase in the money supply.
   b. It will decrease but only if the economy had been in long-run equilibrium before the increase in the money supply.
   c. It will return to whatever the original price level was prior to the increase in the money supply.
   d. It will decrease even if the economy was not in long-run equilibrium before the increase in the money supply.
   e. It will increase even if the economy was not in long-run equilibrium before the increase in the money supply.

Helpful Tips

- Students often confuse the long-run concept of money neutrality with the short-run use of discretionary monetary policy. The idea of money neutrality can seem contradictory to what we learned in Module 31 about central banks' use of monetary policy to increase GDP during recessions and decrease it to combat inflation. How can monetary policy have no effect on real GDP if we just said that the Fed can increase real GDP using monetary policy? The answer is simple: the Fed can influence real GDP in the short run, but not in the long run. In the short run, monetary policy can influence the business cycle. However, the long-run performance of an economy (e.g. its ability to produce goods and services) depends on the fundamentals of the economy: the land, labor, capital, and technology that determine potential output. For a change to have an effect on real GDP in the long run, it has to impact the *LRAS* curve.

Module Notes

It is important to distinguish between the short-run and long-run effects of monetary policy. In the short run, monetary policy can be used to stimulate *AD* and shift it to the right, resulting in an increase in aggregate real output, or monetary policy can be used to contract *AD,* thereby shifting it to the left and leading to a decrease in the level of aggregate real output. In the long run, changes in the quantity of money affect the aggregate price level, but they do not change real aggregate output or the interest rate. Therefore, in the long run, the Federal Reserve can only affect the aggregate price level. So, while short-run stabilization policy is an important function of monetary policy, the Federal Reserve keeps a close eye on the aggregate price level to assure that monetary policy prevents inflation or deflation in the long run. Since the aggregate price level is the only variable that monetary policy can affect in the long run, it is a primary focus of the Fed. Economists refer to this as "monetary neutrality." Money is neutral in its effect on aggregate real output in the long run, since it cannot affect the level of aggregate real output.

The Fed is especially concerned with avoiding deflation – which, in practical terms, means accepting a very low level of inflation. Trying to achieve an inflation rate of zero is difficult and runs the risk of allowing deflation in the economy. For many years it was widely believed that the Fed preferred to maintain inflation at around 2% per year. Beginning in 2012, the Fed has stated explicitly that it will target a rate of inflation of 2% per year.

Can an inflation target lead to price stability in the long run? If people believe, as many do, that the Fed will keep inflation at around 2%, then 2% will serve as an anchor for inflationary expectations. That is, if people believe that inflation will be kept at 2%, then they build 2% inflation into their decisions for the future and wages, prices, interest rates, etc. are determined with the expectation that there will be 2% inflation. This expectation of inflation turns out to be important in the Phillips Curve model - a model discussed in a later module.

MODULE 33 TYPES OF INFLATION, DISINFLATION, AND DEFLATION

BEFORE YOU READ THE MODULE

Summary

This module discusses two phenomena that involve monetary policy, inflation, and deflation.

Module Objectives

Review these objectives before you read the module. Place a "√" on the line when you can do each of the following:

_____**Objective #1.** Use the classical model of the price level

_____**Objective #2.** Explain why efforts to collect an inflation tax by printing money can lead to high rates of inflation and even hyperinflation

_____**Objective #3.** Define the types of inflation: cost-push and demand-pull

WHILE YOU READ THE MODULE

Key Terms

Define these key terms as you read the module:

Classical model of the price level:

Inflation tax:

Cost-push inflation:

Demand-pull inflation:

Practice the Model

1) Use the *AD-AS* model to show demand-pull inflation in an economy that is initially in long-run equilibrium. Label the full employment output Y_f, the initial price level PL_1, the initial real GDP Y_1, the output level with demand-pull inflation Y_2, and the price level with demand-pull inflation PL_2.

2) Use the *AD-AS* model to show cost-push inflation in an economy that is initially in long-run equilibrium. Label the full employment output Y_f, the initial price level PL_1, the initial real GDP Y_1, the output level with cost-push inflation Y_2, and the price level with cost-push inflation PL_2.

List questions or difficulties from your initial reading of the module.

AFTER YOU READ THE MODULE

Fill-in-the-Blanks

Fill in the blanks to complete the following statements. If you find yourself having difficulties, please refer back to the appropriate section in the text.

- Inflation that is caused by significant increases in input prices is known as **1)**_____

  inflation. Inflation that is caused by increases in aggregate demand is known as

  2)_____ inflation.

- The idea that people who hold money end up "paying for" inflation through a reduction in the

  purchasing power of their money holdings is known as a(n) **3)**_____ tax.

- When actual aggregate output is equal to potential output, the actual unemployment rate is

4)_____ the natural rate of unemployment. When the output gap is positive

(an inflationary gap), the unemployment rate is **5)**_____ the natural rate.

When there is a **6)**_____ gap, the unemployment rate is *above* the natural

rate.

Multiple-Choice Questions

Circle the best choice to answer or complete the following questions or incomplete statements. For additional practice, use the space provided to explain why one or more of the incorrect options do not work.

7. After being in long-run equilibrium, an economy experiences inflation and has an unemployment rate higher than the natural rate of unemployment. The economy is experiencing which of the following?
   a. cost-push inflation
   b. demand-pull inflation
   c. expansionary fiscal policy
   d. contractionary fiscal policy
   e. hyperinflation

8. The initial effect of expansionary monetary policy on the price level is due to _____ and the long-run effect of expansionary monetary policy on the price level is due to _____.
   a. demand-pull inflation, cost-push inflation
   b. cost-push inflation, demand-pull inflation
   c. expansionary fiscal policy, demand-pull deflation
   d. demand-pull deflation, demand-push inflation
   e. cost-push inflation, demand-push inflation

Helpful Tips

- Governments can increase the money available to spend either by increasing taxes (an explicit tax increase) or by printing money (an implicit tax increase). An increase in taxes is explicit because there is an actual tax bill that households must pay. For example, when income taxes are increased, households can't buy as much because they have less income to spend. Printing money is an implicit tax on households because, while households don't have to pay an actual tax bill, printing money causes inflation. When there is inflation, households have to pay higher prices, so they can't buy as much with their income – which has the same effect as raising the income tax.

Module Notes

When the aggregate price level rises (that is, there is inflation in the economy), then a given quantity of money will not purchase as much. The real money supply has fallen because the purchasing power of money has gone down. The real money supply is equal to the nominal money supply divided by the aggregate price level. That is, the real quantity of money is equal to M/P. The classical model of the price level is a simplified model in which the real quantity of money, M/P, is always at long-run equilibrium. Even if the money supply (M) increases, the price level will increase by a proportional amount – leading to the idea of money neutrality.

The implication of this is that if governments increase the money supply to pay for goods and services, the real value of money will not change - only the price level will. This poses a tax on the individuals who hold money, because the money they had will now be less valuable.

Inflation can arise for two different reasons: cost-push inflation and demand-pull inflation. Cost-push inflation is due to an increase in the price of an input, such as wages, that has economy-wide importance. Demand-pull inflation is inflation that is caused by an increase in aggregate demand. Thus, an increase in the money supply would cause both demand-pull and cost-push inflation. In the short run, demand-pull inflation would occur as the increase in the money supply leads to a decrease in interest rates, which would increase aggregate demand. The increase in output and accompanying decrease in unemployment would drive up wages in the long run, leading to cost-push inflation.

MODULE 34 INFLATION AND UNEMPLOYMENT: THE PHILLIPS CURVE

BEFORE YOU READ THE MODULE

Summary

This module discusses the short-run trade-off between unemployment and inflation—lower unemployment is associated with higher inflation, and vice versa. This trade-off is represented by the *Short-Run Phillips Curve*. However, the same trade-off does not exist in the long run.

Module Objectives

Review these objectives before you read the module. Place a "√" on the line when you can do each of the following:

_____ **Objective #1.** Use the Phillips curve to show the nature of the short-run trade-off between inflation and unemployment

_____ **Objective #2.** Explain why there is no long-run trade-off between inflation and unemployment

_____ **Objective #3.** Discuss why expansionary policies are limited due to the effects of expected inflation

_____ **Objective #4.** Explain why even moderate levels of inflation can be hard to end

_____ **Objective #5.** Identify the problems with deflation that lead policy makers to prefer a low but positive inflation rate

WHILE YOU READ THE MODULE

Key Terms

Define these key terms as you read the module:

Short-run Phillips curve:

Nonaccelerating inflation rate of unemployment (NAIRU):

Long-run Phillips curve:

Debt deflation:

Zero bound:

Liquidity trap:

Practice the Model

1) In the space below, draw a graph of the Phillips curve model for an economy in long-run macroeconomic equilibrium showing both the short-run Phillips curve (*SRPC*) and the long-run Phillips curve (*LRPC*). Recall that when an economy is in long-run macroeconomic equilibrium, the actual rate of unemployment is equal to the natural rate of unemployment. Be sure to label the current rate of unemployment UR_1. Commonly used abbreviations in macroeconomics for inflation are "inf." and "π" (the Greek letter "pi"). Use the commonly used abbreviation π to denote the current rate of inflation π_1, and the natural rate of unemployment UR_N.

2) In the space below, draw a graph of the Phillips curve model for an economy that is experiencing a recessionary output gap, showing both the short-run Phillips curve (*SRPC*) and the long-run Phillips curve (*LRPC*). Recall that when an economy is experiencing a recessionary output gap, the unemployment rate is higher than the natural rate of unemployment. Be sure to label the current rate of unemployment UR_1, label the current rate of inflation π_1, and label the natural rate of unemployment UR_N.

3) In the space below, draw a graph of the Phillips curve for an economy that is experiencing an expansionary output gap, showing both the short-run Phillips curve (*SRPC*) and the long-run Phillips curve (*LRPC*). Recall that when an economy is experiencing an expansionary output gap, the unemployment rate is lower than the natural rate of unemployment. Be sure to label the current rate of unemployment UR_1, label the current rate of inflation π_1, and label the natural rate of unemployment UR_N.

List questions or difficulties from your initial reading of the module.

AFTER YOU READ THE MODULE

Fill-in-the-Blanks

Fill in the blanks to complete the following statements. If you find yourself having difficulties, please refer back to the appropriate section in the text.

- The short-run Phillips curve shows that there is a **1)**_____ relationship

  between the unemployment rate and inflation rate in the short run. A shift in the short-run Phillips

  curve (*SRPC*) is caused by a change in the expected rate of **2)**_____. If

  people believe that this rate will increase, the *SRPC* will shift to the **3)**_____.

- The unemployment rate at which inflation does not change over time is known as the

  4)_____ or N-A-I-R-U. The Phillips curve is a **5)**_____

  line at the natural rate of unemployment.

- The nominal interest rate can't go below zero. This is known as the zero **6)**_____.

  When nominal interest rates are at this point, conventional monetary policy (buying and selling

  treasury notes) cannot be used to stimulate an economy, a problem known as the

  7)_____.

- Even though economists are concerned about excessive amounts of inflation, a far more worrying

  phenomenon is the opposite problem of **8)**_____.

Multiple-Choice Questions

Circle the best choice to answer or complete the following questions or incomplete statements. For additional practice, use the space provided to explain why one or more of the incorrect options do not work.

9. The long-run Phillips curve shows that
    a. the *SRPC* is straight rather than curved.
    b. there is a negative relationship between inflation and unemployment in the long run.
    c. there is a positive relationship between inflation and unemployment in the long run
    d. there is a negative relationship between inflation and unemployment in both the long run and the short run.
    e. inflation and unemployment are unrelated in the long run.

10. If the actual rate of unemployment is lower than the NAIRU, then people will have expectations of a _____ rate of inflation, which causes the *SRPC* to _____.

    a. higher, shift to the left

    b. lower, shift to the right

    c. higher, move along the curve to the right

    d. higher, shift to the right

    e. lower, move along the curve to the left

Helpful Tips

- Drawing the *SRPC* and the *LRPC* with incorrect slopes is a common mistake. Phillips curves represent the relationship between the unemployment rate and the inflation rate. Conventionally, the vertical axis on a Phillips curve graph measures the rate of inflation and the horizontal axis measures the unemployment rate. A downward-sloping *SRPC* curve shows a negative relationship between unemployment and inflation rate. On a conventional Phillips curve graph, the *LRPC* is a vertical line. A vertical *LRPC* indicates that the unemployment rate and the inflation rate are unrelated and that the unemployment rate does not change in the long run. In the long run, we know that the economy will always produce at potential output, the natural rate of unemployment, and the NAIRU.

- A common error in reasoning is that if inflation is undesirable, then the opposite of inflation – deflation – is a better option. This cannot be further from the truth! As economist Irving Fisher pointed out, deflation can lead to a vicious cycle of decreasing economic output.

Module Notes

This module introduces a new model – the Phillips curve model. Since we have already used several other important models, it is important not to confuse them and to understand how they are related. The Phillips curve shows the relationship between the inflation rate and the unemployment rate. As with all models, it is important to correctly label the axes when drawing a Phillips curve. Typically, the inflation rate is shown on the vertical axis and the unemployment rate is shown on the horizontal axis.

The NAIRU provides a measure of the unemployment rate that corresponds to the economy operating at its potential output level without any inflationary pressures. Economies that adopt policies in order to reduce their unemployment rate below this natural rate will experience inflation: persistent adoption of these policies will generate accelerating inflation.

The Phillips curve model is closely related to the aggregate demand and supply model. Remember that the level of potential output, the natural rate of unemployment, and the NAIRU all occur at the point at which the economy is producing at its maximum. When the economy is operating at full employment, it reaches its potential output and this is where the NAIRU is found. Also, the vertical axes in both the Phillips curve and the *AD-AS* models are used to measure changes in the aggregate price level (inflation). However, the horizontal axis measures unemployment in the Phillips curve model and aggregate output in the *AD-AS* model. Recall that the level of aggregate output and unemployment are inversely related, so when output goes up, more people are employed producing output, and unemployment falls; when output falls, fewer workers are needed and unemployment rises.

Long-run changes are also related in the Phillips curve and *AD-AS* models. Long-run economic growth is shown by a rightward shift of the *LRAS* curve representing an increase in potential output and a decrease in the natural rate of unemployment. This corresponds to a leftward shift of the long-run Phillips curve (showing a decrease in the NAIRU) in the long run.

The short-run Phillips curve (*SRPC*) is used to show the effect of a change in the expected inflation rate in the economy. The *SRPC* illustrates the negative relationship between the inflation rate and the unemployment rate and is drawn with a given level of expected inflation. If expected inflation increases, the *SRPC* shifts upward by the change in the expected inflation rate. In the long run, the economy—no matter what the expected inflation rate—will settle at an unemployment rate equal to the NAIRU; therefore, the long-run Phillips curve (*LRPC*) is a vertical line at the NAIRU.

Debt deflation refers to a situation in which deflation makes existing loan contracts more costly for borrowers: as the real burden of their debt increases, borrowers will decrease their spending. This reduction in aggregate spending is referred to as debt deflation.

The zero bound refers to the lower limit for the nominal interest rate: nominal interest rates cannot fall below zero percent. When an economy finds that its nominal interest rate has fallen to zero, it will no longer be able to use conventional monetary policy to stimulate the economy: monetary policy will be unable to stimulate aggregate spending through decreases in the nominal interest rate because the nominal interest rate cannot be negative. This situation is referred to as a liquidity trap: increasing the money supply, an increase in liquidity, does nothing for the economy since the economy is "trapped" by the inability of the nominal interest rate to fall further.

MODULE | 35 | HISTORY AND ALTERNATIVE VIEWS OF MACROECONOMCS

BEFORE YOU READ THE MODULE

Summary

This module presents a brief overview of the history of macroeconomics.

Module Objectives

Review these objectives before you read the module. Place a "√" on the line when you can do each of the following:

_____**Objective #1.** Explain why classical macroeconomics wasn't adequate for the problems posed
by the Great Depression

_____**Objective #2.** Discuss how Keynes and the experience of the Great Depression legitimized
macroeconomic policy activism

_____**Objective #3.** Define monetarism and identify monetarist views on the limits of discretionary
monetary policy

_____**Objective #4.** Describe how challenges led to a revision of Keynesian ideas and the emergence
of the new classical macroeconomics

WHILE YOU READ THE MODULE

Key Terms

Define these key terms as you read the module:

Keynesian economics:

Macroeconomic policy activism:

Monetarism:

Discretionary monetary policy:

Monetary policy rule:

Quantity Theory of Money:

Velocity of money:

Natural rate hypothesis:

Political business cycle:

New classical macroeconomics:

Rational expectations:

New Keynesian economics:

Real business cycle theory:

Practice the Model

1) Starting with an economy in long-run equilibrium, show the effect of expansionary fiscal policy using an *AD-AS* graph. Label the initial output Y_1, the initial price level PL_1, the output after expansionary fiscal policy Y_2, and the price level after expansionary policy PL_2.

2) Use a graph of the money market to show the effect of the expansionary fiscal policy on the interest rate as a result of the changes in the price level shown in **1)** above. Assume that there is no accompanying increase in the money supply. Use Figure 35.2 in your textbook as your guide.

List questions or difficulties from your initial reading of the module.

AFTER YOU READ THE MODULE

Fill-in-the-Blanks

Fill in the blanks to complete the following statements. If you find yourself having difficulties, please refer back to the appropriate section in the text.

- Before the 1930s, the **1)**_____ model of economics assumed that output was

  fixed and only the price level would adjust, which is represented as a **2)**_____

  aggregate supply curve. However, during the 1930s, economists had an incentive to develop theories

  to guide macroeconomic policy-making as a result of the Great Depression. This led to the

  development of **3)**_____ economics, which focuses on the ability of shifts in

  aggregate demand to change output as well as prices. The main practical consequence of Keynesian

  economics was that it made the use of fiscal policy or monetary policy to smooth business cycles,

  known as **4)**_____, a legitimate undertaking.

- Two schools of thought modified the classical model to account for the challenges faced by

  economies during the great depression, Keynesian economics and Monetarism, both of which

  believed that monetary policy should have been far more aggressive to correct output during the Great

  Depression. A key equation relating the money supply to production, called the quantity theory of

  money, is **5)**_____. In this equation, velocity is assumed to be fixed, which

  means that in order for GDP to increase, the **6)**_____ must also increase.

Multiple-Choice Questions

Circle the best choice to answer or complete the following questions or incomplete statements. For additional practice, use the space provided to explain why one or more of the incorrect options do not work.

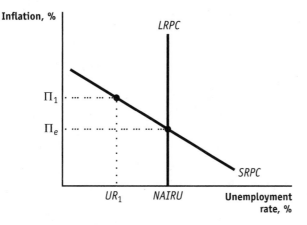

7. Refer to the figure above, in which π_1 is the current rate of inflation and π_e is the expected rate of inflation. According to the natural rate hypothesis, what will happen to inflation if the unemployment rate remains at UR_1, and why?
   a. The unemployment rate will continue to increase because it is below the nonaccelerating inflation rate of unemployment.
   b. The inflation rate will increase because it is not in equilibrium.
   c. The inflation rate will decrease because the unemployment rate will decrease.
   d. The short-run Phillips curve will shift to the right as expected inflation increases.
   e. The unemployment rate will decrease to return to long-run equilibrium.

8. What happens to the demand for money and the interest rate as a result of inflation?

	Demand for money	***Effect on interest rate***
a.	the demand for money will decrease	which will increase the interest rate
b.	the demand for money will decrease	which will decrease the interest rate
c.	the demand for money will increase	which will increase the interest rate
d.	the demand for money will increase	which will decrease the interest rate
e.	the demand for money will not change	but the interest rate will still increase

Helpful Tips

- The distinction between what classical economics believed about the effect of monetary policy on the economy and later schools of thought believed about the effect that monetary policy has on the economy can be summarized well using the quantity theory of money ($M \times V = P \times Y$). In the classical view, the velocity of money is fixed (V), as is output (Y). Therefore, if you increase the money supply (M), the only possibility was for the price level (P) to increase.

Module Notes

This module takes an historical view of macroeconomics, presenting an overview of how modern macroeconomics developed. The module presents some of the alternative macroeconomic theories that have developed over the past 70 years. It is not important to know about each of the schools of thought for the AP® exam, but the material in this module is important for understanding how modern macroeconomic theory has developed and what differences of opinion remain.

To differentiate between generally accepted macroeconomic theory and areas where economists still have significant differences of opinion, return to the distinction between positive and normative economics. Positive economics answers questions about the way the world works and relies heavily on models. For example, "Can expansionary fiscal policy result in an increase in aggregate demand?" The answer to this question can be modeled and tested. Economists have come to a consensus regarding many of the important positive questions in macroeconomics. Normative economics, on the other hand, involves prescription. That is, answering questions about how the economy *should* work. For example, "Should expansionary fiscal policy be used to alleviate recessions?" Here we find considerably more disagreement among economists and no way to determine a "right" or "wrong" answer.

Recall from our earlier discussion of positive versus normative economics that we identified several sources of the differences between economists regarding normative questions. First, economics is unavoidably tied up in politics. Individuals and groups have political opinions and they have an incentive to try to support their political views with the opinions of economists. A second source of differences is individual values. In any diverse group of individuals, reasonable people can differ. This certainly applies to economists. Finally, differences arise from economic modeling. Recall that economic models are simplifications of reality that require assumptions about how the world works. Economists may legitimately disagree about which models and which simplifying assumptions are appropriate. As a result, they arrive at different conclusions.

The goal of an introductory course in macroeconomics (as opposed to political science or philosophy) is to understand how the economy works. Your focus should be on the economic models presented. To fully understand the economic models presented, you also need to understand their simplifying assumptions and how those assumptions affect the model. Given this goal, questions and answers in introductory economics courses will not focus on history, politics, or values. Rather, they will focus on understanding and applying macroeconomic models. This module should help you to understand differences in important macroeconomic models and their effect on our understanding of how the economy works.

MODULE | 36 | CONSENSUS AND CONFLICT IN MODERN MACROECONOMICS

BEFORE YOU READ THE MODULE

Summary

This module explains how the intense debates about macroeconomics in the 1960s, 1970s, and 1980s have led to a broad consensus about several crucial macroeconomic issues.

Module Objectives

Review these objectives before you read the module. Place a "√" on the line when you can do each of the following:

_____**Objective #1.** List and describe the elements of the modern macroeconomic consensus

_____**Objective #2.** Explain the main remaining disputes

WHILE YOU READ THE MODULE

Practice the Model

Draw a correctly labeled Laffer curve. Label the horizontal axis "tax rate (%)" and the vertical axis "tax revenue." Then illustrate two points on your Laffer curve. Label point *A* where a reduction in tax rates would result in a reduction in tax revenues, and point *B* where a reduction in tax rates would result in an increase in tax revenues. Use the FYI box on page 356 in Module 36 of your textbook as your guide.

List questions or difficulties from your initial reading of the module.

Fill-in-the-Blanks

Fill in the blanks to complete the following statements. If you find yourself having difficulties, please refer back to the appropriate section in the text.

- A group of economists called **1)**_____ economists generally believed that

  expansionary monetary policy was ineffective or even harmful in fighting recessions. This differed

  from **2)**_____ economists who believed that expansionary monetary policy may

  help fight recessions and **3)**_____ economists who believed that expansionary

  monetary policy was of doubtful effectiveness. The modern consensus, however, is that expansionary

  monetary policy is usually effective in fighting recessions except in extreme situations such as a

  4)_____ trap.

- The modern consensus on fiscal policy is that it **5)**_____ affect output during

  recessions; however, most economists agree that it should not be used in a **6)**_____

  way. In summary, the modern consensus is that **7)**_____ policy should be the

  primary tool of stabilization policy, **8)**_____ policy should be used sparingly to

  avoid political business cycles, and **9)**_____ banks should be independent and

  insulated from government to avoid political business cycles.

Multiple-Choice Questions

Circle the best choice to answer or complete the following questions or incomplete statements. For additional practice, use the space provided to explain why one or more of the incorrect options do not work.

10. The idea that households will see any increase in government spending as an indication that their taxes will increase in the future, and therefore those households will decrease their current spending in order to pay those taxes is called
    a. new Keynesian economics.
    b. Ricardian equivalence.
    c. new classical macroeconomics.
    d. the Laffer equilibrium.
    e. a Phillips trade off.

222   Module 36: Consensus and Conflict in Modern Macroeconomics

11. The modern consensus on fiscal policy is that it _____ because of the lags that can occur.

   a. should never be used

   b. should not be used in a discretionary way, but can be used in extreme circumstances as long as there is no budget deficit

   c. should always be used as a stabilization tool

   d. should not be used in a discretionary way, but running budget deficits during recessions and budget surpluses during expansions is an appropriate automatic stabilizer

   e. should be used to influence elections

Helpful Tips

- The fact that expansionary fiscal policy is appropriate in some circumstances, but not in others, is a reminder that economics does not attempt to describe something as "bad" or "good," but rather to understand the benefits and consequences of each action. Fiscal policy has its limitations: understanding what those limitations are is critical.

Module Notes

The material presented in this module is not meant to imply that there is complete agreement among economists. As we have seen, economists often disagree. However, disagreements between economists most often arise with regard to normative questions that involve value judgments and/or politics. Over time, economists have reached a general consensus (though not complete agreement) regarding the way the economy works. Over the past 70 years, the economics discipline has grown and developed. Economic theories have been developed, tested, discarded, and refined. While there is still much to learn and the economy is ever-changing, the economics discipline has developed a considerable understanding of the macroeconomy and has created a modern macroeconomic consensus. This consensus should be the focus of your initial study of macroeconomics.

As noted above, disagreements between economists most often arise with regard to normative questions that involve value judgments or political beliefs. Of course you have your own values and political opinions and these will factor into your answers to normative questions. However, the focus in an introductory macroeconomic course is on positive questions and understanding how the economy works. Questions and answers will focus on understanding models and their underlying assumptions rather than history, politics, and philosophies. Once you understand the basics, you will be in a better position to form your own position with regard to normative questions.

Draw the Featured Model: The Phillips Curve

1) In the graph below, draw a short-run Phillips curve for an expected rate of inflation equal to zero labeled $SRPC_0$. The long-run Phillips curve has been drawn for you. Label the point where the short-run Phillips curve intersects the long-run Phillips curve if the expected rate of inflation equals zero.

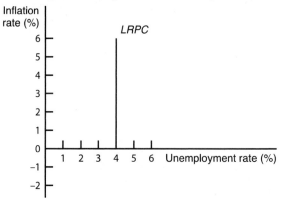

2) Draw a short-run Phillips curve for an expected rate of inflation equal to 2%. The long-run Phillips curve has been drawn for you. Explain why there is a negative portion of the horizontal axis on this graph.

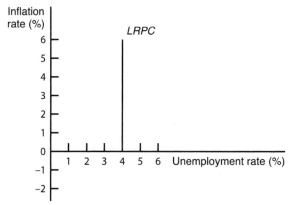

3) Draw a short-run Phillips curve for an expected rate of inflation equal to zero but a current rate of inflation equal to 1%. The long-run Phillips curve has been drawn for you. Label the current rate of unemployment UR_1. Where is the current rate of unemployment relative to the natural rate of unemployment?

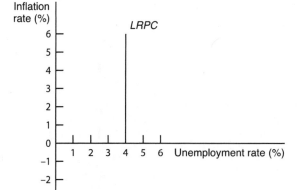

4) Draw the short-run Phillips curve and the long-run Phillips curve for an economy where the natural rate of unemployment is 5%, the expected rate of inflation is 3%, and the current rate of unemployment is 4%. Label the current rate of inflation π_1. What is the current rate of inflation relative to the expected rate of inflation? Show how the difference between the current and expected rate of inflation will affect the short-run Phillips curve.

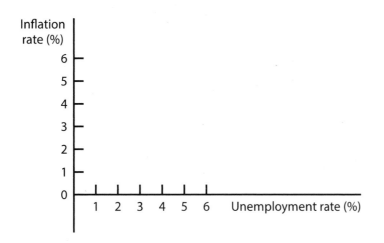

Complete the Exercise

Assume the economy is in long-run equilibrium with an expected inflation rate of 3% and an unemployment rate of 8%.

a. Draw the short-run and long-run Phillips curves and show the long-run equilibrium. Label the point associated with the current rate of unemployment and the current rate of inflation as point *X.*

b. Suppose the actual rate of unemployment decreases to 6%. Show the effect of this change on your graph from part **a.** and label the new point on the short-run Phillips curve as point *Y.* Explain what has happened to the rate of inflation.

c. Now suppose expected inflation rises to 4%. Show what happens to the short-run Phillips curve and the long-run Phillips curve on your graph. Label the new long-run equilibrium as point *Z.*

Problems

1. The following table gives data about Uplandia's real GDP for this year (Year 1) and its projected real GDP for the next two years. Real GDP and the budget deficit are projected to grow 3% per year over the next five years.

    a. Fill in the missing cells in the table.

Year	Real GDP (millions of dollars)	Debt (millions of dollars)	Budget deficit (millions of dollars)	Debt (percentage of real GDP)	Budget deficit (percentage of real GDP)
Year 1	$800	$200	$20	25%	2.5%
Year 2					
Year 3					

    b. Explain what happens to the government's debt–GDP ratio and deficit–GDP ratio when real GDP and the government deficit both grow 5%.

    c. Suppose Uplandia decides to reduce government spending over the next two years. This results in a 1% per year increase in the budget deficit each of the next two years. Assume real GDP continues to grow 3% per year. Fill in the table below based on these assumptions.

Year	Real GDP (millions of dollars)	Debt (millions of dollars)	Budget deficit (millions of dollars)	Debt (percentage of real GDP)	Budget deficit (percentage of real GDP)
Year 1	$800	$200	$20	25%	2.5%
Year 2					
Year 3					

    d. Explain what happens to the government's debt– GDP ratio and deficit–GDP ratio when real GDP grows at 3% per year while the deficit grows at 1% per year.

    e. GDP, deficits, and debt changes are as shown in the following table.

Year	Real GDP (millions of dollars)	Debt (millions of dollars)	Budget deficit (millions of dollars)	Debt (percentage of real GDP)	Budget deficit (percentage of real GDP)
Year 1	$800	$200	$20	25%	2.5%
Year 2	824	222	22	26.94	2.67
Year 3	848.72	246.2	24.2	29.01	2.85

    Explain what happens to the government's debt–GDP ratio and deficit–GDP ratio when real GDP grows at 3% per year while the deficit grows at 10% per year.

f. Compare the growth of real GDP to the growth of the debt to the growth of the debt-real GDP ratio. Can you generalize your findings from this exercise? What general principles does this exercise present?

2. A government is currently operating with a deficit that is growing 4% per year. Assume the economy started with zero debt. If the economy's annual economic growth rate is 5% per year, what will happen to the debt–GDP ratio over time? Explain.

3. **a.** Draw a correctly labeled *AD-AS* graph showing the economy of Macroland in long-run equilibrium. Be sure to include the short-run aggregate supply curve ($SRAS_1$), the long-run aggregate supply curve ($LRAS$), and the aggregate demand curve (AD_1). Label the initial equilibrium aggregate price level (PL_1), initial aggregate output level (Y_1), and potential output (Y_f).

   b. Assume the central bank of Macroland decides to reduce interest rates through open-market operations. Draw a correctly labeled graph of the money market showing the effect of the central bank's monetary policy. Label the initial equilibrium quantity of money and interest rate as M_1 and i_1 and the equilibrium quantity of money and interest rate after the open-market operations as M_2 and i_2.

   c. Explain how the monetary policy action in part **b.** affects real GDP and the price level in the short run. Draw a correctly labeled *AD-AS* graph to illustrate your answer. Label the initial price level and real GDP PL_1 and Y_1, respectively, and the new short-run equilibrium price level and real GDP PL_2 and Y_2.

d. Explain how the monetary policy action in part **b.** affects the price level and real GDP in the long run.

4. **a.** Explain how the Federal Reserve can use monetary policy to expand the economy during a recession.

   b. Explain how the Federal Reserve can use monetary policy to control inflation when the economy is producing an output greater than the potential output level.

5. Evan lends Maggie $10,000 for a year. They agree that Maggie will repay the $10,000 plus $1,000 in interest at the end of the year.

   a. What is the nominal interest rate that Maggie and Evan have agreed to in this contract?

   b. If Evan and Maggie both anticipate that inflation will be 4% for the year, what real interest rate are they trying to achieve in their loan contract?

   c. Suppose the actual inflation rate for the year is 7%. What is the real rate of interest for the contract? Who benefits from the unanticipated inflation? Explain.

   d. Suppose instead that the actual inflation rate for the year is 2%. What is the real interest rate for the contract? Who benefits when the actual inflation rate is below the anticipated rate? Explain.

   e. If you knew what the actual inflation rate was going to be, and it equals the nominal interest rate, would you be willing to be a lender? Explain why or why not.

6. Suppose that both borrowers and lenders anticipate correctly that the inflation rate will increase by 5% over the next year.

   a. What will happen to the real interest rate?

b. What will happen to the nominal interest rate?

c. Use the following graph to illustrate the effect of this anticipated inflation on the loanable funds market.

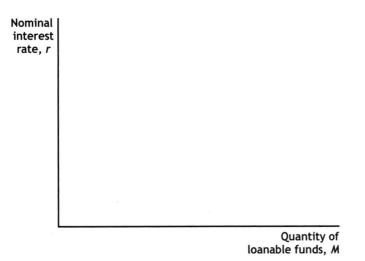

Nominal interest rate, *r*

Quantity of loanable funds, *M*

7. Expansionary monetary policy reduces the nominal interest rate and increases aggregate demand. Explain why expansionary monetary policy does not work in the case of a liquidity trap. Use the following graph to illustrate your answer.

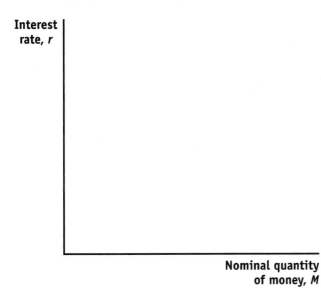

Interest rate, *r*

Nominal quantity of money, *M*

8. Explain why the debt burden increases during a period of deflation and how this relates to debt deflation. Use an initial debt of $1,000, an initial income of $20,000, and deflation of 50% to describe what occurs.

9. Suppose you are given the following information about the economy of Funland.

Unemployment rate	Inflation rate	Expected inflation rate
1%	6%	2%
2	5	2
3	4	2
4	3	2

a. Use the data in the table to draw a short-run Phillips curve labeled $SRPC_1$. Graph the unemployment rate on the horizontal axis and the inflation rate on the vertical axis.

b. Given $SRPC_1$, at what rate of unemployment will inflation equal 0% for this economy? Since the expected rate of inflation is 2%, how will this economy adjust over time to this expected inflation rate? Illustrate this short-run adjustment on your graph and explain your answer.

c. If policymakers effectively change inflationary expectations to 0%, what is this country's NAIRU? Illustrate this NAIRU using a correctly labeled Phillips curve graph and explain your answer.

d. Draw a correctly labeled graph showing Funland's long-run Phillips curve ($LRPC$) and explain its location and slope.

10. The economy of Davia is currently in a recession.

a. Draw a correctly labeled AD-AS graph to represent the current state of the economy of Davia.

b. Assume the expected rate of inflation in Davia is positive. Draw a correctly labeled Phillips curve graph for the economy of Davia. Label the point representing the current state of the economy as point *A*.

c. Assume that as a result of expansionary monetary policy, the economy of Davia returns to long-run equilibrium.

    i. Identify the action that the Federal Reserve took to return the economy to long-run equilibrium.

    ii. Show the effect that the action you describe in part **i.** will have on your graph from part **b.** Label the new level of unemployment as UR_2 and a new level of inflation as π_2. Assume that expectations of inflation have not changed.

11. Assume that the economy of Maxistan is producing an output beyond the full employment level. The nonaccelerating inflation rate of unemployment is 2%, the current rate of inflation is 5%, and the expected rate of inflation is 2%.

a. Draw a correctly labeled *AD-AS* graph that represents the current state of the economy in Maxistan.

b. Draw a Phillips curve graph that shows the current state of the economy in Maxistan labeled point *B*.

c. Suppose the Federal Reserve wants to bring inflation back to 2%. What monetary policy action will the Fed take to reduce inflation?

d. Suppose the Fed undertakes the action you described in part **c.** However, it was unable to bring inflation back down to 2%. Show the point that the economy is now at on the appropriate Phillips curve from part **b.** Label this point *C*.

e. As a result of failing to bring inflation down to the expected rate of 2%, expectations of inflation now adjust to the new rate of inflation associated with point *C* you drew in part **d.** On your graph, show what the effect will be of people incorporating this new, higher rate of inflation in their expectations.

Review Questions

Circle your answer to the following questions.

1. Holding everything else constant, the government's budget balance
   a. tends to increase during a recession, but only if the government expands government spending.
   b. tends to increase during an expansion, even if the government takes no action.
   c. will increase only if the government pursues expansionary fiscal policy, whether or not the economy is in a recession.
   d. tends to decrease during an expansion, even if the government takes no action.
   e. is always equal to zero because the budget must be balanced.

2. When a government decides to spend more than it collects in tax revenue,
   a. it usually borrows the necessary funds.
   b. the budget balance increases.
   c. it runs a budget deficit but reduces its overall level of government debt.
   d. it is forced to sell valuable assets to finance its spending.
   e. the only option is to print more money.

3. Government debt
   a. is always equal to the amount of the deficit.
   b. is the difference between government spending and tax revenue.
   c. always decreases when the tax rate decreases.
   d. is the total amount a government owes, accumulated over time.
   e. is always less than the deficit.

4. The debt–GDP ratio
   a. is a measure of inflation.
   b. provides a measure of government debt relative to the potential ability of the government to collect taxes to cover that debt.
   c. is a measure of unemployment relative to inflation that tells policy makers how much to increase government spending.
   d. is a measure of the difference between taxes collected, government spending, and transfer payments.
   e. is a measure of the relationship between the money supply, the velocity of money, and nominal GDP.

5. An increase in the nominal money supply will
   a. increase the potential output level in the long run, but have no effect on the aggregate price level.
   b. decrease potential output in the long run, but have no effect on the aggregate price level.
   c. lead to a proportionate increase in the aggregate price level.
   d. increase the potential output level in the long run and decrease the aggregate price level by a smaller amount than the increase in the nominal money supply.
   e. lead to an increase in the aggregate price level that is greater than the increase in the nominal money supply.

6. Suppose that an economy experiences an increase in the aggregate output level caused by an increase in aggregate demand. Assuming that the central bank does not engage in monetary policy, which of the following statements is true?
   a. The interest rate in this economy will increase.
   b. The interest rate in this economy will decrease.
   c. The interest rate in this economy will be unaffected by this change in aggregate output.
   d. This change in aggregate output will cause a movement along the money demand curve.
   e. This change in aggregate output will cause the money demand curve to decrease.

7. The chain of events linking expansionary monetary policy to an increase in aggregate demand is
   a. The Fed buys bonds, $\downarrow MS$, $\downarrow i$, $\uparrow$spending on stocks and bonds, $\uparrow$aggregate demand.
   b. The Fed buys bonds, $\uparrow MS$, $\downarrow i$, $\uparrow$spending on stocks and bonds, $\uparrow$aggregate demand.
   c. The Fed sells bonds, $\downarrow MS$, $\downarrow i$, $\uparrow$spending on investment goods such as capital and inventory, $\uparrow$aggregate demand.
   d. The Fed buys bonds, $\uparrow MS$, $\downarrow i$, $\uparrow$spending on investment goods such as capital/inventory, $\uparrow AD$.
   e. The Fed sells bonds, $\uparrow MS$, $\downarrow i$, $\uparrow$spending on investment goods such as capital/inventory, $\uparrow AD$.

8. Holding everything else constant, expansionary monetary policy will
   a. lower the interest rate and cause AD to shift to the right.
   b. lower the interest rate and cause AD to shift to the left.
   c. raise the interest rate and cause AD to shift to the right.
   d. raise the interest rate and cause AD to shift to the left.
   e. raise the interest rate and cause AS to shift to the left.

9. When the economy is producing at a short-run level of aggregate output that is less than potential output, the Fed will most likely engage in what open-market operation?
   a. purchase of Treasury bills
   b. sale of Treasury bills
   c. lowering the discount rate
   d. raising the discount rate
   e. increasing the reserve ratio

10. Inflation targeting means that
   a. the central bank adheres to maintaining a very strict interest rate target and will take actions to hit exactly that target.
   b. the central bank announces the inflation rate that it is trying to achieve and then uses monetary policy to achieve that inflation rate, but there may be a range of acceptable inflation rates or a specific inflation rate that the central bank hopes to achieve.
   c. the central bank will only take actions to lower inflation to that level.
   d. the central bank will only take actions to increase inflation to that level.
   e. the central bank only allows market forces to achieve an inflation target and will not intervene in that market.

11. Suppose the aggregate economy in the short run is operating at an aggregate output level that is greater than the potential output level. Holding everything else constant, what do you anticipate will happen to nominal wages and short-run aggregate supply in the long run given this information?

	Nominal wages will	*SRAS will*
a.	decrease	increase
b.	remain constant	will not change
c.	increase	increase
d.	decrease	decrease
e.	increase	decrease

12. Money is neutral in the _____, assuming that the velocity of money is _____.
   a. long run, increasing
   b. long run, decreasing
   c. long run, constant
   d. short run, increasing
   e. short run, decreasing

13. In periods of high inflation, the short-run *AS* curve
   a. adjusts quickly by shifting to the right.
   b. adjusts slowly, if at all, and will eventually shift to the left.
   c. is insensitive to the high inflation and is therefore unaffected by the high inflation.
   d. adjusts swiftly and shifts to the left due to rising nominal wages.
   e. None of the above statements is true.

14. When there is unexpected inflation in an economy, then
   a. real GDP will decrease in the economy in the long run.
   b. real income will decrease in the economy in the long run.
   c. borrowers benefit while lenders lose.
   d. lenders benefit while borrowers lose.
   e. the real quantity of money increases.

15. All else equal, an increase in the money supply when there is demand-pull inflation and an output gap
   a. will increase the unemployment rate, moving it closer to the natural rate of unemployment.
   b. will decrease the unemployment rate, moving it closer to the natural rate of unemployment.
   c. will have no effect on the rate of unemployment, since unemployment is not part of the *AD-AS* model.
   d. will decrease the unemployment rate, moving it farther away from the natural rate of unemployment.
   e. will increase the unemployment rate, moving it farther away from the natural rate of unemployment.

16. A negative supply shock, such as an increase in the price of an input to production, would initially cause
   a. an increase in the rate of inflation, causing a movement to the left on the short-run Phillips curve
   b. an increase in the rate of inflation, causing a shift to the right of the short-run Phillips curve.
   c. an increase in the rate of inflation, causing a shift to the right of the long-run Phillips curve.
   d. a decrease in the rate of inflation, causing a shift to the right of the short-run Phillips curve.
   e. a decrease in the rate of inflation, causing a movement to the right on the short-run Phillips curve.

17. Which of the following statements is true?
    a. The short-run Phillips curve is a vertical line with the horizontal intercept equaling the NAIRU.
    b. The short-run Phillips curve depicts the negative relationship between the unemployment rate and the inflation rate.
    c. An economy with a low rate of unemployment is an economy that has a shortage of labor and other resources, which leads to falling prices.
    d. The long-run Phillips curve adjusts to take expectations of inflation into account.
    e. The long-run Phillips curve adjusts when there are changes in the current rate of unemployment.

18. Which of the following best captures the idea of the "zero bound"?
    a. The natural rate of unemployment is equal to zero.
    b. If the real rate of interest is 4% and the expected rate of inflation is -4%, the nominal rate of interest is 0%; however, if the real rate of interest is 4% and the expected rate of inflation decreases to -5%, the nominal rate of interest will still be equal to zero.
    c. A central bank will buy bonds until the amount of reserves that a cash has on hand is equal to zero, because only at this point will the target rate of inflation be reached.
    d. When the money supply is equal to the velocity of money, the value of real GDP will be equal to zero
    e. If the rate of inflation as shown by the CPI is less than zero, the actual rate of inflation is zero because the inflation rate can never be negative.

Use the following graph to answer Questions 19 through 21. In this graph, SRPC₁ is the short-run Phillips curve for this economy when the expected inflation rate equals 0%.

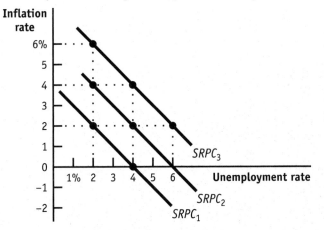

19. The short-run Phillips curve (*SRPC*) equals $SRPC_2$ when the expected inflation rate equals
    a. 0%.
    b. 2%.
    c. 4%.
    d. 6%.
    e. cannot be determined from the graph

20. Suppose the inflation rate is 4% and this economy finds that its unemployment rate equals 3%. What is the NAIRU for this economy?
    a. 0%
    b. 2%
    c. 4%
    d. 6%
    e. cannot be determined without more information

21. Suppose the policymakers decide to pursue an unemployment rate of 2%. This will
    a. cause accelerating inflation in the long run, which will cause the *LRPC* to shift to the left.
    b. lead to rightward shifts in the *LRPC*, due to accelerating inflation in the long run.
    c. cause equilibrium wage rates to fall.
    d. lead to rightward shifts of the *SRPC* due to decelerating inflation in the long run.
    e. lead to rightward shifts of the *SRPC* due to accelerating inflation in the long run.

22. Governments that run large deficits can
    a. reduce the size of the deficit by decreasing taxes.
    b. reduce the size of the deficit by increasing spending.
    c. finance the deficit by printing money.
    d. finance the deficit by decreasing the money supply.
    e. reduce the size of the deficit by loaning funds in the loanable funds market.

23. Disinflation in an economy
    a. is incorporated into expectations of inflation quickly.
    b. has no impact on production.
    c. has no impact on unemployment.
    d. is the same as deflation.
    e. is incorporated into expectations of inflation slowly.

24. Which of the following statements is true for the modern consensus in macroeconomics?
    a. Prices are flexible in the long run but are likely to be sticky in the short run; in the long run, the macroeconomy will produce at the full employment level of output.
    b. Prices are sticky in the long run but are likely to be flexible in the short run; in the long run, the macroeconomy will produce at the full employment level of output.
    c. Prices are flexible in the long run but are likely to be sticky in the short run; in the long run, the macroeconomy will produce beyond the full employment level of output.
    d. Prices are flexible in the long run but are likely to be sticky in the short run; in the long run, the macroeconomy will produce less than the full employment level of output.
    e. Prices are sticky in the long run but are likely to be flexible in the short run; in the long run the macroeconomy will produce less than the full employment level of output.

25. When the central bank uses a formula that determines its actions, this is called
    a. monetarism.
    b. a monetary policy rule.
    c. discretionary monetary policy.
    d. discretionary fiscal policy.
    e. an automatic stabilizer.

26. The hypothesis that states that inflation eventually gets built into expectations, so that any attempt to keep the unemployment rate above the natural rate will lead to an ever-rising inflation rate, is known as
    a. the natural rate hypothesis.
    b. Phelps hypothesis.
    c. monetarism.
    d. the Laffer hypothesis.
    e. Ricardian equivalence.

Section ⑦ Economic Growth and Productivity

Overview

This section presents long-run growth, the factors that economists believe determine the pace at which long- run growth takes place, and how government policies can help or hinder growth. It also discusses the environmental sustainability of long- run growth.

Featured Model/Graph: *PPC* and *AD-AS*

This section does not present a new model, but it does reiterate how economic growth is represented in two of the models we have already developed: **the *PPC*** and the ***AD-AS* model**.

MODULES IN THIS SECTION

Module 37   **Long-Run Economic Growth**

Module 38   **Productivity and Growth**

Module 39   **Growth Policy: Why Economic Growth Rates Differ**

Module 40   **Economic Growth in Macroeconomic Models**

BEFORE YOU TACKLE THE TEST

Draw the Featured Model

Complete the Exercise

Problems

Review Questions

MODULE 37   LONG-RUN ECONOMIC GROWTH

BEFORE YOU READ THE MODULE

Summary

This module analyzes the sources of long-run economic growth and presents data illustrating how much the U.S. economy has grown over time. It also discusses how large the gaps are between wealthy countries like the United States and countries that have yet to achieve comparable growth.

Module Objectives

Review these objectives before you read the module. Place a "√" on the line when you can do each of the following:

_____ **Objective #1.** Interpret measures of long-run economic growth

_____ **Objective #2.** Describe how real GDP has changed over time

_____ **Objective #3.** Explain how real GDP varies across countries

_____ **Objective #4.** Identify the sources of long-run economic growth

_____ **Objective #5.** Explain how productivity is driven by physical capital, human capital, and technological progress

WHILE YOU READ THE MODULE

Key Terms

Define these key terms as you read the module:

Rule of 70:

Labor productivity or productivity:

Physical capital:

Human capital:

Technology:

Practice the Model

1) Recall that the components of aggregate demand are C – consumption spending, I – investment spending, G - government spending, and X - M – net exports. An increase in one of these components will cause an increase in aggregate demand, which is shown as a shift to the right of the aggregate demand curve. Draw a correctly labeled graph of aggregate demand and show the effect of an increase in investment spending. Label the original AD curve AD_1 and the new AD curve AD_2.

2) The $LRAS$ curve depends on the stock of the inputs of production: labor, capital, natural resources, and technology. Therefore, an increase in any one of these will shift the $LRAS$ curve to the right. Draw a correctly labeled graph of aggregate supply and show the effect of an increase in the stock of capital.   Label the original AS curve AS_1 and the new AS curve AS_2.

List questions or difficulties from your initial reading of the module.

AFTER YOU READ THE MODULE

Fill-in-the-Blanks

Fill in the blanks to complete the following statements. If you find yourself having difficulties, please refer back to the appropriate section in the text.

• The total value of an economy's production of final goods and services in a given year is its

1)_____.   When we calculate the value of production in *real* terms, we have

excluded the effect of changes in the **2)**_____ level. And when we want to

account for changes in population over time, we use **3)**_____, the key statistic

used to track economic growth.

- The mathematical formula that tells us how long it takes real GDP per capita, or any other variable that grows gradually over time, to double is called the rule of **4)**_____.

- There has been an increase in **5)**_____ in an economy when the amount of output produced by the average worker increases. Productivity is calculated as **6)**_____.

Multiple-Choice Questions

Circle the best choice to answer or complete the following questions or incomplete statements. For additional practice, use the space provided to explain why one or more of the incorrect options do not work.

7. Jessica is 17 years old. She lives in a country with a 10% rate of growth, as measured by average annual increase in real GDP per capita. How old will Jessica be when the size of the economy she lives in is twice as large as it currently is?
   a. 50
   b. 24
   c. 75
   d. 20
   e. 17.7

8. Jessica has a pen pal, Jennifer, who lives in another country. Jennifer's economy grows at 5% per year. Jennifer's economy will take _____ more years to double than Jennifer's.
   a. 5
   b. 10
   c. 7
   d. 28
   e. 30

9. Higher rates of growth can be explained by which of the following?
   a. depreciation of the stock of capital
   b. lower output per worker
   c. advances in technology
   d. higher input prices
   e. expansionary fiscal policy

Helpful Tips

- Remember that "technology" refers to the way that resources are combined to produce output. An advance in technology is a new and better way to produce. One example of an advance in technology is digging a ditch with a tractor rather than with a shovel. While technological advances can lead to changes in computers, iPhones, and other "tech" devices, the term "technological change" refers to how those and other devices are used to produce output. An improvement in technology is an improvement in how any of the resources, land, labor, or capital is used to produce output.

- Just because there has been an increase in GDP does not mean that there has been economic growth. Recall that an economy, at least temporarily, can operate past its potential output. Economic growth occurs when that potential output has permanently increased.

Module Notes

When studying economic growth, it's important to understand the difference between a change in level and a rate of change. When we say that real GDP "grew," we mean that the level of real GDP increased. For example, suppose U.S. GDP was \$13.86 trillion in 2006 and \$14.48 trillion in 2007. The difference between these two years, \$620 billion, is the amount GDP grew. \$13.86 trillion and \$14.48 trillion represent the level of GDP in each year. The rate of change between these two years is found by using the formula "$\frac{new-old}{old} \times$ 100" which gives the growth rate. The growth rate, which is the rate of change in GDP between these two years, is $[(14.48-13.86)/13.86] \times 100 = 4.47\%$. If GDP grows at that *same rate* over the next year, the level of GDP in 2008 is found as follows:

\$14.48 trillion + (4.47% $\times$ \$14.48 trillion) = \$15.127 trillion

However, when economists are talking about economic growth over a period of years, they are usually not talking about the same rate of change going on into the future indefinitely. Instead, they are almost always talking about changes in that rate of growth. So, for example, if an economist says that "the U.S. growth rate fell in 2009," that would mean that the *rate of growth* fell from 4.47%. In fact, the growth rate in 2009 fell to 0.11% , less than 1%! And when economists say "U.S. growth accelerated during the early 2000s," they are saying that the growth rate increased year after year, for example going from 2% to 5% to 6%.

Real GDP per capita is a key statistic for measuring economic growth. Real GDP (not nominal GDP) is used to measure economic growth, since real GDP focuses on the increase in the quantity of goods and services being produced and not on the effects of an increase in the aggregate price level. Real GDP per capita provides a measure of the average standard of living in a country.

It is important to understand and know the sources of long-run economic growth. Economic growth arises because of increases in productivity, or output per worker. This increase in productivity is due to increases in human capital per worker, physical capital per worker, and/or technological advance. Economic growth is enhanced by high levels of saving which results in increased investment in capital goods, a strong educational system, adequate infrastructure, well supported research and development, political stability, and appropriate levels of government intervention in the economy.

Productivity increases when physical capital per worker, human capital per worker, or technology increases. Increases in productivity are the primary source of economic growth over time. It is important to understand what productivity is and how an economy's productivity can be improved, as discussed in the next module.

MODULE 38 PRODUCTIVITY AND GROWTH

BEFORE YOU READ THE MODULE

Summary

This module shows how an aggregate production function can be used to analyze economic growth. It also presents the convergence hypothesis.

Module Objectives

Review these objectives before you read the module. Place a "√" on the line when you can do each of the following:

_____**Objective #1.** Illustrate changes in productivity using an aggregate production function

_____**Objective #2.** Discuss how growth has varied among several important regions of the world and explain why the convergence hypothesis applies to economically advanced countries

WHILE YOU READ THE MODULE

Key Terms

Define these key terms as you read the module:

Aggregate production function:

Diminishing returns to physical capital:

Growth accounting:

Total factor productivity:

Convergence hypothesis:

Practice the Model

The nation of Tem had a real GDP of $100 million and the nation of Met had a real GDP of $10 million last year. This year, both countries have experienced a $1 million increase in GDP and both countries have a population of 10,000.

1) What is the current GDP in each country? What is the growth rate of GDP in each country?

2) What is the doubling time for GDP in each country?

3) Suppose that both countries continue to increase real GDP with the same rate of growth as you found above. What happens to the difference in size between the two countries over time? Use your answer to explain convergence theory.

List questions or difficulties from your initial reading of the module.

AFTER YOU READ THE MODULE

Fill-in-the-Blanks

Fill in the blanks to complete the following statements. If you find yourself having difficulties, please refer back to the appropriate section in the text.

- There are three main reasons why U.S. worker productivity has increased over time. First, workers

  have more equipment and machinery, or **1)**_____ capital, to work with. Second,

  workers are better educated and so possess more **2)**_____ capital. Finally, modern

  firms have the advantage of a century's accumulation of technical advancements, reflecting

  3)_____.

- The aggregate **4)**_____ shows how productivity depends on the quantities of physical capital per worker and human capital per worker as well as the state of technology. Increases in physical capital represent movements **5)**_____the productivity curve or aggregate production function, while an increase in technology will **6)**_____ the aggregate production function. Typically, when the amount of human capital per worker and the state of technology are held fixed, each successive increase in the amount of physical capital per worker leads to a smaller increase in productivity. This phenomenon is known as **7)**_____ to physical capital.

- The amount of output that can be produced with a given amount of factor inputs is known as **8)**_____ productivity.

Multiple-Choice Questions

Circle the best choice to answer or complete the following questions or incomplete statements. For additional practice, use the space provided to explain why one or more of the incorrect options do not work.

9. The purpose of growth accounting is
   a. to measure growth rates in various components in GDP.
   b. to measure employment and the relationship between employment and the price level.
   c. to measure changes in the price level and the relationship between the price level and unemployment.
   d. to attempt to figure out how much each component of the aggregate production function contributes to growth.
   e. to calculate the tax revenues earned from economic growth.

10. Suppose two countries have identical amounts of physical capital per worker but different amounts of real GDP per worker. Which of the following could explain the difference in real GDP per worker?
    a. There are differences in the number of workers.
    b. One country has higher productivity per worker than another.
    c. The price level is different in each country.
    d. One country is experiencing diminishing returns to physical capital and the other is not.
    e. One country has higher human capital per worker.

Helpful Tips

- Don't memorize details of the specific case studies in the textbook. The AP® exam will test basic economic concepts rather than specific cases. Instead, focus on the economic concepts that explain *why* East Asia, Africa, and Latin America experienced different rates of growth and how the differences in these regions affect the aggregate production function.

- Diminishing returns is an important economic concept with a very intuitive meaning. Think about studying for an exam as an input to the production of a good (the grade on an exam). The first few hours of studying in a day are likely very productive. However, the payoff (in terms of a higher grade) of studying an additional hour likely goes down more and more the longer you study. For instance, the additional payoff you get from going from studying for 11 hours to 12 hours is nowhere near as high as the additional payoff you get from going from studying for zero hours to one hour.

- Understanding diminishing returns is important because it is a critical concept for understanding aggregate production functions. First of all, diminishing returns apply to all countries and all production functions. We cannot explain that a country has a different amount of output per worker than another by saying that one has diminishing returns and the other does not – it is true of both countries. This leads us to the second reason why understanding diminishing returns is important in understanding aggregate production functions – we can measure diminishing returns to capital only if other factors like technology and human capital per worker are held constant. Therefore, if two countries have different output per worker but have the same rate of capital, it must mean that at least one of those other factors (technology and human capital per worker) must be different and that explains the difference in output per worker.

Module Notes

Diminishing returns to physical capital is an "other things equal" statement. That is, holding the amount of human capital per worker and the technology fixed, each successive increase in the amount of physical capital per worker results in a smaller increase in real GDP per worker. If each successive increase in the amount of physical capital per worker results in larger and larger increases in real GDP per worker, technology and human capital have probably changed

But diminishing returns does not mean negative returns! Real GDP per worker will not ever fall as more and more physical capital is added (the worst adding physical capital can do is not change real GDP per worker). Rather, the *increase* in real GDP per worker gets smaller and smaller, but it remains at or above zero. So an increase in physical capital per worker will never reduce productivity. But due to diminishing returns, at some point increasing the amount of physical capital per worker is so small that it is not worth the cost of the additional physical capital.

MODULE 39 GROWTH POLICY: WHY ECONOMIC GROWTH RATES DIFFER

BEFORE YOU READ THE MODULE

Summary

This module investigates why growth rates differ across countries and across periods of time.

Module Objectives

Review these objectives before you read the module. Place a "√" on the line when you can do each of the following:

_____**Objective #1.** Discuss the factors that explain why long-run growth rates differ so much among countries

_____**Objective #2.** Explain the challenges to growth posed by scarcity of natural resources, environmental degradation, and efforts to make growth sustainable

WHILE YOU READ THE MODULE

Key Terms

Define these key terms as you read the module:

Research and development or R&D:

Infrastructure:

Sustainable:

Practice the Model

Infrastructure, like capital, is not a one-time expenditure. It requires ongoing spending to maintain. For instance, if you build a bridge, that bridge will require maintenance and repairs to keep it operational. Suppose a country maintains the same level of government expenditures, but spends zero on infrastructure maintenance, causing the stock of capital to decrease in the long run. Draw a correctly labeled *AD-AS* graph to illustrate what happens when there is a decrease in the economy's stock of capital that provides the underpinnings of economic activity on the equilibrium price level and real GDP.

List questions or difficulties from your initial reading of the module.

AFTER YOU READ THE MODULE

Fill-in-the-Blanks

Fill in the blanks to complete the following statements. If you find yourself having difficulties, please refer back to the appropriate section in the text.

- Economies grow when they increase their physical capital stock through **1)**_____ spending, add to their **2)**_____ capital through education, or benefit from scientific advances that lead to **3)**_____ progress. Spending by the private sector or the government to create new technologies and implement their use is known as **4)**_____ spending.

- Governments can spur economic growth by spending on the parts of the economy's physical capital that provide an underpinning for economic activity, known as **5)**_____. The government can also spur private investment spending by providing an efficient **6)**_____ system that links savers with investors. Governments also facilitate economic growth through spending on education to develop the economy's **7)**_____ capital and providing political stability and **8)**_____ rights. Economic growth that occurs in spite of a scarcity of natural resources is said to be **9)**_____ growth.

Multiple-Choice Question

Circle the best choice to complete the following incomplete statement. For additional practice, use the space provided to explain why one or more of the incorrect options do not work.

10. Most economists believe that sustainable growth
   a. is based on increasing the number of workers
   b. is based on increasing the stock of capital.
   c. can continue as long as more natural resources are discovered.
   d. can continue in spite of resource scarcity.
   e. is limited by legal restrictions.

Helpful Tips

- Economic growth is expressed as a shift to the right of the *LRAS* curve. However, the *LRAS* curve can also shift to the left. If a stock of a resource decreases, such as a decrease in the stock of capital, this will cause the *LRAS* curve to decrease, representing a decrease in the potential output of an economy.

Module Notes

In the United States during the 1960s, increased awareness of declining environmental quality led to the start of a growing environmental movement that is often associated with creation of the first Earth Day in 1970. Before this time, neither the discipline of economics nor the country was very focused on environmental issues. But the growing environmental movement has led both the economists and the country to think more about the environment in recent decades.

Early in the environmental movement, many assumed that there was a trade-off between economic growth and environmental quality. According to this view, you could draw a production possibility curve with a trade-off between environmental quality and other goods and services. If this was true, the only way to protect the environment would be to restrict economic growth, and economic growth could only come at a cost to the environment.

However, since that time, economists have come to realize that there is not a strictly negative relationship between economic growth and environmental quality. It is possible to continue long-run economic growth while protecting the environment through technological progress and market-based incentives.

MODULE [40] ECONOMIC GROWTH IN MACROECONOMIC MODELS

BEFORE YOU READ THE MODULE

Summary

This module explains how to evaluate the effects of long-run growth policies using the production possibilities curve and the aggregate demand and supply model.

Module Objectives

Review these objectives before you read the module. Place a "√" on the line when you can do each of the following:

_____**Objective #1.** Explain how long-run economic growth is represented in macroeconomic models

_____**Objective #2.** Model the effects of economic growth policies

WHILE YOU READ THE MODULE

Key Term

Define the following key term as you read the module:

Depreciation:

Practice the Model

1) Draw a correctly labeled *AD-AS* graph to show an increase in real GDP, without economic growth.

2) Draw a correctly labeled *AD-AS* graph to show both an increase in real GDP and economic growth. Explain the difference between this graph and your graph in 1).

3) Draw a correctly labeled production possibilities curve graph to illustrate an economy that produces two goods: butter and guns. Identify an initial efficient point on your graph. Now assume the economy increases its production of butter. Label a new efficient point that illustrates this change. Label the initial production combination on the *PPC* point *A* and the new production combination point *B*.

4) On the same graph you drew in 3), illustrate economic growth. Label a point *C* that shows the economy producing more butter without giving up gun production.

List questions or difficulties from your initial reading of the module.

AFTER YOU READ THE MODULE

Fill-in-the-Blanks

Fill in the blanks to complete the following statements. If you find yourself having difficulties, please refer back to the appropriate section in the text.

- On a production possibilities curve graph, economic growth is shown by an

  1)_____ shift of the *PPC*. This shift will result from an increase in physical or

  human **2)**_____ or **3)**_____ progress. Over time, physical

  capital will wear out. This is known as **4)**_____ and it will shift the *PPC* inward if

  the capital is not replaced. A movement **5)**_____ the same *PPC* does not represent

  economic growth, but instead illustrates a different, but still efficient, combination of goods.

- In the aggregate supply and demand model, economic growth is shown as a rightward shift of the

  6)_____ curve. This shift represents an increase in the economy's level of

7)_____ output. If depreciation of capital occurs without any replacement, then the

LRAS curve will shift **8)**_____.

Multiple-Choice Questions

Circle the best choice to answer or complete the following questions or incomplete statements. For additional practice, use the space provided to explain why one or more of the incorrect options do not work.

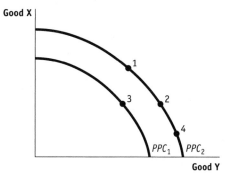

9. Refer to the figure above. Which movement represents economic growth? A movement from
   a.   1 to 2
   b.   2 to 1
   c.   4 to 2
   d.   3 to 2
   e.   4 to 3

10. Refer to the figure above. Which point represents an economy that is experiencing an unemployment rate higher than the natural rate of unemployment?
   a.   1
   b.   2
   c.   3
   d.   4
   e.   Either 1 or 2

Helpful Tips

• An increase in GDP is not necessarily economic growth. Economic growth means that an economy's potential output has changed. Therefore, short-run fluctuations in *AD* or *SRAS* do not create economic growth. Economic growth is represented in the *AD-AS* model *only* by an increase in the *LRAS* curve.

Module Notes

It is important to distinguish long-run changes from short-run fluctuations due to the business cycle. Both the production possibilities curve and the aggregate demand and supply model can help us do this. Recall that the production possibility model shows an efficient level of production on a production possibilities curve (that is, a point inside a *PPC* would indicate that not all resources are being used efficiently). In the production possibilities curve model, if the economy experiences a macroeconomic fluctuation due to the business cycle—such as unemployment due to a recession--production falls to a point inside the production possibilities curve. On the other hand, long-run growth will appear as an outward shift of the production possibilities curve.

In the aggregate demand and supply model, fluctuations of actual aggregate output around potential output are illustrated by shifts of the short-run aggregate supply curve or the aggregate demand curve. In the case of short-run fluctuations due to the business cycle, adjustments in nominal wages will eventually bring the actual level of real GDP back to the potential level. So if *SRAS* or *AD* change, in the long run the economy will return to a production consistent with the *LRAS*, which represents long-run potential output. Long-run economic growth, on the other hand, is represented by a rightward shift of the long-run aggregate supply curve and corresponds to an increase in the economy's level of potential output.

Draw the Featured Model: *PPC* and *AD-AS*

Show economic growth in the *PPC* and *AD-AS* graphs that follow.

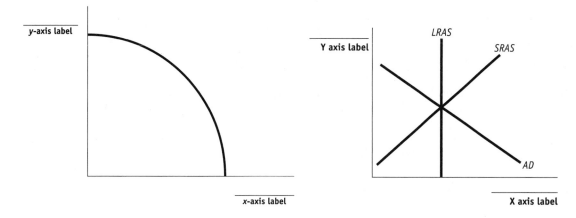

Complete the Exercise

How will each of the following changes shift the *PPC* and the *LRAS* (⟶, ⟵, or not at all)?

	PPC	LRAS

1. An economy adds $100 in new capital, but loses $200 through depreciation.

2. Government education programs lead to increases in human capital.

3. Research and development spending lead to technological progress.

4. A war reduces a country's political stability.

Problems

1. You are given the following information about the country of Macronesia.

Year	Nominal GDP	CPI	Real GDP	Population
2010	$19 billion	95		1.0 million
2011	20 billion	100		1.05 million
2012	23.0 billion	110		1.08 million

   a. Calculate the missing values in the table. Round to the nearest billion. For instance, 18,829,000 would be rounded to 19 billion.

   b. What is the base year for the economy represented in the previous table? How did you identify the base year?

c. Use the completed table from part a. to calculate the missing values in the following table. You will find it helpful to define real GDP in millions (for example, 14.8 billion is 14,800 million), since population is expressed in millions.

Year	Real GDP per capita
2010	
2011	
2012	

d. Let's compare the percentage changes in some of the variables we are working with in this problem. Use the following table to organize your calculations.

Year	Percentage change in nominal GDP	Percentage change in real GDP	Percentage change in population	Percentage change in real GDP per capita
2010				
2011				
2012				

e. In order for real GDP per capita to increase over time, what must be true about the relationship between the percentage change in real GDP and the percentage change in population?

f. Why do we focus on computing real GDP per capita instead of nominal GDP per capita?

2. Suppose real GDP per capita in Fun Land is $10,000 in 2009. Economists in Fun Land predict steady increases in real GDP in Fun Land of 7% a year for the foreseeable future.

a. According to the rule of 70, how many years will it take for Fun Land's real GDP per capita to double?

b. To verify your answer in part a., compute the values for real GDP per capita in the following table.

Year	Real GDP per capita
2009	$10,000
2010	
2011	
2012	
2013	
2014	
2015	
2016	
2017	
2018	
2019	

c. Is your value for real GDP per capita for 2019 equal to $20,000? If it differs, does this surprise you? Explain your answer.

3. The economy of Macro States has 100 workers. The table below gives the output of Macro States at various amounts of capital when technology and human capital per worker are held constant.

a. Complete the table below by calculating real GDP per worker (Y/L) and physical capital per worker (K/L) for the given levels of physical capital and output. Round (K/L) to the nearest hundredth and (Y/L) to the nearest whole number.

K	Workers	Output (Y)	Capital Per Worker (K/L)	Output per Worker (Y/L)
$0	$100	$0		
20	100	$447		
40	100	$632		
60	100	$775		
80	100	$894		
100	100	$1,000		
200	100	$1,414		
400	100	$2,000		

b. Plot Macro States' aggregate production function in the space provided below, where physical capital per worker is measured on the x-axis and real GDP per worker is measured on the y-axis.

c. As physical capital per worker increases, what happens to real GDP per worker?

4. Suppose that Macro States increases its level of technology and human capital per worker relative to its economic condition in problem 3. Now, Macro States' economists estimate that the aggregate production per amount of capital is given in the following table:

K	Workers	Output	K/L	Y/L
$0	$100	$0	0	
20	100	$2,236	0.2	
40	100	$3,162	0.4	
60	100	$3,873	0.6	
80	100	$4,472	0.8	
100	100	$5,000	1	
200	100	$7,071	2	
400	100	$10,000	4	

a. Complete the table above. Round (K/L) to the nearest hundredth and (Y/L) to the nearest whole number.

b. Relative to the aggregate production function you plotted in problem 3b, what do you anticipate will happen to the graph of Macro States' aggregate production function because of this increase in human capital per worker and technology?

c. Compare productivity in Macro States in the initial situation to its new situation, assuming that Macro States has $100 worth of physical capital.

d. Why are increases in productivity important?

5. The nations of Alle and Newo currently have a real GDP per capita of $20,000 and $40,000, respectively. Alle's economy has an average annual growth rate of 3% and Newo has an average annual growth rate of 2%. The size of an economy any number of years from now can be calculated using the equation $X_0(1 + r)^t$, where X_0 is the initial value, r is the rate of growth, and t is the number of years from now.

a. Compute real GDP per capita for both Alle and Newo 10 years from now. The calculation has been started for you for Alle using the values for r, t, and X_0 for Alle:

Alle: Newo:
$20,000 $(1+.03)^{10} =$

b. Compute real GDP per capita for both Alle and Newo 100 years from now.

c. Initially, Alle's real GDP per capita is 50% of Newo's real GDP per capita. After 10 years, what is the relationship of Alle's real GDP per capita to Newo's real GDP per capita in percentage terms? What is this relationship after 100 years?

6. Many people worry that the world may run out of important resources like oil and that this depletion of a vital resource will bring an end to economic growth. Why do many economists *not* believe in this particular perspective?

7. Economists argue that the problems presented by widespread climate destruction can only be resolved through government intervention as well as cooperation among different governments. Why do they hold this view?

Review Questions

Circle your answer to the following questions.

1. Real GDP per capita is
  a. the value of real GDP divided by the number of units of capital in an economy in a given time period.
  b. always increasing over time for any given economy.
  c. the value of real GDP divided by population for a given country.
  d. always greater than nominal GDP.
  e. always decreasing over time for any given economy.

2. The economy of Nosaj had an increase in real GDP of 5% and the population increased by an unknown amount. Which of the following statements is definitely true?
  a. Real GDP per person increased.
  b. Real GDP per person decreased.
  c. Real GDP per person stayed constant.
  d. Real GDP per person may have increased, decreased, or stayed the same.
  e. Real GDP per person is unrelated to population.

3. Which of the following best reflects the doubling time of the U.S. economy, based on the average rate of growth between 1910 and 2010?
   a. 50 years
   b. 33 years
   c. 67 years
   d. 100 years
   e. 20 years

4. Let g be the rate of growth (in percent) of real GDP. The "rule of 70" is used to show that
   a. a healthy economy doubles every 70 years.
   b. an economy's doubling time is $70 + g$.
   c. a country that grows at $g = 10\%$ will double in 70 years.
   d. doubling time for any economy is 70 years if the real GDP grows at the same rate as the population.
   e. the doubling time in years of an economy is $70/g$.

5. Which of the following has historically been most important in driving long-run economic growth?
   a. rising labor productivity or output per worker
   b. putting more people to work
   c. being a relatively rich country initially
   d. the availability of abundant natural resources
   e. controlling population growth

6. Which of the following statements is true of the aggregate production function?
   a. An aggregate production function indicates how output per worker depends on the level of physical capital per worker, human capital per worker, and the state of technology.
   b. Holding everything else constant, an increase in human capital per worker reduces the level of output per worker.
   c. Holding everything else constant, a decrease in physical capital per worker increases the level of output per worker.
   d. Holding everything else constant, a decrease in the state of technology reduces output per worker.
   e. An aggregate production function indicates how output per worker depends on capital only.

7. Suppose the amount of human capital per worker and the state of technology are held constant. As physical capital per worker increases, each additional increase in physical capital per worker leads to
   a. greater increases in output per worker.
   b. greater decreases in output per worker.
   c. smaller increases in output per worker.
   d. smaller decreases in output per worker.
   e. identical increases in output per worker.

8. An economy increases its level of physical capital per worker by increasing the level of investment spending. This can be achieved by
   a. having domestic residents spend more of their income on consumption spending.
   b. having domestic residents spend less of their income on consumption spending while increasing their domestic saving.
   c. lending to residents of other countries.
   d. decreasing consumption spending without changing domestic savings.
   e. decreasing domestic savings.

9. Which of the following statements is true about incomes around the world?
   a. The United States produced twice as much in 2010 as it did in 1910.
   b. As of 2010, China was as wealthy as the United States was in 1910.
   c. Despite dramatic growth in India over the past 30 years, India was still poorer in 2010 than the United States was in 1910.
   d. High income countries are found only in North America.
   e. All low income countries are in Africa.

10. Suppose real GDP in Macroland was $500 billion in 2012 and $650 billion in 2013. Then the growth rate of real GDP in Macroland between 2012 and 2013 was
    a. 50%.
    b. 5%.
    c. 150%.
    d. 15%
    e. 30%

11. Which of the following statements is true about the role of infrastructure?
    a. Countries with low levels of infrastructure typically experience low rates of economic growth.
    b. Infrastructure is primarily provided by private companies.
    c. Basic public health measures, like clean water, are not considered part of an economy's infrastructure.
    d. Convergence theory holds when there are differences in infrastructure.
    e. Low capital infrastructure is an issue for many poor countries, but poor health infrastructure is not.

12. Long-run economic growth requires
    a. the imposition of bureaucratic restrictions on business and household activity.
    b. political stability and respect for property rights.
    c. extensive government intervention in markets in the form of import restrictions, government subsidies, and protection of firms from competitive economic pressures.
    d. private capital accumulation, but not infrastructure development.
    e. private capital accumulation, but not human capital development.

13. Which of the following statements is true?
    a. Today there is approximately $30,000 worth of physical capital per average U.S. private-sector worker.
    b. There have been no improvements in the education of the American population in the past 50 years.
    c. Modest innovations can result in large technological gains for an economy.
    d. The typical U.S. worker produces about the same amount of goods today as the typical U.S. worker produced 100 years ago.
    e. The typical U.S. worker produces fewer goods today than the typical U.S. worker did 100 years ago.

14. Which of the following would represent economic growth on an *AD-AS* graph?
    a. an increase in the *LRAS* curve
    b. an increase in the *SRAS* curve
    c. an increase in the *AD* curve
    d. an increase in both the *AD* and *SRAS* curve
    e. Growth cannot be represented on an *AD-AS* graph.

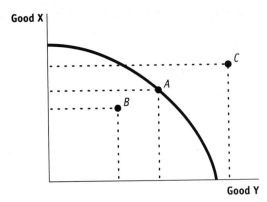

15. Refer to the figure above. An economy moves from a combination of goods represented by point *A* to a combination of goods represented by point *B*. The economy is
    a. operating at the natural rate of unemployment.
    b. operating with an unemployment rate of zero.
    c. experiencing an increase in unemployment.
    d. experiencing a decrease in unemployment.
    e. increasing its natural rate of unemployment.

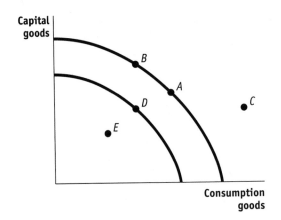

16. Refer to the figure above. If the economy shown moves from the production represented by point *A* to the production represented by point *D*, then the economy will have
    a. a higher level of unemployment.
    b. an accumulation of more capital.
    c. an increase in the stock of technology.
    d. an inefficient amount of production.
    e. no change in the rate of unemployment.

Section ⑧ The Open Economy: International Trade and Finance

Overview

This section presents the key issues in open-economy macroeconomics: the determinants of a country's balance of payments, the factors affecting exchange rates, the different forms of exchange rate policy adopted by various countries, and the relationship between exchange rates and macroeconomic policy.

Featured Model/Graph: The Foreign Exchange Market

The supply and demand model is again featured in this section. It is used to analyze the foreign exchange market. Foreign currency is bought and sold in the foreign exchange market where the quantity of the currency exchanged and the equilibrium price of the currency, also known as the exchange rate, are determined by the interaction of supply and demand.

MODULES IN THIS SECTION

Module 41   **Capital Flows and the Balance of Payments**

Module 42   **The Foreign Exchange Market**

Module 43   **Exchange Rate Policy and Macroeconomic Policy**

Module 44   **Barriers to Trade**

Module 45   **Putting it All Together**

BEFORE YOU TACKLE THE TEST

Draw the Featured Model

Complete the Exercise

Problems

Review Questions

MODULE 41 CAPITAL FLOWS AND THE BALANCE OF PAYMENTS

BEFORE YOU READ THE MODULE

Summary

This module explains how economists keep track of international transactions using balance of payment accounts similar to the national income and product accounts studied in Section 3.

Module Objectives

Review these objectives before you read the module. Place a "√" on the line when you can do each of the following:

_____**Objective #1** Explain the meaning of the balance of payments accounts

_____**Objective #2** Identify the determinants of international capital flows

WHILE YOU READ THE MODULE

Key Terms

Define these key terms as you read the module:

Balance of payments accounts:

Balance of payments on the current account (also called the current account):

Balance of payments on goods and services:

Merchandise trade balance (also called the trade balance):

Balance of payments on the financial account (also called the financial account):

Practice the Model

The nation of Atem and the nation of Tema are trading partners with no restrictions on capital flows between them. The table below describes the quantity demanded and supplied of loanable funds in each country at various interest rates:

Interest rate	Quantity demanded of LF in Atem	Quantity supplied of LF in Atem	Surplus or shortage in Atem at that interest rate	Quantity demanded of LF in Tema	Quantity supplied of LF in Tema	Surplus or shortage in Tema at that interest rate
2	120	80	$40 (shortage)	180	100	$80 (shortage)
3	110	90	$20 (shortage)	170	110	$60 (shortage)
4	100	100	$0	160	120	$40 (shortage)
5	90	110	$20 (surplus)	150	130	$20 (shortage)
6	80	120	$40 (surplus)	140	140	$0
7	70	130	$60 (surplus)	130	150	$20 (surplus)

Assume the international equilibrium interest rate is 5%. Fill in the blanks in the side-by-side graphs of the market for loanable funds for each country shown below. Indicate for each country the capital inflows or outflows based on the information in the table.

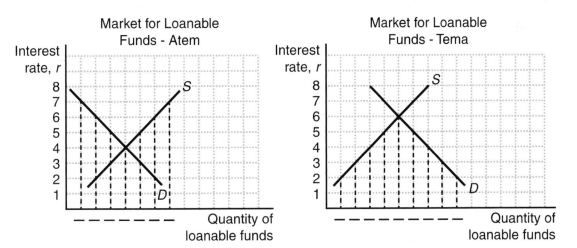

List questions or difficulties from your initial reading of the module.

AFTER YOU READ THE MODULE

Fill-in-the-Blanks

Fill in the blanks to complete the following statements. If you find yourself having difficulties, please refer back to the appropriate section in the text.

• A country's transactions with other countries is summarized in the **1)**_____

accounts. Transactions that don't create liabilities (such as purchases and sales of goods and services,

transfer payments, and factor income) are considered part of the **2)**_____ account.

The most important part of the current account is the difference between the value of exports and the value of imports during a given period, known as the balance of payments on 3)_____. Transactions that involve the sale or purchase of assets that create future liabilities (for example, a bond), are considered part of the 4)_____ account. The current account and the financial account must sum to 5)_____. The sale and purchase of assets is modeled using the market for 6)_____; therefore, a change in the balance of payments in a country will have an effect on the market for loanable funds for each of the countries involved in the sale and purchase of those assets.

Multiple-Choice Questions

Circle the best choice to answer or complete the following questions or incomplete statements. For additional practice, use the space provided to explain why one or more of the incorrect options do not work.

7. If a country has an increase in exports, the country's _____ will increase, and its _____ will decrease.
   a. trade balance; financial account
   b. current account; financial account
   c. financial account; current account
   d. trade balance; current account
   e. financial account; trade balance

8. If imports exceed exports, what will happen to the current account and the financial account?

	Effect on current account	*Effect on financial account*
a.	increase	decrease
b.	decrease	decrease
c.	increase	increase
d.	decrease	increase
e.	no effect	increase

9. If the value of assets sold to foreigners increases, what is the effect on the current account and the financial account in that economy?

	Effect on current account	*Effect on financial account*
a.	increase	decrease
b.	decrease	decrease
c.	increase	increase
d.	decrease	increase
e.	no change	increase

Helpful Tips

- When assets are exchanged, this has an impact on the market for loanable funds, not the money market. A good way to remember the distinction is to consider the case in which a country is running a current account deficit; for instance, it is buying more foreign goods and services than it is selling. The only way this is possible is if another country <u>lends its savings;</u> therefore, this is the loanable funds market, rather than the money market.

- The current account and the financial account always add up to zero, $CA + FA = 0$; therefore, $CA = -FA$. So if CA increases, FA must decrease.

Module Notes

In this section, we expand our study of the economy to include the rest of the world. But, "the rest of the world" has been there all along! We saw it when we studied comparative advantage, in the circular-flow diagram, and as X and IM as contributors to GDP. We live in an interconnected world, and it is impossible to study macroeconomics without considering the relationships between national economies. At the beginning, we assumed away international trade and finance so that we could understand the simplified model. It is crucial that we now integrate the international sector into our understanding of the economy.

You will want to be thoroughly familiar with the terminology and the relationships represented in the balance of payments. The balance of payments shows the flow of money between national economies. It illustrates why the balance of payments on current account must equal the balance of payments on financial account. It illustrates the relationship in a domestic economy between the payments from the rest of the world for goods and services, factor income, and transfers, and payments to the rest of the world for goods and services, factor income, and transfers.

MODULE 42 THE FOREIGN EXCHANGE MARKET

BEFORE YOU READ THE MODULE

Summary

The financial account reflects the movement of capital and the current account reflects the movement of goods and services. As we saw in Module 41, the current account and the financial account offset each other. Actions in the foreign exchange market are what ensure this balance. This module looks at how the exchange rate, determined in the foreign exchange market, assures balance in the balance of payments.

Module Objectives

Review these objectives before you read the module. Place a "√" on the line when you can do each of the following:

_____Objective #1. Explain the role of the foreign exchange market and the exchange rate

_____Objective #2. Discuss the importance of real exchange rates and their role in the current account

WHILE YOU READ THE MODULE

Key Terms

Define these key terms as you read the module:

Foreign exchange market:

Exchange rates:

Appreciates:

Depreciates:

Equilibrium exchange rate:

Real exchange rates:

Purchasing power parity:

Practice the Model

The currency of Canada is the dollar and the currency of Japan is the Yen. As a result of an increase in exports from Canada to Japan, the demand for the Canadian dollar increases. In a correctly labelled graph of the foreign exchange market for the Canadian dollar, show the effect of the increase in the demand for the Canadian dollar on the dollar/Yen exchange rate. Use the symbol $ to stand for the Canadian dollar and the symbol ¥ to stand for the Japanese Yen. Use Figure 42.2 in your textbook as your guide.

List questions or difficulties from your initial reading of the module.

AFTER YOU READ THE MODULE

Fill-in-the-Blanks

Fill in the blanks to complete the following statements. If you find yourself having difficulties, please refer back to the appropriate section in the text.

- Currencies are exchanged for each other in the **1)**_____ market. The price at

  which currencies trade is known as the **2)**_____ rate.

- An increase in the financial account in the United States will lead to a(n) **3)**_____

  in the demand for the U.S. dollar, which will lead to a(n) **4)**_____ in the

  exchange rate. Because of the change in the exchange rate, U.S. goods become more expensive,

  which will cause **5)**_____ to decrease. This then causes a decrease in the U.S.

  current account balance. This is an example of why the current account and the financial account

  always move in **6)**_____ directions.

- The nominal exchange rate at which a given basket of goods and services would cost the same amount in each country is called **7)**_____. This nominal exchange rate will change over time if countries have different rates of **8)**_____.

Multiple-Choice Questions

Circle the best choice to answer or complete the following questions or incomplete statements. For additional practice, use the space provided to explain why one or more of the incorrect options do not work.

9. The real exchange rate between the U.S. dollar and the Japanese Yen (expressed as Yen per dollar) for the U.S. dollar, in Japanese Yen, would increase if
   a. the price level in the United States increased relative to the price level in Japan.
   b. the price level in Japan increased relative to the price level in the United States.
   c. the nominal exchange rate of the U.S. dollar decreased.
   d. the price level in Japan decreased relative to the price level in the United States.
   e. the interest rate in the United States decreased.

Helpful Tips

- A common error in foreign exchange markets is to incorrectly state the price of a currency. The price of one currency is always expressed in terms of another currency. This makes sense: if you are buying dollars with dollars, you aren't really exchanging currency. Therefore, if you are talking about the market for dollars, the exchange rate (the "price") of dollars will always be in some other currency (Yen, yuan, pesos, etc.)

- When you say that a currency appreciates, you are saying that it takes more of another currency to buy the same amount. For instance, if the dollar appreciates relative to the peso, then it will take more pesos to purchase a dollar. Similarly, if a dollar depreciates, it takes fewer pesos to purchase a dollar.

Module Notes

Suppose someone says, "The U.S. exchange rate is up." What does that mean? It isn't clear: it ultimately depends on how they are expressing the value of currency. For this reason, it is more precise to say that a currency has either appreciated (that it is worth more, in terms of other currencies), or depreciated (is worth less, in terms of other currencies).

It is important to understand what an exchange rate is and how changes in the exchange rate affect the country's balance of payments. An exchange rate is the price of one currency in terms of another currency. When a country's exchange rate increases, or appreciates, this makes its domestically produced goods relatively more expensive than goods produced by other economies. This will decrease exports and increase imports for the domestic economy: the balance of payments on current account will decrease, while the balance of payments on financial account will increase.

MODULE 43 EXCHANGE RATE POLICY AND MACROECONOMIC POLICY

BEFORE YOU READ THE MODULE

Summary

This module looks at government policies that have been adopted to influence exchange rates, called exchange rate regimes.

Module Objectives

Review these objectives before you read the module. Place a "√" on the line when you can do each of the following:

_____**Objective #1.**   Explain the difference between fixed exchange rates and floating exchange rates

_____**Objective #2.**   Describe the effects of currency devaluation and revaluation under a fixed exchange rate regime

_____**Objective #3.**   Explain how macroeconomic policy affects exchange rates under a floating exchange rate regime

_____**Objective #4.**   Discuss the considerations that lead countries to choose different exchange rate regimes

WHILE YOU READ THE MODULE

Key Terms

Define these key terms as you read the module:

Exchange rate regime:

Fixed exchange rate:

Floating exchange rate:

Exchange market intervention:

Foreign exchange reserves:

Foreign exchange controls:

Devaluation:

Revaluation:

Practice the Model

Japan and Canada are trading partners with no restrictions on capital flows between them. The following table shows the quantity of Japanese Yen (¥) demanded and the quantity of Japanese Yen supplied at various exchange rates. The current exchange rate on the international market is $2.50 per Yen. Use the values in the table to answer the questions that follow.

Exchange rate ($ per ¥)	Quantity demanded of ¥	Quantity supplied of ¥	Shortage or surplus of ¥
$1	¥400	¥150	Shortage of ¥250
$1.5	¥350	¥225	Shortage of ¥125
$2	¥300	¥300	No surplus or shortage of Yen
$2.5	¥250	¥375	Surplus of ¥125
$3	¥200	¥450	Surplus of ¥250

1) Draw a correctly labeled graph of the market for Yen. Label any surplus or shortage that exists at the fixed exchange rate. Use Figure 43.1 in your textbook as your guide.

2) What action will Japan need to take in order to maintain this fixed exchange rate?

List questions or difficulties from your initial reading of the module.

AFTER YOU READ THE MODULE

Fill-in-the-Blanks

Fill in the blanks to complete the following statements. If you find yourself having difficulties, please refer back to the appropriate section in the text.

- An exchange rate regime is a **1)**_____ governing policy toward the exchange rate. A **2)**_____ exchange rate is an exchange rate that is kept by a government at or near a particular target, while a **3)**_____ exchange rate is a rate that a government allows to go wherever the exchange rate market takes it.

- A government cannot just set a fixed rate by law; it must actively engage in **4)**_____ in order to maintain a fixed rate. Most countries maintain stocks of foreign currency, called **5)**_____, that they can use to buy their own currency to support its price. A government may buy its own currency on the international market if it wants to maintain a fixed exchange rate that is **6)**_____ the international equilibrium exchange rate. A country might want to have a fixed exchange rate if it wants to protect its economy from fluctuations in **7)**_____. A fixed exchange rate is also a good signal that a country will not engage in inflationary policies, because inflation makes a fixed exchange rate **8)**_____ to maintain. However, the tradeoff of a fixed exchange rate is that it limits the ability of a country to use **9)**_____ policy to stabilize the economy.

Multiple-Choice Questions

Circle the best choice to answer or complete the following questions or incomplete statements. For additional practice, use the space provided to explain why one or more of the incorrect options do not work.

Use the figure on the next page to answer questions 10 and 11.

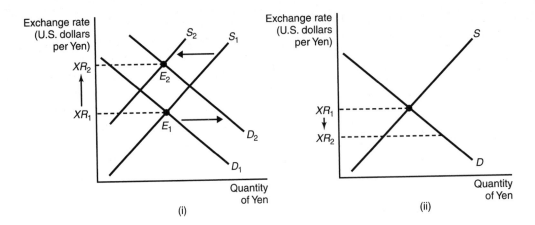

(i)

(ii)

10. A movement from XR_1 to XR_2 in graph (ii) is consistent with which of the following?
   a. a devaluation of the Yen
   b. a devaluation and appreciation of the Yen
   c. appreciation and a revaluation of the Yen
   d. appreciation of the Yen
   e. a revaluation of the Yen

11. What has happened to the value of the Yen in graph (i), and which policies could have caused this?

	Value of the Yen	*Policy*
a.	revaluation	The United States changed from a floating exchange rate regime to a fixed exchange rate regime.
b.	appreciation	The United States has increased its money supply.
c.	depreciation	The United States has decreased its money supply.
d.	revaluation	The United States has lowered taxes on savings, increasing the supply of loanable funds.
e.	appreciation	The United States has decreased its money supply.

Helpful Tips

- Changes in a country's balance of payments or *AD-AS* are not isolated events. They will always impact the foreign exchange market. The foreign exchange market is linked to monetary policy and the balance of payments accounts. Be sure to remember that anything that changes foreigners' purchase of goods, services, and assets will impact the demand for a nation's currency, because foreigners must use that nation's currency to purchase them. For example, if the Japanese want to purchase goods and services or assets from the United States, they need dollars. On the other hand, anything that changes domestic purchases of goods, services, and assets will impact the supply of currency in the foreign exchange market. For example, if people in the United States buy more goods and assets in the United States, they will use more dollars domestically and have fewer dollars available to supply to the foreign exchange market.

- The distinction between fixed and floating exchange rate regimes and the advantages and disadvantages associated with either type is important for understanding the foreign exchange market.

Module Notes

When countries use a floating exchange rate regime, the foreign exchange market determines the exchange rate. With a floating exchange rate, you can use the supply and demand model of a country's currency to analyze how changes (in, for example, interest rates) affect exchange rates the same way you used the supply and demand model to analyze changes in markets for goods and services we developed early on. Any change that affects a determinant of the demand or supply of a country's currency will shift the relevant curve and move the market to a new equilibrium. The determinants of the demand and supply of a country's currency are listed below:

Supply	Demand
Domestic residents buying in other countries	Foreigners buying domestically
- Goods	- Goods
- Services	- Services
- Assets	- Assets

A change in a determinant of demand or supply will shift the demand or supply curve and lead to a new equilibrium exchange rate.

In a fixed exchange rate regime, a country must respond any time a change affects the foreign exchange market. Without a government response, a change in a determinant of demand or supply will shift the demand or supply curve and lead to a new equilibrium exchange rate. To keep the exchange rate fixed, the government must take an action to counteract the effect of any change that affects the equilibrium exchange rate in the market. In the case of either a floating or a fixed exchange rate regime, this model of the exchange rate has the same underlying principles as the supply and demand model of a market for a good or service.

MODULE 44 BARRIERS TO TRADE

BEFORE YOU READ THE MODULE

Summary

This module looks at reasons why a country may enact barriers to trade, and the tools it has available if it wants to restrict international trade.

Module Objectives

Review these objectives before you read the module. Place a "√" on the line when you can do each of the following:

_____Objective #1. Explain the pros and cons of protectionism

_____Objective #2. Illustrate the effects of a tariff and an import quota

WHILE YOU READ THE MODULE

Key Terms

Define these key terms as you read the module:

Protectionism:

Tariffs:

Import quota:

Practice the Model

The figure on the next page represents the market for televisions in the United States. The current equilibrium price of televisions in the United States is $200 and 40,000 televisions are sold at that price. The current world price of televisions is $125.

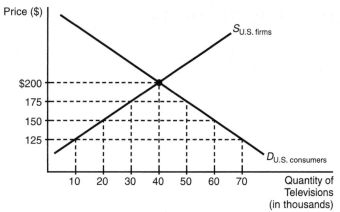

1) What is the quantity of televisions supplied by firms in the United States if the United States is a closed economy?

2) On the figure above, draw the supply curve that represents the international supply of televisions if foreign firms can supply an unlimited number of televisions at the world price. Label this curve Supply$_W$. Use Figure 44.2 in your textbook as your guide.

3) What is the total number of televisions that would be sold in the United States if the economy were open? How many of these are produced by firms in the United States? How many are imported?

4) Now suppose that the United States imposes a tariff of $50 per television set. On the same graph you used in part 2) above, draw the supply curve that represents the foreign supply of televisions with a $50 tariff. Label this curve Supply$_{WT}$.

5) As a result of the tariff, how many televisions will be sold in the United States? How many will be produced by firms in the United States? How many will be imported? What is the total amount of tariff revenue collected?

List questions or difficulties from your initial reading of the module.

AFTER YOU READ THE MODULE

Fill-in-the-Blanks

Fill in the blanks to complete the following statements. If you find yourself having difficulties, please refer back to the appropriate section in the text.

- The practice of limiting trade to protect domestic industries is called **1)**_____.

  Despite the fact that specialization and trade have the potential to benefit consumers by making more goods available, some countries may limit trade on some products for a period of time. They do this

so that they can attain comparative advantage without having to compete with countries with

2)_____ prices. One way of providing protection from imports that also

provides revenues for governments is/are 3)_____, which is a tax on imports.

Another way of restricting trade is to impose a limit on the quantity of a good that can be imported,

called a(n) 4)_____. Trade barriers are rarely one sided. One problem with

enacting a trade barrier against goods from another country is that the other country will likely

5)_____ by enacting its own barrier against importing goods.

Multiple-Choice Questions

Circle the best choice to answer or complete the following questions or incomplete statements. For additional practice, use the space provided to explain why one or more of the incorrect options do not work.

Use the following figure to answer questions 6 and 7:

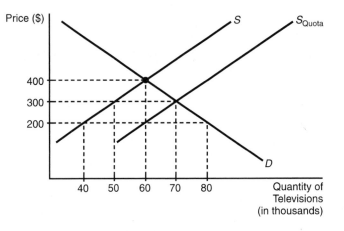

6. Refer to the preceding figure. Without any barriers to trade, _____ televisions are sold, at a price of $_____, and _____ televisions are imported.

	Televisions sold	Price of televisions	Number imported
a.	60,000	$400	0
b.	30,000	$200	80,000
c.	60,000	$200	0
d.	80,000	$200	40,000
e.	80,000	$400	60,000

7. Refer to the preceding figure. The graph shows an import quota that results in _____ televisions being sold in the United States at a price of $300 and _____ televisions allowed to be imported.

	Televisions sold in the United States	*Televisions imported*
a.	40,000	40,000
b.	70,000	20,000
c.	70,000	70,000
d.	50,000	50,000
e.	50,000	40,000

Helpful Tips

• Be careful not to confuse quotas and tariffs. Import quotas are restrictions on quantity. Tariffs are taxes placed on goods that are imported, and therefore change the price of a good. A good way to remember them is quantity and quota both start with "Q" and taxes and tariff both start with "T."

Module Notes

This module presented reasons why a country might want to restrict trade, and two of the ways it might do so. Previous modules explained that specialization and trade can make more goods available to consumers. When the international price of a good is lower than the domestic price of a good, consumers are able to buy more of that good, at a lower price, if trade is open. Trade barriers prevent this benefit of trade and are seldom one-sided. When one country enacts trade barriers against another country's goods, it is likely to be answered with trade barriers in that country for its own exports. For these reasons, many economists believe that there are potentially substantial benefits for lowering, if not eliminating, trade barriers between countries.

MODULE 45 PUTTING IT ALL TOGETHER

BEFORE YOU READ THE MODULE

Summary

This module shows you how to use the models developed in the text to analyze different scenarios and evaluate alternative policy recommendations.

Module Objectives

Review these objectives before you read the module. Place a "√" on the line when you can do each of the following:

_____**Objective #1.** Use macroeconomic models to conduct policy analysis

_____**Objective #2.** Improve your approach to free-response macroeconomics questions

When faced with analyzing the macroeconomy, we have seen how breaking a question up into its components (starting point, event, response, short-run effects, long-run effects) can make the task more manageable. Here are some additional tips to make your analysis more efficient and effective.

What is the question?

We have seen that macroeconomic analysis can be very complex. It is easy to go off on tangents when you are thinking about all of the related issues. Make sure that you keep the question you are trying to answer, exactly as it is being asked, at the front of your mind as you consider different scenarios. Pay close attention to exactly what is asked of you. Were you asked to draw a graph, identify, or explain? Were you asked a simple yes/no or increase/decrease question? Be sure you provide the answer to what was asked – if you are asked to "graph" or "show" something, you need to draw a graph showing what is asked. On the other hand, if you are asked to describe, identify, explain, or indicate whether something has increased or decreased, you must answer using words or symbols, not a graph. After you complete your analysis, check to make sure you have answered each of the specific questions that were asked. Also, there is no point to adding explanations or information that wasn't the focus of the scenario/questions. There are no bonus points for extraneous information. Adding superfluous details takes time and may end up confusing you or lead you to contradict a correct answer you had already given.

Use symbols and abbreviations in explanations

Using commonly recognized symbols can save you time and make your answer more concise. You can expect any economists evaluating your analysis to understand typical "economics shorthand." For example, an economist will know what GDP, P, or Q stand for. You can also use symbols to more quickly and clearly convey your analysis. For example, if you are asked to explain how an increase in the money supply will affect the aggregate demand curve, you could write out your answer in words, for example:

> *An increase in the money supply causes the interest rate to fall, which results in an increase in spending on investment goods such as capital, which leads to a rightward shift in the aggregate demand curve.*

You could also answer using symbols and abbreviations:

$$\uparrow MS \rightarrow \downarrow r \rightarrow \uparrow I \rightarrow \uparrow AD$$

One note of caution: be sure you are correctly using commonly accepted symbols or letters that stand for economic concepts. For instance, the lower case letter r typically stands for the nominal interest rate, although you can use i as well. Inflation has several accepted abbreviations (or you can write out the whole word), but using "I" for inflation is unacceptable because it typically refers to the interest rate, not inflation.

Keep going

Analyzing a scenario involves several steps, and there are a number of connections between the conclusions from one step and the analysis in the next step. It is not uncommon to become uncertain about whether you have made a mistake on a previous step, which makes you wonder if you should change direction or stop altogether. If you are unsure about your analysis at any step, don't just give up or change direction. Continue with your answer through the entire scenario. For example, suppose you are given a situation in which you need to determine what happens to the real interest rate, but you aren't completely sure. You are then asked what will happen to the investment portion of GDP if the real interest rate changes *as you specified*. Whether or not you are sure that the real interest rate increases, you can show you understand that IF the interest rate increased, spending on investment goods such as capital would fall. Even if you make a mistake early on, you will still have the opportunity to show that you understand other parts of the analysis.

Draw the Featured Model: The Foreign Exchange Market

1) The following graphs show the market for genos (the currency of Genovia, abbreviated G) and the market for Genovia's trading partner Patia, whose currency is the pat (P). The current equilibrium exchange rate is 3 genos per pat and 1/3 pat per geno. However, some of the labels of each graph are missing. Fill in the missing labels on each graph.

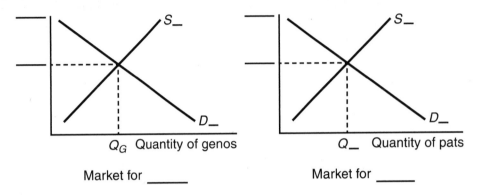

Market for _____   Market for _____

2) Draw correctly labeled side-by-side graphs of the market for pesos and the market for U.S. dollars. On each graph, show the initial equilibrium exchange rate and the effect on it in each market if U.S. investors decide to invest more in Mexico.

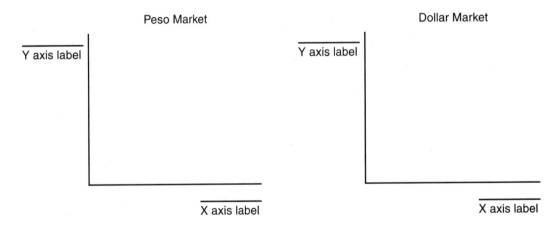

Complete the Exercise

Assume that Canada and Albania are the only two countries in the world, and that there are no barriers to trade. The currency of Canada is the Canadian dollar ($) and the currency of Albania is the lek (L). For each of the following scenarios, i) indicate the effect on the real exchange rate for each currency and ii) indicate the country that will have an increase in the demand for its currency.

(HINT: Start with an exchange rate of 10 lek per dollar and a price index of 100 in each country. Using these numbers, the real exchange rate $RER_\$ = ER(inLek)x\dfrac{PL_{Canada}}{PL_{Albania}} = RER_\$ = 10Lx\dfrac{100}{100} = 10L$ and

$RER_L = \dfrac{1}{10}\$x\dfrac{100}{100} = \dfrac{1}{10}\$$. So if a question indicated that inflation in Canada was 5%, the real

exchange rate of the dollar would then be $RER_\$ = 10Lx\dfrac{105}{100} = 10.5L$, and the real exchange rate of the lek would be $RER_L = \frac{1}{10}\$x\frac{100}{105} = .0952\$$. Therefore, the RER of the Canadian dollar increased and the RER of the Albanian lek decreased.)

_____ 1. Inflation is 3% in Canada and 5% in Albania and the nominal dollar-lek exchange rate stays the same.

_____ 2. Inflation is 3% in Albania and 8% in Canada; the price of the Canadian dollar falls from 10 to 8 Albanian lek.

_____ 3. Inflation is 4% in Canada and 2% in Albania; the price of the lek falls from 1/10 of a Canadian dollar to 1/20.

_____ 4. Inflation is 5% in Canada and 4% in Albania; the price of the Albanian lek rises from 1/10 of a Canadian dollar to 1/2 of a Canadian dollar.

Problems

1. Use the information in the following table to answer this question.

	Payments from foreigners (millions of dollars)	Payments to foreigners (millions of dollars)	Sales of assets to foreigners (millions of dollars)	Purchases of assets from foreigners (millions of dollars)
Goods	$200	$80	--	--
Services	50	20	--	--
Factor income	70	10	--	--
Transfer payments	10	20	--	--
Official sales and purchases	--	--	$100	$300
Private sales and purchases	--	--	80	80

a. Provide a definition or an equation for each of the following items.

(i.) Merchandise trade balance:

(ii.) Balance of payments on goods and services:

(iii.) Net international factor income:

(iv.)   Net international transfer payments:

(v.)   Balance of payments on current account:

(vi.)   Balance of payments on financial account:

b. Given the previous information, compute the value of each of the terms given in part **a.**

c. Explain why the sum of the balance of payments on current account and the balance of payments on financial account must equal zero.

2. The following graphs represent the loanable funds market in Macroland and Funland, the only two economies in the world.

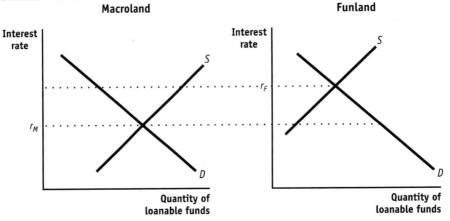

Macroland   Funland

Residents in Macroland and Funland believe that foreign assets and liabilities are as good as domestic assets and liabilities.

a. Given the two graphs, which country is likely to attract capital? Why?

b. Given the Macroland graph, what do you predict will happen to the interest rate in Macroland over time? Explain your answer.

c. Given the Funland graph, what do you predict will happen to the interest rate in Funland over time? Explain your answer.

d. Briefly describe the capital flows between Macroland and Funland.

3. a. The following table reflects the exchange rates between three currencies in June.

Calculate the missing values in the table.

	U.S. Dollars	Indian Rupee	Malaysian Ringget
1 U.S. dollar exchanged for			2.5
1 Indian rupee exchanged for	0.02		
1 Malaysian ringget exchanged for			

b. Suppose that the above exchange rates change in July as shown in the following table. Calculate the missing values.

	U.S. Dollars	Indian Rupee	Malaysian Ringget
1 U.S. dollar exchanged for	1	40	10
1 Indian rupee exchanged for		1	
1 Malaysian ringget exchanged for			1

c. Which currencies appreciated against the U.S. dollar?

d. Which currencies depreciated against the U.S. dollar?

e. Holding everything else constant, what do you expect will happen to the level of U.S. exports to India and Malaysia?

f. Did the ringget depreciate or appreciate against the rupee? Explain.

g. Will Malaysia export more or fewer goods to India? Explain.

h. As a result of the change you indicated in part **g.**, what will happen to Malaysia's GDP (all else equal)? Explain.

4. Suppose you are shown the information in the following table. Assume net international transfers and factor income equal zero for this problem.

Funland purchases of Macroland dollars in the foreign exchange market to buy Macroland goods and services	3.0 million Macroland dollars
Funland total purchases in the foreign exchange market of Macroland dollars	5.0 million Macroland dollars
Macroland sales of Macroland dollars in the foreign exchange market to buy Funland assets	1.5 million Macroland dollars
Macroland sales of Macroland dollars in the foreign exchange market to buy Funland goods and services	3.5 million Macroland dollars

a. Given this information, compute the values in the following table.

Funland purchases of Macroland dollars in the foreign exchange market to buy Macroland assets	
Total sales of Macroland dollars in the foreign exchange market	
Macroland balance of payments on current account	
Macroland balance of payments on financial account	

Now suppose that capital flows to Macroland from Funland decrease and this causes Macroland's currency to depreciate against Funland's currency, holding everything else constant.

b. How will this change affect the demand and supply of Macroland dollars in the foreign exchange market? Use the following graph to illustrate your answer.

Exchange rate
(Funland dollars
per Macroland
dollar)

Quantity of
Macroland dollars

c. How will this depreciation affect Macroland's balance of payments on current account? Explain.

d. How will this depreciation affect Macroland's balance of payments on financial account? Explain.

5. Suppose initially the nominal exchange rate is 20 Macroland dollars per 1 Funland dollar, and the aggregate price index in both countries has a value of 100.

   a. What is the real exchange rate expressed as Macroland dollars per Funland dollar?

   b. Suppose the real exchange rate increases to 25 Macroland dollars per Funland dollar when the aggregate price index in Funland increases to 150. Assuming the nominal exchange rate is unchanged, what is the aggregate price index in Macroland?

   c. Suppose the aggregate price index in Funland is 150 and the aggregate price index in Macroland is 125. If the nominal exchange rate increases to 25 Macroland dollars per Funland dollar, what is the real exchange rate?

   d. If the real exchange rate measured as Macroland dollars per Funland dollar increases, holding everything else constant, what happens to the level of exports and imports in Macroland?

6. Suppose that currently the cost of a standardized market basket in Macroland is 300 Macroland dollars, while the same market basket in Funland costs 150 Funland dollars.

   a. If purchasing power parity holds for the two countries, what must the nominal exchange rate, expressed as Macroland dollars per Funland dollar, equal? Explain your answer.

   b. If the actual nominal exchange rate equals 4 Macroland dollars per 1 Funland dollar, what do you expect will happen to the nominal exchange rate over the long run, holding everything else constant? Explain your answer.

7. Compare and contrast the advantages and disadvantages of a fixed exchange rate regime and a floating exchange rate regime.

8. Suppose Macroland has adopted a fixed exchange rate regime and wishes to target the exchange rate to U.S. $2.25 for each Macroland dollar.

  a. The following figure represents the current situation in Macroland.

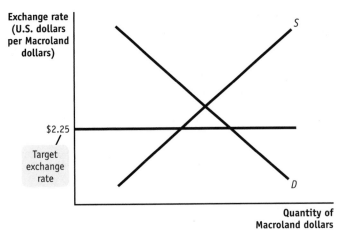

  Describe the situation depicted in this figure, given that Macroland would like to maintain a fixed exchange rate of U.S. $2.25.

  b. Given the graph in part **a.**, what policies are available to Macroland if it is determined to maintain the exchange rate at U.S. $2.25? Explain each option.

  c. The following figure represents the situation in Macroland six months later.

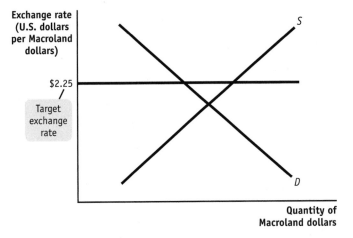

  Describe the situation depicted in this graph, given that Macroland would like to maintain a fixed exchange rate of U.S. $2.25.

d. Given the graph in part **c.**, what policies are available to Macroland if it is determined to maintain the exchange rate at U.S. $2.25? Explain each option.

9. Consider each of the following transactions and identify how the transaction would be categorized in the U.S. balance of payments accounts. For each transaction, identify whether it would be counted as part of the balance of payments in the current account or the financial account. Lastly, identify whether the transaction will increase or decrease the relevant account.

   a. An American company purchases machinery that is produced in Germany by a German company.

   b. An American donates money to the foreign group organizing an international sporting event in another country.

   c. A French citizen purchases cheese produced in the United States.

   d. An American purchases 100 shares of a Swiss company.

Review Questions

Circle your answer to the following questions.

1. Which of the following statements is true?
   a. The balance of payments on goods and services is the difference between the value of imports and the value of exports during a given period.
   b. The merchandise trade balance includes the sale of goods as well as financial assets.
   c. A country's international transactions are tracked by the balance of payments accounts.
   d. The current account is equal to the financial account.
   e. The current account is equal to zero if the financial account is positive.

2. Suppose the balance of payments on the financial account for a country equals -$15 million. Which of the following statements is true about the balance of payments on the current account?
   a. It must equal $15 million.
   b. It must equal $10 million.
   c. It must be less than $15 million.
   d. It must be greater than $15 million.
   e. We cannot determine the balance of payments on the current account without more information.

3. Does the balance of payments track the flow of payments from one country to the rest of the world, the flow of payments into a country from the rest of the world, and the flow of payments for goods and services, factor income, and transfers in the BOP account?

	Flow of payments into a country from the rest of the world, as well as the flow of payments from the country to the rest of the world	Flow of payments for goods and services, factor income, and transfers in the balance of payments on current account	Flow of payments for goods and services, factor income, and transfers in the balance of payments on the BOP account
a.	yes	no	yes
b.	yes	yes	no
c.	no	yes	yes
d.	no	no	no
e.	yes	yes	yes

4. Country 1 and country 2 are open to trade and capital flows between them. If the interest rate in the loanable funds market is higher in country 1 than it is in country 2, which of the following should we expect to occur, all else equal?
    a. Capital will flow from country 2 to country 1 until the interest rates are zero in both countries.
    b. Capital will flow from country 1 to country 2 until the interest rates are equal in both countries.
    c. The supply of loanable funds will increase in country 1 and decrease in country 2 but interest rates will not change.
    d. The supply of loanable funds will increase in country 1 and decrease in country 2, but there will be no flow of capital.
    e. Capital will flow from country 2 to country 1, and the supply of loanable funds will increase in country 1 and decrease in country 2.

5. Country 1 and country 2 are trading partners with no restrictions on capital flows between them. The government of country 1 increases government spending, which it finances through borrowing. What will happen to capital flows between the countries and the exchange rate of country 1's currency as a result of the increased government spending?

	Effect on capital flows	Effect on exchange rate of country 1
a.	no effect	no effect
b.	increased capital flows into country 1	no effect
c.	decreased capital flows into country 1	no effect
d.	increased capital flows into country 1	depreciate
e.	increased capital flows into country 1	appreciate

Answer questions 6 and 7 using the following information. Country A is initially in long-run macroeconomic equilibrium. The central bank of country A increases the money supply, which lowers the interest rate. As a result of the lower interest rate, aggregate demand in country A increases.

6. What will be the effect of these actions on imports, the current account balance, and the financial account balance?

	Effect on imports	Effect on current account	Effect on financial account
a.	increase	increase	increase
b.	increase	increase	decrease
c.	decrease	increase	increase
d.	decrease	no effect	no effect
e.	decrease	decrease	increase

7. What will be the effect on the exchange rate of for country A's currency, and why?

	Effect on exchange rate	Explanation
a.	no effect	An increase in aggregate demand has no impact on foreign exchange markets.
b.	increase	There will be an increase in the supply of country A's currency.
c.	decrease	There will be an increase in the supply of country A's currency.
d.	decrease	There will be an decrease in the supply of country A's currency.
e.	decrease	There will be no change in the supply of country A's currency.

8. Which of the following statements is true?
   a. When a country's currency undergoes a real depreciation, this causes exports to fall and imports to rise.
   b. Nominal exchange rates almost always equal the purchasing power parity rate.
   c. The current account is affected by changes in the nominal exchange rate as well as the real exchange rate.
   d. When a currency undergoes a real depreciation, this causes exports to increase and imports to decrease.
   e. Nominal exchange rates have no effect on real exchange rates.

9. If a government wishes to fix the value of a currency above its equilibrium value in the foreign exchange market, it can
   a. engage in monetary policy to reduce interest rates, thereby increasing capital flows into its country.
   b. reduce the supply of its currency by limiting the right of its citizens to buy foreign currencies.
   c. engage in selling its currency through exchange market intervention.
   d. engage in buying its currency through exchange market intervention.
   e. simply set a new exchange rate, and no further action is necessary to maintain the higher exchange rate.

10. Suppose that in the foreign exchange market there is a shortage at the target exchange rate. We know that
    a. the supply of the country's currency is greater than the demand for that country's currency.
    b. it is possible to maintain the target exchange rate without exchange market intervention.
    c. maintaining a fixed exchange rate will enhance the ability of the government to pursue stabilization policy.
    d. it is impossible to maintain the target exchange rate unless the government engages in exchange market intervention, changes monetary policy, adjusts foreign exchange controls, or pursues some combination of these three policies.
    e. the country has allowed its currency to appreciate.

11. A fixed rate regime
    a. reduces uncertainty for businesses about the value of a currency.
    b. exposes a country to a potential bias toward inflationary policies.
    c. reduces the amount of foreign currency a country must hold.
    d. creates an incentive to pursue monetary policy to help stabilize the country's economy.
    e. clears the market for a currency without intervention.

12. A potential effect of devaluation of a currency, all else equal, is that
    a. foreign goods will become more attractive, which will lead to an increase in imports and a decrease in aggregate demand.
    b. foreign goods will become less attractive, which will lead to an increase in imports and a decrease in aggregate demand.
    c. foreign goods will become more attractive, which will lead to an increase in imports and an increase in aggregate demand.
    d. foreign goods will become less attractive, which will lead to a decrease in imports and an increase in aggregate demand.
    e. foreign goods will become less attractive, which will lead to a decrease in imports and a decrease in aggregate demand.

13. When a country pursues an expansionary monetary policy, this will have what effect on the level of investment spending, the demand for that country's currency, and the supply of that country's currency?

	Investment spending	*Demand for that country's currency*	*Supply of that country's currency*
a.	increase	decrease	increase
b.	decrease	decrease	decrease
c.	increase	increase	increase
d.	decrease	increase	decrease
e.	decrease	decrease	increase

14. The United States and Malaysia are trading partners. The Central Bank of Malaysia increases the money supply. What will be the effect on the price level in the United States, the unemployment rate in the United States, and the value of the dollar?

	Effect on price level	*Effect on unemployment rate*	*Effect on the value of the dollar*
a.	increase	decrease	appreciate
b.	decrease	increase	appreciate
c.	no effect	increase	no effect
d.	no effect	decrease	depreciate
e.	increase	increase	no effect

15. Which of the following represents a payment from foreigners to the hypothetical economy called Macropedia?
    a. the dollar value of corn Macropedia imports from Cornucopia
    b. the dollar value of bicycles Macropedia exports to Pedal Land
    c. the fees engineering firms in Islandville receive for bridge designs they provide to the foreign country of Macropedia
    d. a citizen of Macropedia sells an asset to Gabeland
    e. transfer payments from a citizen of Macropedia to a family in Saliland

16. Foreign exchange reserves are
    a. funds of one country's currency held by another country.
    b. funds of a country's currency that the government holds in case it needs money unexpectedly.
    c. funds that can be used by a country to maintain a fixed exchange rate above the equilibrium, but not below.
    d. funds that can be used by a country to maintain a fixed exchange rate below the equilibrium, but not above.
    e. used to change the money supply.

17. Which of the following statements is true?
    a. The sum of the balance of payments on current account *(CA)* and the balance of payments on financial account *(FA)* cannot equal zero.
    b. The balance of payments account illustrates the concept that the flow of funds into a country's economy must equal the flow of funds out of that country's economy.
    c. A country that exports more than it imports must by definition have negative capital inflows.
    d. The sum of the balance of payments on current account *(CA)* and the balance of payments on financial account *(FA)* must equal two.
    e. The current account is always greater than the financial account.

18. Because of capital flows, most countries now
    a. both owe money to other countries and are lenders to other countries.
    b. owe to other countries, but are not lenders to other countries.
    c. lend to other countries, but do not owe other countries.
    d. neither owe to other countries nor borrow from other countries.
    e. maintain the same capital flows in and out every year.

19. Suppose the loanable funds market in Macroland is currently in equilibrium. Holding everything else constant, if capital inflows increase to Macroland, this will cause what change to the equilibrium interest rate and quantity of loanable funds?

	Effect on Equilibrium interest rate	*Effect on loanable funds*
a.	decrease	increase
b.	increase	decrease
c.	decrease	decrease
d.	increase	increase
e.	no change	no change

20. Suppose the loanable funds market in Macroland is currently in equilibrium. Holding everything else constant, if businesses in Macroland increase the level of their investment spending that is financed by borrowing, this will cause a shift
    a. in the supply of loanable funds curve to the right and a movement along the demand for loanable funds curve.
    b. in the supply of loanable funds curve to the left and a movement along the demand for loanable funds curve.
    c. in the demand for loanable funds curve to the right and a movement along the supply of loanable funds curve.
    d. in the demand for loanable funds curve to the left and a movement along the supply of loanable funds curve.
    e. No change, since the loanable funds market is in equilibrium

21. Which of the following statements is true?
    a. Fast growing economies often have less of a demand for loanable funds than do slower growing economies since fast growing economies often have greater investment opportunities.
    b. The supply of loanable funds in any particular country is impacted by the country's private savings rate: some countries have higher savings rates than do other countries.
    c. Between 1996 and 2007, the United States provided huge capital outflows to much of the rest of the world.
    d. Between 1996 and 2007, the United States provided huge capital outflows to Japan only.
    e. In 2013, private savings in Japan was less than in the United States.

22. The economy of Maxistan is currently in long-run macroeconomic equilibrium. The government of Maxistan increases government spending. All else equal, which of the following are likely results of this action on the real exchange rate and economic growth?

	Effect on real exchange rate	*Will economic growth occur?*
a.	increase	yes
b.	increase	no
c.	decrease	yes
d.	decrease	no
e.	no change	no

23. Suppose that Mexico and the United States have a floating exchange rate regime and currently the exchange rate is one U.S. dollar to 5 Mexican pesos. If the exchange rate changes to one U.S. dollar to 10 Mexican pesos, then the peso has
    a. appreciated against the dollar.
    b. depreciated against the dollar.
    c. devalued against the dollar.
    d. revalued against the dollar.
    e. ceased to be exchanged.

24. Maxistan has a fixed exchange rate regime for its currency, the peso, and the current equilibrium exchange rate is at its target. As a result of political instability in its trading partner, Ile, there is an increase in the size of capital flows into Maxistan. What is the effect on the exchange rate in Maxistan, and will Maxistan need to intervene to maintain the fixed exchange rate?

	Effect on the exchange rate in Maxistan	*Intervention needed?*
a.	depreciate	no
b.	appreciate	no
c.	no change	no
d.	appreciate	yes – Maxistan needs to buy up excess pesos.
e.	depreciate	yes – Maxistan needs to buy up excess pesos.

25. Holding everything else constant, if the U.S. dollar rises against the Mexican peso, then
    a. .U.S. goods will look cheaper to Mexico.
    b. U.S. goods will look more expensive to Mexico.
    c. U.S. goods will look more expensive to Mexico, but Mexican goods will not seem to have changed.
    d. Mexico's goods will look more expensive to the United States.
    e. Mexico's goods will look more expensive to the United States, but U.S. goods will not seem to have changed.

Preparing for the AP® Macroeconomics Exam

I.   Overview

II.   Sample Schedule

III.   The AP® Course Outline

IV.   Planning Your Test Preparation and Review

V.   Reviewing for the AP® Macroeconomics Exam

VI.   Test-taking Tips

VII.   Practice Tests

I. OVERVIEW

The AP® Macroeconomics exam is the culmination of all of your efforts in macroeconomics. There are incentives to do well on this exam. For example, many colleges and universities recognize success on the AP® Macroeconomics exam as the equivalent of a macroeconomics course. This means that you receive credit for a college course and are one course closer to graduating, pay tuition for one less college course, and are eligible to take more advanced courses for which macroeconomics is a prerequisite. Since many institutions give priority registration to students with more credit hours, AP® credit can help you get your preferred college classes. So, for these (and a variety of other) reasons, you want to make sure you do your best on the AP® exam. Doing your best requires that you have a plan to prepare and review for the exam. The material that follows is designed to help you as you prepare for and take the AP® Macroeconomics exam.

You will not be alone in your endeavor. Every year the number of students attempting the AP® Macroeconomics exam grows. As of 2014, more than 217,000 students like you took the AP® Macroeconomics exam, an increase of more than 40% from 2010. A little more than 1/2 of those taking the exam scored a 3 or higher in 2014, the grade that many colleges and universities accept for college credit.

As of 2014, there were more than 30 different AP® courses, and each exam follows its own format. The AP® Macroeconomics exam consists of two parts (which are described in more detail in Section IV).

- **Multiple-Choice Questions**
  The multiple-choice section has 60 questions. You are allowed 70 minutes to complete this section and it counts as 2/3 of your AP® exam score.

- **Free-Response Questions**
  The free-response section has 1 long question and 2 short questions. You are allowed 60 minutes to complete this section and it counts as 1/3 of your AP® exam score.

According to the College Board, AP® test scores carry the following recommendations:

AP® SCORE	QUALIFICATION	OUR TRANSLATION
5	Extremely well qualified	Oh yeah!
4	Well qualified	Most likely college credit
3	Qualified	Maybe college credit
2	Possibly qualified	Hmmm… probably not
1	No recommendation	Ugh!

Maximizing your performance on any AP® exam requires a well thought out preparation and review plan. Following is a suggested schedule for preparing for your AP® Macroeconomics exam. Keep in mind that this suggested schedule will need to be modified to fit your individual circumstances. In particular, you will need to adjust the schedule based on any other AP® exams and activities that you will also have during this very busy time of year!

II. SAMPLE SCHEDULE

What follows is a general guide for creating a plan to prepare and review for the AP® Macroeconomics exam. While each student's approach will differ, consider these suggestions for creating your own plan to maximize your performance on the exam!

1. *At the start of your AP® Macroeconomics course – know what's ahead*
During the first few weeks of your class, take some time to familiarize yourself with the course outline and AP® exam information. It will be helpful to have a general idea about the topics you will study and the format of the AP® exam for Macroeconomics. AP® Macroeconomics exams are not the same as AP® exams in other disciplines and you want to be aware of the differences so that your approach to the class best prepares you to succeed on the exam. The AP® course outline and format of the exam are outlined in Section III.

2. *During your AP® Macroeconomics course – keep the exam in mind*
As you progress through each section of material, periodically refer to sample AP® exam questions to get an idea of course expectations. It is important to understand the level at which the material will be tested and to see how questions testing that material are typically written. You can find sample exam questions --both multiple choice and free response--in your textbook, in the sections that follow, and on the College Board's AP® Central website.

3. *Six weeks before the exam – start gearing up!*
Approximately 6 weeks before the exam, you should begin planning for your exam preparation and review. Depending on what other exams and commitments you have, you may need to start your preparation right away or you may wait until the exam date is closer. Remember that AP® exams for all subjects are given over a two-week period. The economics exams are given during the second week. So, if you are taking other AP® exams, you will need to complete most of your exam preparations before AP® exams begin, more than a week before the AP® Macroeconomics exam is scheduled.

4. *Five weeks before the exam – get into the thick of preparing*
About 5 weeks before your exam (end of March, beginning of April), you should use the diagnostic test provided in the following section to determine how much additional studying you will need and what specific areas you should emphasize as you allocate your additional study time. Follow the instructions provided to take the diagnostic test and use the score sheet and guidelines to help you determine your study and review schedule. At this point, there will still be several weeks of class left and therefore some

content will still need to be covered in class. Make sure that your plan includes this material and allows time for you to learn, practice, and review it.

5. *The week before the AP exam – finalize your preparation*

During the week preceding the exam (around the last week in April), you should be finished studying for the exam and spend your available time reviewing. At this stage, you should be reminding yourself of things you have already learned and reviewing the topics that you had the most trouble mastering or remembering. The study sheets included in the following sections are a great way to review the most important models, formulas, and graphs you will need to understand for the exam. At this point, you can use one of the practice tests included below to help you get used to the exam process and format.

6. *A night or two before the exam – rest and review*

Schedule time for one last review of the course material to make sure it is fresh in your mind. You may want to use the second practice test at this point. You can take the practice test as another mock exam, use it to review, or work through it with a study group. Your final review session should not be too long or intense (you have already done the hardest work!); it is *not* the time to try to learn new concepts. Make sure you arrange to get a good night's sleep the night before the exam, have a good breakfast the morning of the exam, have everything you need to take to the exam with you, and get to your exam site early on the day of your exam!

III.   THE AP® COURSE OUTLINE

The course outline for AP® Macroeconomics is provided below. This outline shows the content areas covered in the course and the percentage of the course/exam devoted to that material.

Content area (percentage of the exam – Multiple-Choice section)

I.   Basic Economic Concepts   (8-12%)
   A.   Scarcity, choice, and opportunity costs
   B.   Production possibilities curve
   C.   Comparative advantage, specialization, and exchange
   D.   Demand, supply, and market equilibrium
   E.   Macroeconomic issues: business cycle, unemployment, inflation, growth

II.   Measurement of Economic Performance   (12-16%)
   A.   National income accounts
        1.   Circular flow
        2.   Gross Domestic Product
        3.   Components of gross domestic product
        4.   Real versus nominal gross domestic product
   B.   Inflation measurement and adjustment
        1.   Price indices
        2.   Nominal and real values
        3.   Costs of inflation
   C.   Unemployment
        1.   Definition and measurement
        2.   Types of unemployment
        3.   Natural rate of unemployment

III. National Income and Price Determination   **(10-15%)**
    A.   Aggregate demand
        1. Determinants of aggregate demand
        2. Multiplier and crowding out effects
    B.   Aggregate supply
        1. Short-run and long-run analyses
        2. Sticky versus flexible wages and prices
        3. Determinants of aggregate supply
    C.   Macroeconomic equilibrium
        1. Real output and price level
        2. Short and long run
        3. Actual versus full-employment output
        4. Business cycle and economic fluctuations

IV. Financial Sector   **(15-20%)**
    A.   Money, banking, and financial markets
        1. Definition of financial assets: money, stocks, bonds
        2. Time value of money (present and future value)
        3. Measures of money supply
        4. Banks and creation of money
        5. Money demand
        6. Money market and the equilibrium nominal interest rate
    B.   Loanable funds market
        1. Supply of and demand for loanable funds
        2. Equilibrium real interest rate
        3. Crowding out
    C.   Central bank and control of the money supply
        1. Tools of central bank policy
        2. Quantity Theory of Money
        3. Real versus nominal interest rates

V. Stabilization Policies   **(20-30%)**
    A.   Fiscal and monetary policies
        1. Demand-side effects
        2. Supply-side effects
        3. Policy mix
        4. Government deficits and debt
    B.   The Phillips curve
        1. Short-run and long-run Phillips curve
        2. Demand-pull versus cost-push inflation
        3. Role of expectations

VI. Economic Growth   **(5-10%)**
    1.   Definition of economic growth
    2.   Determinants of economic growth
        1. Investment in human capital
        2. Investment in physical capital
        3. Research and development, and technological progress
    3.   Growth policy

VII. **Open Economy: International Trade and Finance** (10-15%)
   A. Balance of payments accounts
       1. Balance of trade
       2. Current account
       3. Financial account (formerly known as capital account)
   B. Foreign exchange market
       1. Demand and supply of foreign exchange
       2. Exchange rate determination
       3. Currency appreciation and depreciation
   C. Imports, exports, and financial capital flows
   D. Relationships between international and domestic financial and goods markets

IV. EXAM FORMAT

The AP® Macroeconomics test is divided into two sections. The first section is comprised of 60 multiple-choice questions and the second is three free-response questions. The multiple-choice section counts for two-thirds of the overall exam grade weight, and the free-response counts for one-third of the overall exam grade weight. The number of questions you will be asked from each section of the course outline corresponds to the percentages provided in the course outline. For example, VI. Economic Growth.... 5 - 10% means that anywhere from three to six questions will be asked on the multiple-choice section over this topic.

Multiple-Choice

You will have 70 minutes to complete the sixty questions on the multiple-choice section of the exam. Each multiple-choice question has five answer choices, only one of which is correct. The 70 minutes you are allotted to complete the multiple-choice section translates to 70 seconds per question. For each question answered correctly, you earn one point. No deductions are made for an incorrect response. This means that if you are unsure about the answer to a question, then your best strategy is to make an educated guess. You should always answer all of the multiple-choice questions – there is no penalty for guessing, but you are always wrong if you leave an answer blank! You are trying to rack up as many points as possible. So when in doubt, give it your best shot and guess; you just might get lucky. The worst thing that can happen is that no point will be earned.

Unlike tests that you might take in a class, the AP® exams do not use all of the above, none of the above, or true/false type questions. Instead, the multiple-choice questions you will encounter will come in several different formats. The most common question type asks you to either define or classify concepts learned in macroeconomics. The next most common question type is best described as cause and effect format. Far less common are questions that ask you to calculate an answer or interpret a graph.

Free-Response

The second section of the AP® Macroeconomics exam is made up of free-response questions. Sixty minutes is allocated to the free-response section. Be careful to follow the instructions on where to write your answers for the free-response questions. Only answers written in the space designated for answers will be graded. Anything you write in other spaces on the exam will not be considered by graders.

The free-response section is divided into three separate questions. The first question is the longest and most comprehensive of the three. You should allocate roughly half of your time, about 25 minutes, to answering it. The second and third free-response questions are shorter and typically test a particular area of the course outline. You should allocate roughly a quarter of the time available, or about 12 - 13 minutes, to each of the shorter questions. Allocate and monitor your time carefully so that you are able to provide at least a basic response to each question.

When you answer free-response questions, keep the following in mind:

- Answer each part of the question and provide exactly what the question asks for. Responding to the question asked is crucial. If you skip a part of the question or do not provide the specific answer that is requested, you will not receive any points for that part of the question.

- Be concise. Usually a complete sentence or two is all that is needed to explain an answer. Sometimes only a single word is needed.

- Match your answer to the verb in the prompt. There are four verbs that you will see in free-response questions, and each is asking for something specific. "Show" means use a correctly labeled diagram to illustrate your answer. "Explain" means you need to use words to demonstrate the economic reasoning or chain of events. "Identify" means provide a specific answer, and any elaboration is unnecessary. "Calculate" means you need to perform a mathematical calculation and show your work.

V. PLANNING YOUR TEST PREPARATION AND REVIEW

The following test is designed to help you assess the strengths and weaknesses in your knowledge of AP® Macroeconomics. The test is comprised of 60 multiple-choice questions, each with 5 answer choices, and follows the format of an AP® Macroeconomics exam multiple-choice section. This test is for diagnostic purposes and does not include free-response questions.

Try to replicate AP® exam conditions when you take this diagnostic test: allow yourself 70 minutes to take the test, do not use your textbook or notebook, and do all calculations by hand. The use of a calculator is not permitted on the AP® exam, so do not use one on this test either. If you are uncertain of the correct answer, make an educated guess.

The answers, along with explanations, are provided for you to review once you have completed and graded your diagnostic test. In addition, the answer key correlates each question with a section on the AP® Course Outline. When you are finished, take time to review the answers to the questions you missed and assess which areas of the course outline you have mastered and which you need to review. Use your results to allocate your study time before the AP® exam. Good luck!

Diagnostic Test

1. Which fiscal policy would be most appropriate for combating inflation?
   a. increase taxes and transfer-payments
   b. raise the reserve requirement
   c. the open market purchase of treasury securities by the Federal Reserve
   d. increase taxes and decrease government spending
   e. decrease taxes and decrease government spending

2. If the government increases its defense spending, the opportunity cost is
   a. zero.
   b. irrelevant.
   c. the dollar amount of the spending increase.
   d. the next best alternative use for the money spent on defense.
   e. the dollar amount by which taxes are increased to pay for the defense spending.

3. Depreciation of the Thai Baht in the foreign exchange market could be due to which of the following?
   a. an increase in Thailand's imports from China
   b. a decrease in the price level in the United States
   c. an increase in the demand for Thailand's financial assets
   d. a decrease in real interest rates in China
   e. an increase in Thailand's exports to India

4. Economic growth is best illustrated by a
   a. leftward shift in the production possibilities curve.
   b. rightward shift of the short-run Phillips curve.
   c. rightward shift of the aggregate demand curve.
   d. rightward shift of the long-run aggregate supply curve.
   e. decrease in the slope of the money demand curve.

5. If the combination of goods or services being produced in an economy lies on the production possibilities curve, then
   a. any increase in the production of one of the goods or services incurs an opportunity cost in terms of the other good or service.
   b. the combination of goods or services produced is not productively efficient.
   c. a tariff would increase the capacity of the economy to produce efficiently.
   d. available resources are idle.
   e. the opportunity cost of the two goods being produced must be equal.

6. Unanticipated inflation will have what impact on the following groups?

	Borrowers paying fixed-interest rates	Savers earning fixed-interest rates	Financial institutions issuing fixed-interest loans
a.	better off	better off	better off
b.	better off	worse off	worse off
c.	worse off	worse off	better off
d.	better off	better off	worse off
e.	worse off	worse off	worse off

7. If the money supply is constant, then an increase in money demand will result in which of the following?

	Nominal Interest Rate	Quantity of Money
a.	Increase	Decrease
b.	Decrease	Increase
c.	No change	No change
d.	Increase	No change
e.	Increase	Increase

8. According to the preceding graph, an increase in input prices will most likely cause the price level and employment to change in which of the following ways?

	Price level	Employment
a.	Increase	Increase
b.	Decrease	Increase
c.	Decrease	Decrease
d.	Increase	No change
e.	Increase	Decrease

9. Which type of unemployment would not exist if fiscal and monetary policy effectively eliminated the business cycle?
   a. frictional
   b. cyclical
   c. seasonal
   d. structural
   e. part-time

10. If the marginal propensity to consume is greater than one, then
   a. households are saving all of their income.
   b. the marginal propensity to save must be zero.
   c. households are dissaving.
   d. the spending multiplier is negative.
   e. banks hold additional excess reserves.

11. If the current rate of unemployment is less than the natural rate of unemployment, an appropriate stabilizing monetary policy would be to
   a. lower the required reserve ratio.
   b. raise taxes.
   c. lower taxes.
   d. purchase bonds on the open market.
   e. raise the discount rate.

12. Which of the following combinations of fiscal and monetary policy would effectively reduce capital investment while not reducing output?

	Fiscal policy	*Monetary policy*
a.	Expansionary	Contractionary
b.	Expansionary	Expansionary
c.	Contractionary	No change
d.	Contractionary	Contractionary
e.	Contractionary	Expansionary

13. If the real interest rate in the United States increased relative to the real interest rate in Belgium while domestic prices remained unchanged, then the United States dollar would
    a. appreciate, making Belgian exports to the United States more expensive.
    b. appreciate, making United States imports from Belgium more expensive.
    c. appreciate, making Belgian imports from the United States cheaper.
    d. appreciate, making United States imports from Belgium cheaper.
    e. depreciate, making United States exports to Belgium cheaper.

14. If an economy is experiencing a significant recession, then which of the following will cause employment to increase and interest rates to decrease?
    a. The Federal Reserve raises the discount rate.
    b. The government reduces spending while raising taxes.
    c. The Federal Reserve buys treasury securities on the open market.
    d. The Federal Reserve raises the reserve requirement.
    e. The government increases spending and reduces taxes.

15. An increase in which of the following would most likely hinder economic growth?
    a. personal savings
    b. gross private investment
    c. the government's budget deficit
    d. capital formation
    e. bond purchases by the Federal Reserve

16. Money is classified as inconvertible fiat when it
    a. is not backed by a valuable commodity.
    b. is backed by gold.
    c. acts as a source of intrinsic value.
    d. lacks portability.
    e. does not function as a medium of exchange.

17. A criticism of expansionary fiscal policy to stimulate the economy and contractionary monetary policy to restrict the economy is that they
    a. lead to demand-pull inflation.
    b. result in lower interest rates.
    c. create cost-push inflation.
    d. lead to higher interest rates.
    e. result in permanent increases in the money supply.

18. In the long run, increases in the money supply result in which of the following changes in the price level and unemployment?

	Price level	Unemployment
a.	Increase	Increase
b.	Increase	Decrease
c.	Decrease	No change
d.	Increase	No change
e.	No change	Increase

19. Crowding out is best described as a(n)
    a. increase in capital investment at the expense of government spending.
    b. decrease in net exports resulting from appreciation of the currency.
    c. increase in both inflation and unemployment.
    d. decrease in gross private investment resulting from government borrowing.
    e. rightward shift of the money supply.

20. If the real interest rate in China increases relative to that of the rest of the world, capital flow and the value of the Chinese currency should change in which of the following ways?

	Capital flow	Currency
a.	Out from China	Appreciate
b.	Into China	Appreciate
c.	Into China	Depreciate
d.	Out from China	Depreciate
e.	No change	No change

21. Which of the following is a combination of fiscal and monetary policy designed to offset the effects of a recession in an economy?
    a. increase taxes and reduce government spending
    b. lower the discount rate and buy treasury bonds
    c. reduce taxes and buy treasury bonds
    d. decrease government spending and the required reserve ratio
    e. increase taxes and sell treasury bonds

22. Natalie is classified as a part-time worker. Jane has a full-time job but is searching for a better job. Nate is not working and not actively looking for a job but was thinking about looking for work. Bella is not working and has applied for three jobs in the past week. Of these four people, who would be counted as unemployed?
    a. Nate and Bella
    b. Bella and Jane
    c. Jane, Nate, and Bella
    d. Jane
    e. Bella

23. Which of the following best describes the sequence of events that occurs when the Federal Reserve sells Treasury securities on the open market?
    a. $MS\uparrow, i\downarrow, C\uparrow, I\uparrow, AD\uparrow, Y\uparrow, PL\uparrow$
    b. $MS\uparrow, i\downarrow, C\downarrow, I\downarrow, AD\downarrow, Y\downarrow, PL\downarrow$
    c. $MS\downarrow, i\uparrow, C\downarrow, I\downarrow, AD\downarrow, Y\downarrow, PL\downarrow$
    d. $MS\downarrow, i\downarrow, C\downarrow, I\downarrow, AD\downarrow, Y\downarrow, PL\downarrow$
    e. $MS\downarrow, i\uparrow, C\uparrow, I\uparrow, AD\uparrow, Y\uparrow, PL\uparrow$

24. Assume that autonomous consumption is $500 and that the marginal propensity to consume is 0.9. If disposable income increases by $1,000, then saving will increase by how much?
    a. $450
    b. $900
    c. $1,500
    d. $50
    e. $100

25. Assume that all input prices are flexible. A decrease in labor productivity will have which of the following effects on output, price level, and real wages?

	Output	*Price level*	*Real wages*
a.	Increase	Increase	Increase
b.	Decrease	Decrease	Increase
c.	Decrease	Increase	Increase
d.	Decrease	Increase	Decrease
e.	Decrease	Decrease	Decrease

26. If the money supply increases by 5 percent, then which of the following must also increase by 5 percent for the real gross domestic product to remain unchanged?
    a. nominal interest rates
    b. real interest rates
    c. nominal exchange rates
    d. the average price level
    e. the income velocity of money

27. Which of the following will occur in a competitive market if the price exceeds the equilibrium price?
    a. The price will increase to eliminate the surplus.
    b. The price will decrease to eliminate the surplus.
    c. The price will decrease to eliminate the shortage.
    d. Demand will decrease.
    e. Supply will decrease.

28. The inverse relationship between price level and real gross domestic product is shown by the
    a. aggregate demand curve.
    b. demand for loanable funds.
    c. short-run Phillips curve.
    d. short-run aggregate supply curve.
    e. production possibilities curve.

29. If consumers spend $0.90 for each extra $1.00 of disposable income, then a $50 billion increase in government spending financed by a $50 billion increase in taxes will have which of the following effects on the economy? Aggregate demand will
    a. increase by $500 billion.
    b. decrease by $500 billion.
    c. increase by $450 billion.
    d. decrease by $450 billion.
    e. increase by $50 billion.

30. A decrease in the government's budget surplus will most likely result in which of the following?
    a. increased tax revenues
    b. decreased government spending
    c. higher interest rates
    d. a decrease in the international value of the dollar
    e. an increase in unemployment

31. Which of the following would cause the Japanese yen to appreciate relative to the euro?
    a. an increase in Japanese household income
    b. a decrease in Japanese interest rates relative to European interest rates
    c. an increase in Japan's average price level
    d. a decrease in Japanese household income
    e. a decrease in European household income

32. Demand-pull inflation is caused by which of the following?
    a. increased short-run aggregate supply
    b. decreased short-run aggregate supply
    c. increased aggregate demand
    d. decreased aggregate demand
    e. rightward shift of the short-run Phillips curve

33. Which of the following is true if the nominal interest rate is 5 percent and inflation unexpectedly increases from 2 percent to 3 percent?
    a. The nominal interest rate of 5% benefits savers at the expense of borrowers.
    b. The nominal interest rate of 5% is now too high.
    c. The real interest rate has increased from 7% to 8%.
    d. The real interest rate benefits fixed-rate borrowers at the expense of fixed-rate lenders.
    e. The real interest rate remains unchanged.

34. Which of the following would lead to an increase in the United States' aggregate price level?
    a. There is an increase in personal income taxes.
    b. Banks lend out less of their excess reserves.
    c. Full-time employees are reclassified as part-time employees according to a new government definition.
    d. Households increase their savings.
    e. A significant tax is placed on all capital investment in new technology.

35. An increase in labor productivity will cause the
    a. aggregate demand curve to shift left.
    b. aggregate demand curve to shift right.
    c. long-run aggregate supply curve to shift left.
    d. long-run aggregate supply curve to shift right.
    e. short-run aggregate supply curve to shift left.

36. Which is most likely to occur if the Federal Reserve acts to combat recession with open-market operations?
    a. The discount rate will increase.
    b. Aggregate demand will shift to the left.
    c. Bond prices will increase.
    d. The money supply will decrease.
    e. Government spending will decrease.

37. Which action by government will shift short-run aggregate supply to the left?
    a. the open-market sale of bonds by the Federal Reserve
    b. increase in the discount rate
    c. decrease in personal income taxes
    d. increase in government spending
    e. increase in business taxes

38. Assume that the Federal Reserve buys $100 billion worth of treasury securities on the open market. If the required reserve ratio is 20 percent, what is the maximum amount of new loans the banking system can create?
    a. $20 billion
    b. $80 billion
    c. $100 billion
    d. $400 billion
    e. $500 billion

Questions 39 - 41 are based on the diagram below, which shows the choices in production of two countries, Orville and Huey, producing two goods, airplanes and helicopters. Both countries have the same amount of resources and are using all of their available resources.

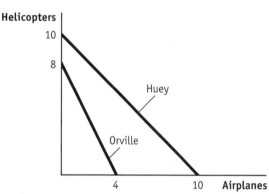

39. Before specialization and trade, the opportunity cost of producing 1 helicopter in Huey and Orville is which of the following?

	Huey	**Orville**
a.	1 airplane	10 airplanes
b.	8 airplanes	2 airplanes
c.	1 airplane	0.5 airplane
d.	0.5 airplane	2 airplanes
e.	1 airplane	2 airplanes

40. Which of the following statements best describes absolute advantage or comparative advantage for these two countries?
    a. Huey has a comparative advantage in helicopters and Orville has a comparative advantage in airplanes.
    b. Huey has a comparative advantage in helicopters and Orville has an absolute advantage in helicopters.
    c. Huey has absolute and comparative advantages in both airplanes and helicopters.
    d. Huey has a comparative advantage in airplanes and Orville has absolute disadvantages in both.
    e. Huey has an absolute advantage in both and Orville has a comparative advantage in airplanes.

41. According to the theory of comparative advantage, Orville would find it advantageous to
   a. export airplanes and import helicopters.
   b. import both helicopters and airplanes.
   c. export both airplanes and helicopters.
   d. import airplanes and export helicopters.
   e. not trade because Huey has absolute advantages in both airplanes and helicopters.

42. A decrease in personal income taxes will most likely cause aggregate demand and short-run aggregate supply to change in which of the following ways?

	Aggregate demand	*Short-run aggregate supply*
a.	Increase	No change
b.	Increase	Decrease
c.	Decrease	Increase
d.	Decrease	No change
e.	Decrease	Decrease

Disposable income = $9 trillion
Imports = $3 trillion
Household Savings = $1 trillion
Government Expenditures = $3 trillion
Exports = $2 trillion
Gross Private Investment = $2 trillion

43. Based on the information in the table above, how much is gross domestic product?
   a. $20 trillion
   b. $14 trillion
   c. $16 trillion
   d. $12 trillion
   e. $5 trillion

44. If firms face increased per unit production costs, then the short-run aggregate supply curve, short-run Phillips curve, and inflation will change in which of the following ways?

	SRAS will shift to the	*Short-run Phillips curve*	*Inflation*
a.	right	shift to the right	increase
b.	right	shift to the left	decrease
c.	right	no change	increase
d.	left	shift to the left	decrease
e.	left	shift to the right	increase

45. Aggregate demand and aggregate supply would simultaneously decrease because of an increase in which of the following?
   a. household savings
   b. the M2
   c. business taxes
   d. disposable income
   e. inflation expectations

46. An increase in the government's budget deficit will have which of the following effects on the exchange rate and net exports?

	Exchange rate	Net exports
a.	appreciate	decrease
b.	appreciate	increase
c.	appreciate	no change
d.	depreciate	increase
e.	depreciate	decrease

47. According to the graph above, which of the following is true about this economy in the long run?
   a. Expansionary monetary policy will restore this economy to its long-run equilibrium.
   b. The long-run aggregate supply curve will shift to the left to restore the long-run equilibrium.
   c. The economy depicted is already in a long-run equilibrium and therefore will not change.
   d. A combination of increased government spending and an increase in the money supply could shift aggregate demand to the right and restore long-run equilibrium.
   e. Wages will increase as they adjust to the new price level and the short-run aggregate supply curve will shift to the left and restore long-run equilibrium.

48. Assuming that input prices are flexible, an economy in recession will experience which of the following changes in output and price level in the long run?

	Output	Price level
a.	Increase	Increase
b.	No change	Increase
c.	Increase	No change
d.	Increase	Decrease
e.	Decrease	Increase

49. Assuming a system of flexible exchange rates, an open-market sale of bonds by the Federal Reserve while other countries do nothing will most likely have which of the following effects on the rate of inflation and the international value of the United States dollar?

	Inflation rate	International value of the United States dollar
a.	Decrease	Appreciate
b.	Decrease	Depreciate
c.	Increase	Appreciate
d.	Increase	Depreciate
e.	Increase	No change

50. The discount rate is the
   a. interest rate the Federal Reserve charges member banks for overnight loans.
   b. interest rate banks charge their best commercial customers.
   c. interest rate banks charge other banks for overnight loans.
   d. percentage of demand deposits that banks may not lend to customers.
   e. difference between the nominal interest rate and the real interest rate.

Labor Market in Kumbiktu (in thousands of persons)	
Population	240
Labor Force	200
Employed	180

51. Based on the information in the table above, what is the unemployment rate for Kumbiktu?
   a. 25%
   b. 30%
   c. 10%
   d. 8.3%
   e. 11.1%

52. Which of the following would lead to economic growth?
   a. a decrease in personal savings
   b. a decrease in taxes on personal savings
   c. an increase in government spending paid for by borrowing in the loanable funds market
   d. a decrease in spending on research and production
   e. an increase in political instability

53. If the marginal propensity to save is 0.2, then a $40 billion decrease in taxes could cause a maximum increase in output of how much?
   a. $8 billion
   b. $32 billion
   c. $200 billion
   d. $160 billion
   e. $250 billion

54. An increase in labor productivity will shift the
   a. short-run aggregate supply to the left.
   b. short-run aggregate supply to the right.
   c. aggregate demand to the right.
   d. aggregate demand to the left.
   e. long-run aggregate supply to the left.

55. In the long run, decreases in aggregate demand lead to which of the following changes in unemployment and the price level?

	Unemployment	*Price level*
a.	No change	Decrease
b.	Decrease	No change
c.	Decrease	Decrease
d.	Increase	Increase
e.	Increase	No change

56. Assume that the required reserve ratio is 10 percent. If Jumanja deposits $50 in cash into her checking account, what is the maximum change in demand deposits possible in the banking system?

a. $45
b. $50
c. $500
d. $450
e. $5

57. If the United States' rate of economic growth increases relative to its trading partners, then the United States' imports and exports will most likely change in which of the following ways if exchange rates are fixed?

	Imports	*Exports*
a.	Increase	Decrease
b.	Decrease	Decrease
c.	Decrease	Increase
d.	Increase	Increase
e.	No change	No change

58. Which of the following would be counted as part of gross domestic product for this year?

a. the purchase of corporate stock
b. the sale of a treasury bond
c. the purchase of a new domestically produced tractor
d. daycare services provided by stay-at-home fathers for their own children
e. the purchase of a twenty-year-old house

59. A shift in the aggregate demand curve corresponds to

a. a shift in the long-run Phillips curve.
b. a shift in the short-run Phillips curve.
c. a decrease in the slope of the short-run Phillips curve.
d. movement along an existing short-run Phillips curve.
e. an increase in the slope of the short-run Phillips curve.

60. Which of the following would cause a leftward shift in the short-run aggregate supply curve?

a. an increase in the expected price level
b. an increase in the available capital stock
c. a decrease in interest rates
d. a decrease in the nominal wage rate
e. an increase in the exchange rate

Place a "√" by the questions you answered correctly.

 # Correct in each section

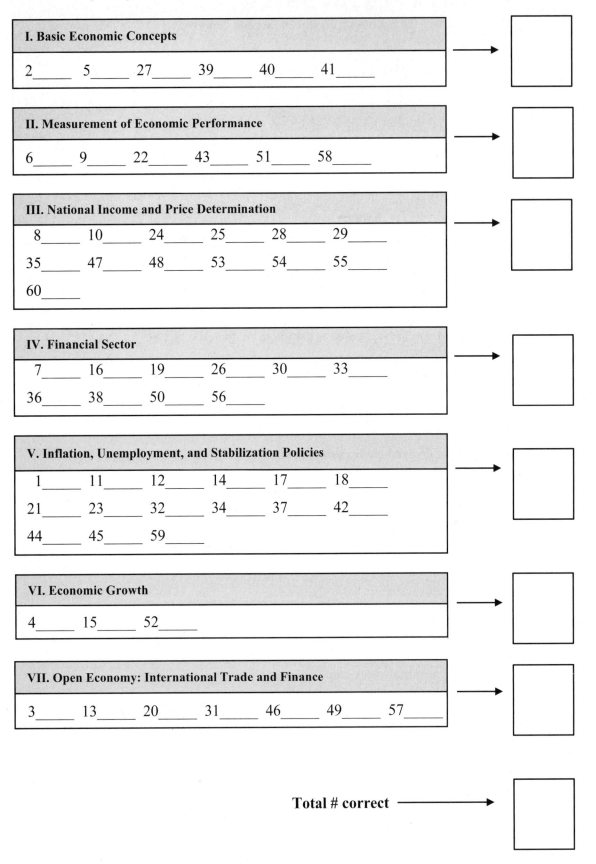

I. Basic Economic Concepts

2_____   5_____   27_____   39_____   40_____   41_____

II. Measurement of Economic Performance

6_____   9_____   22_____   43_____   51_____   58_____

III. National Income and Price Determination

8_____   10_____   24_____   25_____   28_____   29_____

35_____   47_____   48_____   53_____   54_____   55_____

60_____

IV. Financial Sector

7_____   16_____   19_____   26_____   30_____   33_____

36_____   38_____   50_____   56_____

V. Inflation, Unemployment, and Stabilization Policies

1_____   11_____   12_____   14_____   17_____   18_____

21_____   23_____   32_____   34_____   37_____   42_____

44_____   45_____   59_____

VI. Economic Growth

4_____   15_____   52_____

VII. Open Economy: International Trade and Finance

3_____   13_____   20_____   31_____   46_____   49_____   57_____

Total # correct ⟶

Use your scores on the diagnostic test to determine how to prepare for the AP® Exam

Start by determining the percent of the questions that you answered correctly. Your total # correct divided by 60 is the percent of questions you answered correctly:

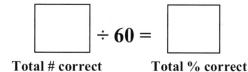

Total # correct   **Total % correct**

To get an idea of how much you will need to study for your AP® exam, you can compare your performance to students who took the most recently released AP® Macroeconomics exam. For instance, of students who scored a "3" on the AP® Macroeconomics exam (the minimum score to receive college credit), roughly 80% scored between 31 and 60 on the multiple-choice section. Roughly two-thirds of those scoring a "3" scored between 31 and 36 on the multiple-choice section. So if your score was below 50% on this diagnostic test, you need to allocate additional time to studying for the AP® exam, beyond the review time that all students need to spend in order to do well on the exam. If you scored above 50%, you should still plan to spend time studying the sections for which you most need to improve your performance, as well as taking time to review all of the sections in the week leading up to the exam.

Next, determine how to allocate your study time to each section of material by evaluating your score in each section. First, find the percent of the questions you answered correctly in each section by dividing the number you answered correctly by the number of questions in the section. Spend more time studying the material in those sections in which the percent you answered correctly is less than your total percent correct and less time studying the sections in which the percent you answered correctly is greater than your total percent correct. Next, look at how much each section is weighted on the AP® exam. Spend more time studying those sections that are given a higher weight on the exam.

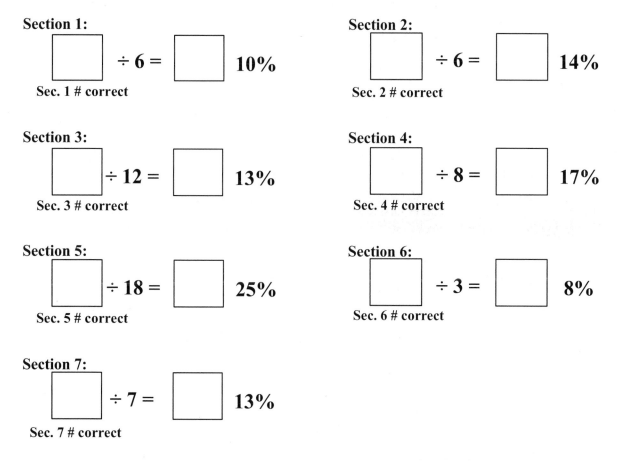

Section 1:

$\boxed{}$ ÷ 6 = $\boxed{}$ **10%**

Sec. 1 # correct

Section 2:

$\boxed{}$ ÷ 6 = $\boxed{}$ **14%**

Sec. 2 # correct

Section 3:

$\boxed{}$ ÷ 12 = $\boxed{}$ **13%**

Sec. 3 # correct

Section 4:

$\boxed{}$ ÷ 8 = $\boxed{}$ **17%**

Sec. 4 # correct

Section 5:

$\boxed{}$ ÷ 18 = $\boxed{}$ **25%**

Sec. 5 # correct

Section 6:

$\boxed{}$ ÷ 3 = $\boxed{}$ **8%**

Sec. 6 # correct

Section 7:

$\boxed{}$ ÷ 7 = $\boxed{}$ **13%**

Sec. 7 # correct

ANSWERS AND EXPLANATIONS
(Note that the section on the course outline is indicated in parentheses.)

1. d. - Increasing taxes and decreasing government spending reduces aggregate demand and therefore the price level and inflation. (V.)
2. d. - Opportunity cost is the next best alternative use of a resource. (I.)
3. a. - As Thailand imports more from China, the supply of the rupee increases, causing Thailand's currency to depreciate. (VII.)
4. d. - Economic growth is illustrated by either an increase in the production possibilities curve or the long-run aggregate. (VI.)
5. a. - If an economy is producing at the production possibilities curve, then outside of economic growth any increase in the production of one good comes at the cost of a decrease in the production of the alternative good. (I.)
6. b. - Savers and lenders at fixed rates are harmed by unanticipated inflation because the interest rate they are earning does not reflect the additional cost of the higher inflation (II.)
7. d. - An increase in money demand increases the nominal interest rate, but because the money supply curve is vertical, no change to the quantity of money occurs. (IV.)
8. e. - An increase in input prices causes the short-run aggregate supply curve to shift left, resulting in an equilibrium at a higher price level and a lower level of output and thus employment. (III.)
9. b. - Cyclical unemployment is associated with downturns in the business cycle. (II.)
10. c. - Dissaving occurs when consumption exceeds disposable income. (III.)
11. e. - Raising the discount rate is the appropriate monetary policy response to an inflationary gap in the economy. (V.)
12. a. - Expansionary fiscal and contractionary monetary policies result in higher interest rates without necessarily reducing output. (V.)
13. d. - A higher real interest rate creates demand for the dollar, causing it to appreciate and making foreign goods relatively less expensive. (VII.)
14. c. - When the Federal Reserve buys bonds on the open market, banks are left with more excess reserves which can be lent. This results in lower interest rates and more investment and interest-sensitive consumption, which increases aggregate demand and therefore employment. (V.)
15. c. - An increase in the government's budget deficit would increase the demand for loanable funds and, therefore, the real interest rate. In turn, this would reduce investment in capital. (VI.)
16. a. - Inconvertible fiat means that money's value derives from government mandate and people's willingness to accept it. (IV.)
17. d. - Over the business cycle, if expansionary fiscal policy is used during recessions and contractionary monetary policy is used to offset inflation, then over time interest rates will 'ratchet' upward. (V.)
18. d. - In the long run, an increase in the money supply only increases the price level and has no impact on real output or unemployment. (V.)
19. d. - Crowding out refers to the decrease in gross private investment that results from deficit-induced higher interest rates. (IV.)
20. b. - The higher interest rate attracts foreign savings and creates a demand for the currency. (VII.)

21. c. - Reducing taxes is the fiscal policy that increases disposable income and consumption, while buying treasury bonds is the open-market operation that leads to lower interest rates and hence more investment and interest-sensitive consumption. (V.)

22. e. – Only Bella is counted as unemployed because she is actively looking for work and not employed. Jane is employed, so she is not counted as unemployed even if she is looking for a better job. Nate is not considered to be in the workforce because he is not currently looking for work and therefore is not counted as being unemployed. (II.)

23. c. - The sale of treasury bonds reduces the money supply which results in a higher interest rate. This results in lower levels of consumption and investment and, therefore, aggregate demand decreases leading to a lower level of output and a lower price level. (V.)

24. e. - Given the marginal propensity to consume of 0.9, the marginal propensity to save is 0.1. If disposable income increases by $1,000, then 10% of this change will be saved or $100. (III.)

25. d. - Decreases in labor productivity result in a decrease in the short-run aggregate supply, which leads to less output, a higher price level, and therefore lower real wages. (III.)

26. d. - Using the monetary equation of exchange ($MV = PQ$), a 5% increase in the money supply holding velocity (V) and real gross domestic product (Q) constant must result in a 5% increase in price level (P). (IV.)

27. b. - A price above the market equilibrium induces competitive sellers to reduce prices; as price falls, consumers respond by purchasing more, thus clearing the surplus. (I.)

28. a. - The aggregate demand curve is the inverse relationship between price level and real GDP. (III.)

29. e. - Spending financed by an equal amount of taxation results in a balanced budget multiplier of 1. (III.)

30. c. - A decrease in the government's budget surplus reduces the overall supply of loanable funds which results in a higher equilibrium real interest rate. (IV.)

31. d. - A decrease in Japan's household income would result in less yen being supplied in foreign exchange as Japanese households imported fewer European goods. This would cause the yen to appreciate. (VII.)

32. c. – Demand-pull inflation occurs when aggregate demand shifts to the right. (V.)

33. d. - The real interest rate would fall from 3% to 2%, benefitting borrowers and harming lenders. (IV.)

34. e. - A tax on capital investment in technology would reduce productivity and therefore short-run aggregate supply. This would lead to a higher price level. (V)

35. d. - Increased productivity has the effect of increasing the long-run aggregate supply. (III.)

36. c. - The Federal Reserve will engage in the open-market purchase of bonds, which would result in an increase in demand for bonds, driving up their price. (IV.)

37. e. - An increase in business taxes raises the unit cost of production for business and reduces the short-run aggregate supply curve. (V.)

38. e. - $500 billion in new loans are capable of being created as the $100 billion dollar increase in excess reserves is multiplied by the reciprocal of the required reserve ratio of 20%. (IV.)

39. c. - Huey gives up 1 airplane for each helicopter produced, while Orville gives up 0.5 airplane for each helicopter produced. (I.)

40. d. - Huey has a comparative advantage in airplanes because the opportunity cost is 1 helicopter as opposed to 2 for Orville. Orville has absolute disadvantages in both because Huey is capable of producing more airplanes and helicopters. (I.)

41. d. - Orville has a comparative advantage in helicopters and would benefit by specializing in their production and importing airplanes from Huey. (I.)

42. a. - A decrease in personal income taxes would increase households' disposable income, resulting in more consumption and leading to an increase in aggregate demand. A decrease in personal income taxes would have no direct effect on short-run aggregate supply. (V.)

43. d. - Real GDP = Consumption + Investment + Government Spending + Net Exports. Consumption = Disposable income - Savings. Net Exports = Exports - Imports, so... [DI ($9 trillion) – S ($1 trillion)] + Ig ($2 trillion) + G ($3 trillion) + [X ($2 trillion) – M ($3 trillion)] = $12 trillion. (II.)

44. e. - Increased production costs result in a leftward shift in short-run aggregate supply, a rightward shift in the short-run Phillips curve, and an increase in inflation. (V.)

45. c. - Increased business taxes would increase unit production cost and also reduce the incentive to invest, which would result in decreases in short-run aggregate supply and aggregate demand. (V.)

46. a. - Increased deficits increase the demand for loanable funds, resulting in higher real interest rates. This attracts foreign saving, resulting in appreciation of the currency. In turn, this drives down net exports, as exports become relatively more expensive and imports become relatively cheap. (VII.)

47. e. - In the long run, output above full employment results in higher nominal wages, which reduces short-run aggregate supply. (III)

48. d. - In the long run, a recession results in lower input prices, which leads to an increase in short-run aggregate supply. This reduces the price level while increasing output. (III.)

49. a. - The sale of bonds decreases the money supply, resulting in a higher interest rate. The higher interest rate will lead to lower inflation, which leads to appreciation of the currency (VII.)

50. a. - The discount rate is the interest rate the Fed charges member banks for borrowing reserves overnight. (IV.)

51. c. - The unemployment rate is equal to the number of unemployed persons divided by the labor force. The number of unemployed persons equals the labor force minus the employed. 20 unemployed divided by 200 in the labor force equals 10% unemployment. (II.)

52. b. A decrease in taxes on personal savings will increase the supply of loanable funds. This will cause the real interest rate to decrease, which will lead to an expansion of the capital stock. This expansion of the capital stock will cause the *LRAS* curve to shift to the right. (VI.)

53. d. - The tax multiplier = *MPC/MPS* = 0.8 / 0.2 = 4. 4 × $40 billion = $160 billion. (III.)

54. b. - Increased labor productivity results in lower unit production costs, thus increasing short-run aggregate supply. (III.)

55. a. - In the long run, *AD* intersects *LRAS* at a lower price level at full employment output. (III.)

56. c. - $50 cash originally converted into demand deposit + $450 in loans created and redeposited = $500 in new demand deposits. (IV.)

57. a. - Assuming exchange rates are fixed, imports increase and exports decrease as the faster growing economy consumes more foreign and domestic production. (VII.)

58. c. - The tractor is the only thing listed that is a new, final, domestically produced good for which a market transaction took place. (II.)

59. d. - Shifts in aggregate demand result in a trade-off between inflation and unemployment, which is illustrated by movements along the short-run Phillips curve (V.)

60. a. - An increase in the expected price level results in higher unit production costs, which reduces short-run aggregate supply (III.)

VI. REVIEWING FOR THE AP® MACROECONOMICS EXAM

This section gives you some important tools to use in answering both the multiple-choice and free-response questions on the AP® Macroeconomics exam. It includes Key Formulas, Commonly Used Abbreviations, A Guide to Graphs, and a special guide to the Free-Response Section.

The Formulas of Macro

There will be both multiple-choice and free-response questions on the AP® Macroeconomics exam that require calculations. For example, you may be required to calculate GDP, the unemployment rate or any of the multipliers you have studied. To answer calculation questions, you will need to remember and understand some important formulas.

One of the best ways to prepare for the AP® exam is to answer released free-response questions and to practice answering as many multiple-choice questions as you can. As you begin, keep the following list of key macroeconomic formulas handy and use it as a guide. But make sure that you practice and review enough that you can recall and apply these formulas without a guide when you take the AP® exam.

Key Macroeconomics Formulas

Expenditure Approach to Real GDP
Real GDP = consumption + investment + government spending + net exports
$$RGDP = C + I_G + G + X_N$$

Income Approach to Real GDP
Real GDP = Rent + Wages + Interest + Profits
$$RGDP = r + w + i + p$$

Labor Force
LF = # Employed + # Unemployed
$$LF = E + U$$

Labor Force Participation Rate

$$\text{Labor force participation rate} = \frac{\text{Labor Force}}{\text{Working Age Population}} \qquad LFPR = \frac{LF}{pop}$$

Unemployment Rate

$$UR = \frac{\text{\# Unemployed}}{\text{Labor Force}} \qquad UR = \frac{U}{LF}$$

Inflation Rate (CPI is Consumer Price Index)

$$\text{Infl } R = \left(\frac{\text{New } CPI - \text{Old } CPI}{\text{Old } CPI} \right) \times 100$$

GDP Deflator

$$GDP_{Defl} = \left(\frac{\text{Nominal } GDP}{\text{Real } GDP} \right) \times 100$$

Converting Nominal GDP to Real GDP

$$RGDP = \left(\frac{\text{Nominal GDP}}{CPI} \right) \times 100 \qquad RGDP = \left(\frac{\text{Nominal GDP}}{GDPDefl} \right) \times 100$$

Real Interest Rate

Real interest rate = Nominal interest rate – Inflation rate

$r\% = i\% - \pi\%$

Nominal Interest Rate

Nominal interest rate = Real interest rate + Expected inflation rate

$i\% = r\% + \pi^{exp}\%$

Marginal Propensity to Save

$$MPS = \frac{\text{Change in saving}}{\text{Change in disposable income}}$$

Marginal Propensity to Consume

$$MPC = \frac{\text{Change in consumption}}{\text{Change in disposable income}}$$

Spending Multiplier

$$\text{Mult}_{\text{spend}} = \frac{1}{1 - MPC} \text{ or } \frac{1}{MPS}$$

Tax Multiplier

$$\text{Mult}_{\text{tax}} = \frac{-MPC}{1 - MPC} \text{ or } \frac{-MPC}{MPS}$$

Money Multiplier

$$\text{Mult}_{\text{m}} = \frac{1}{\text{required reserve ratio}}$$

Note: this ignores households holding onto cash instead of making deposits and banks holding onto excess reserves; with these considerations,

$$\text{Mult}_m = \frac{1 + \text{currency ratio}}{\text{currency ratio} + \text{required reserve ratio} + \text{excess reserve ratio}}.$$

Even without adding in the currency ratio, you could change this to $\dfrac{1}{\text{reserve ratio}}$ where "reserve ratio" accounts for both required and excess reserves.

Multiple Deposit Expansion

- Required reserve = amount of deposit × required reserve ratio
- Maximum amount a single bank can loan = change in excess reserves caused by a deposit
- Change in loans throughout banking system =
  initial change in excess reserves × Multiplier $_{\text{money}}$
- Change in money supply = change in loans throughout banking system + $ amount of any OMOs

Monetary Equation of Exchange

- Money Stock × Income Velocity of Money = Nominal GDP
- Money Stock × Income Velocity of Money = Price Level × Real GDP
- $MV = PQ$ or $MV = PY$

The Commonly Used Abbreviations of Macro

Abbreviations can be used to make your answers clearer and more concise. They also save you time when writing your answers. But you need to make sure that any abbreviations you use are standard in economics or cannot be easily misinterpreted. Use these abbreviations to avoid any confusion:

AD-AS model:

Price Level: *PL* (on your vertical axis)
Real Gross Domestic Product: Real GDP or *Y* (on your horizontal axis)
Short-Run Aggregate Supply: *SRAS* (make sure it is upward-sloping)
Long Run Aggregate Supply: *LRAS* (make sure it is vertical)
Aggregate Demand: *AD* (make sure it is downward-sloping)

Money Market:

Interest rate: *r* or *i* (on your vertical axis, make sure it is *i* and <u>not</u> I!)
Quantity of money: Q_m (on your horizontal axis)
Demand for money: *MD* or D_m (make sure it is downward-sloping)
Supply of money: *MS* or S_m (make sure it is vertical)

Market for Loanable Funds: Interest rate: *r* (on your vertical axis)
Quantity of Loanable Funds: Q_{LF} (on your horizontal axis)
Demand for Loanable Funds: *D* or D_{LF} (make sure it is downward-sloping)
Supply of Loanable Funds: *S* or S_{LF} (make sure it is upward-sloping)

Foreign Exchange Market:

Price of Currency A/Currency B per currency A (for instance, if you are talking about the market for dollars, and dollars are being exchanged for yen, the abbreviation would be "Yen/$" or "Yen per dollar" as your label on the vertical axis)

Quantity of Currency A: $Q_{Currency\ A}$ (for instance, if you are talking about the market for dollars, and dollars are being exchanged for yen, the abbreviation would be $Q_\$$ as your label on the horizontal axis)

Demand for Currency A: D or $D_{currency\ A}$ (for instance, if you are talking about the market for dollars, and dollars are being exchanged for yen, the abbreviation would be $D_\$$ on your downward-sloping curve)

Supply for Currency A: S or $S_{currency\ A}$ (for instance, if you are talking about the market for dollars, and dollars are being exchanged for yen, the abbreviation would be $S_\$$ on your upward-sloping curve)

Equilibrium exchange rate: XR, ER or e

Equilibrium quantity exchanged: q

Phillips Curve:

Inflation: π or inf (on your vertical axis). Do not use "i" for inflation.
Unemployment rate: UR (on your horizontal axis)
Short-Run Phillips Curve: $SRPC$ (make sure it is downward-sloping)
Long-Run Phillips curve: $LRPC$ (make sure it is vertical at the natural rate of unemployment)
Natural rate of unemployment: NRU or $NAIRU$

Graphs

The AP® Macroeconomics exam requires you to understand and correctly draw the important graphs you have studied throughout the course. There are seven key graphs that you need to be able to draw correctly and use to answer questions. The following pages are designed to help you learn these graphs and show you some variations you may see on the AP® exam.

Correct labeling of the axes on your graphs is especially important. Each graph needs a label for the vertical axis, a label for the horizontal axis, and a label for each curve. You will also need to identify the equilibrium point(s) on each graph. It is very important to indicate equilibrium points on the axes of the graph, and not only on an interior point in your graph. Also, be sure that you understand what causes changes in the various diagrams and the resulting effects on the variables represented on both the vertical and horizontal axes of each graph. Rest assured that you will be required to draw and analyze at least four different graphs on the free-response section of the exam.

To prepare for the AP® Macroeconomics exam, practice answering free-response questions that require you to draw graphs. You can find sample free-response questions on previous exams released by the College Board and in your textbook. Make sure that you also look at answer keys and scoring guidelines provided to make sure you are answering correctly and that you understand how your AP® exam is scored.

You should also get into the habit of using graphs to help you answer questions even when a graph is not required. For example, drawing a supply and demand graph can often help you answer multiple-choice questions that involve the supply and demand model. And a graph can often be used to help explain an answer to a free-response question, even if a graph is not explicitly required. Remember – a picture can be worth a thousand words!

Understanding how to use economic models is central to any economics course and therefore it is central to the AP® Macroeconomics exam. So, if you understand and can apply the models presented in this section, then you will have gone a long way in striving for a 5!

The Production Possibilities Curve

The production possibilities curve illustrates trade-offs and opportunity cost incurred as a result of scarce factors of production.

The concave shape shown here indicates that the opportunity cost of producing more consumer/capital goods is increasing.

In the graph on top, an economy that is fully employing all of its available resources by currently producing at point A and that wishes to produce at point B instead must sacrifice 2 units of capital goods in order to gain about 1 1/2 units of consumer goods. Points A and B both represent an economy that is fully employing all of its resources.

The bottom graph illustrates the effect of an increase in available factors of production, the quality of those factors of production, increased technology, or increased productivity.

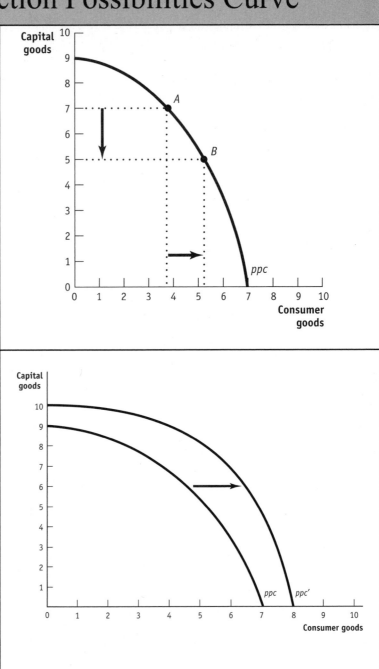

Helpful hints for *PPC*s:
- Make sure you label your axes correctly.
- Use arrows to indicate the direction of change.
- Make sure the shape of your *PPC* matches your prompt – linear for constant opportunity costs and concave for increasing opportunity costs. If the shape is not indicated, use the concave curve.

Supply & Demand

The supply & demand model illustrates producers' willingness and ability to produce a good or service (supply) combined with consumers' willingness and ability to consume a good or service (demand). The intersection of these two functions determines the equilibrium price and equilibrium quantity

Changes in Demand

Δ in M.E.R.I.T. .:

ΔD

$\uparrow D$ right $\rightarrow P\uparrow$ & $Q\uparrow$

$\downarrow D$ left $\rightarrow P\downarrow$ & $Q\downarrow$

Changes in Supply

Δ in N.I.C.E.J.A.G.T.

ΔS

$\uparrow S$ right$\rightarrow P\downarrow$ & $Q\uparrow$

$\downarrow S$ left $\rightarrow P\uparrow$ & $Q\downarrow$

Changes in both Supply and Demand (? Means indeterminant):

$\uparrow S$ & $\uparrow D \rightarrow P$? & $Q\uparrow$

$\uparrow S$ & $\downarrow D \rightarrow P\downarrow$ & Q?

$\downarrow S$ & $\uparrow D \rightarrow P\uparrow$ & Q?

$\downarrow S$ & $\downarrow D \rightarrow P$? & $Q\downarrow$

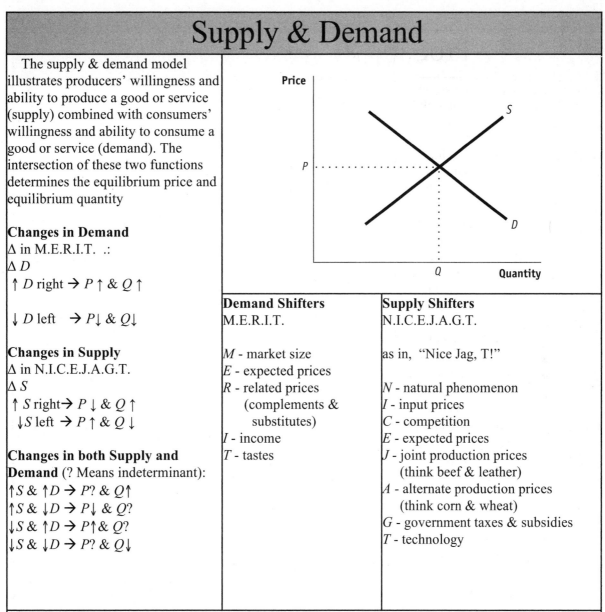

Demand Shifters
M.E.R.I.T.

M - market size
E - expected prices
R - related prices
    (complements & substitutes)
I - income
T - tastes

Supply Shifters
N.I.C.E.J.A.G.T.

as in, "Nice Jag, T!"

N - natural phenomenon
I - input prices
C - competition
E - expected prices
J - joint production prices
    (think beef & leather)
A - alternate production prices
    (think corn & wheat)
G - government taxes & subsidies
T - technology

Helpful hints for Supply and Demand graphs:
- Even if it looks like both price and quantity change when both supply and demand are changing simultaneously, remember that either price or quantity will be indeterminant. It does not "Stay the same"!
- Use arrows to show the direction of shifts. Use numbers to show the order of shifts (for instance D_1 is your initial curve, D_2 is your new curve).
- Make sure you show equilibrium price and quantity on the axes, <u>not on the interior of the graphs</u>. To make sure this is clear to the person grading your exam, draw dotted lines connecting the intersection point to the price axis and the quantity axis.

Foreign Exchange Market

This is the market that brings together people who need to buy or sell one currency in exchange for the currency of another country.

The equilibrium price is referred to as an exchange rate and is denoted as *e*.

The graph to the right illustrates the market for the E.U. euro in terms of the U.S. dollar.

Exchange rates are determined by

Relative S.T.R.I.N.G.
Relative Speculation
Relative Tastes
Relative Rates (interest)
Relative Inflation
Relative Net Exports
Relative Growth

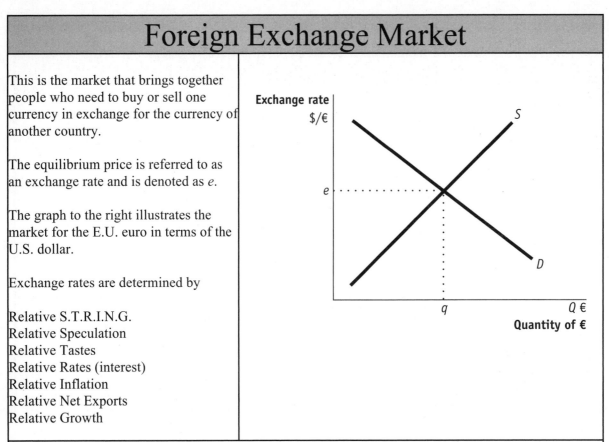

Helpful hints for the Foreign Exchange Market:
- Make sure it is obvious to the reader that you are in the foreign exchange market, as opposed to any other market.
- Make sure the price of a currency is not itself! For instance, if we are in the market for euros, we do not want "Euros" or "Euros per dollar" on the vertical axis.
- Make sure you label your equilibrium exchange rate on the vertical axis. Use a dotted line from the intersection of supply and demand to the vertical axis to make it clear that you understand that the equilibrium refers to an exchange rate, not just an intersection point on a curve.
- Use arrows to make the direction of any shift, and any change in the equilibrium, very clear.

Loanable Funds Market

This is the market that brings together savers and borrowers. Savers supply loanable funds and borrowers demand them.

The equilibrium price which equates savings to borrowing is the real interest rate ($r\%$).

Saving and borrowing go by different names depending on which sector of the economy is doing the saving and borrowing.

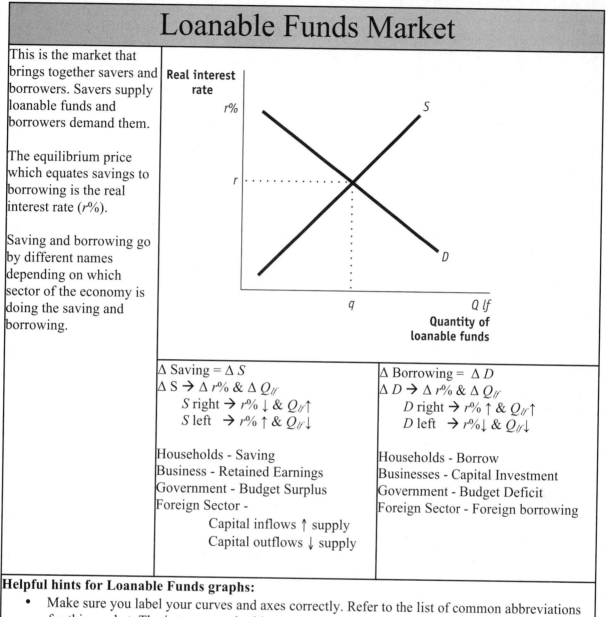

Δ Saving = Δ S

Δ S → Δ $r\%$ & Δ Q_{lf}

    S right → $r\%$ ↓ & Q_{lf}↑

    S left → $r\%$ ↑ & Q_{lf}↓

Households - Saving
Business - Retained Earnings
Government - Budget Surplus
Foreign Sector -
    Capital inflows ↑ supply
    Capital outflows ↓ supply

Δ Borrowing = Δ D

Δ D → Δ $r\%$ & Δ Q_{lf}

    D right → $r\%$ ↑ & Q_{lf}↑

    D left → $r\%$↓ & Q_{lf}↓

Households - Borrow
Businesses - Capital Investment
Government - Budget Deficit
Foreign Sector - Foreign borrowing

Helpful hints for Loanable Funds graphs:
- Make sure you label your curves and axes correctly. Refer to the list of common abbreviations for this market. The interest rate in this market is "r" for "real interest rate."
- When drawing shifts, use arrows to make the direction of the shift clear.
- When showing an equilibrium, show these on the axes, not on the internal portion of the graph.

Money Market

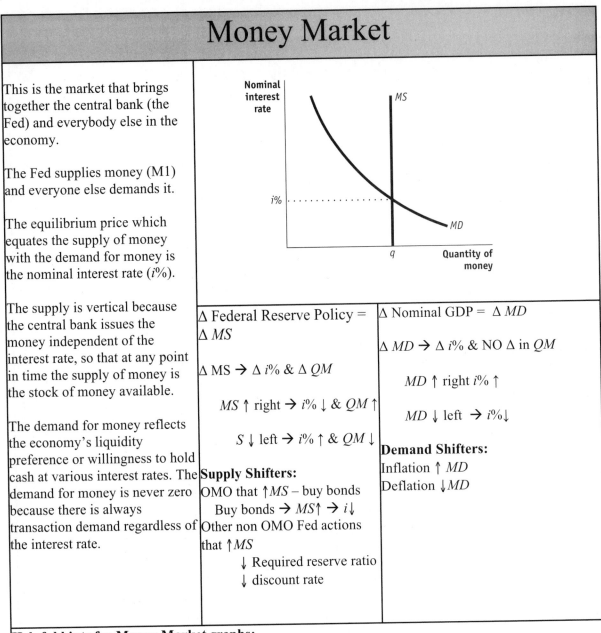

This is the market that brings together the central bank (the Fed) and everybody else in the economy.

The Fed supplies money (M1) and everyone else demands it.

The equilibrium price which equates the supply of money with the demand for money is the nominal interest rate ($i\%$).

The supply is vertical because the central bank issues the money independent of the interest rate, so that at any point in time the supply of money is the stock of money available.

The demand for money reflects the economy's liquidity preference or willingness to hold cash at various interest rates. The demand for money is never zero because there is always transaction demand regardless of the interest rate.

Δ Federal Reserve Policy = Δ MS

Δ MS → Δ $i\%$ & Δ QM

   MS ↑ right → $i\%$ ↓ & QM ↑

   S ↓ left → $i\%$ ↑ & QM ↓

Supply Shifters:
OMO that ↑MS – buy bonds
   Buy bonds → MS↑ → i↓
Other non OMO Fed actions
that ↑MS
   ↓ Required reserve ratio
   ↓ discount rate

Δ Nominal GDP = Δ MD

Δ MD → Δ $i\%$ & NO Δ in QM

   MD ↑ right $i\%$ ↑

   MD ↓ left → $i\%$↓

Demand Shifters:
Inflation ↑ MD
Deflation ↓MD

Helpful hints for Money Market graphs:
- Make sure your money supply curve is vertical.
- Make sure you use the correct labels. See the list of commonly used abbreviations for this graph: *MS, MD, QM, i*
- Use arrows to indicate any change of direction.
- Remember that equilibriums should be labeled on the axis, not internally.

Aggregate Supply and Aggregate Demand

The aggregate supply and aggregate demand model illustrates the economy as a whole. Aggregate supply represents producers' willingness and ability to produce all of the output of the nation at various price levels. Aggregate demand reflects the private, public, and foreign sectors' willingness and ability to purchase the output at various price levels.

Notice in the graph that there are two aggregate supply curves. SRAS refers to the short-run aggregate supply. LRAS refers to long-run aggregate supply. In the short run, firms willingly produce more output as price level changes, because inflexible input prices allow firms to experience profits. In the long run, input prices adjust to change in the price level, so firms have no incentive to vary output as price level changes.

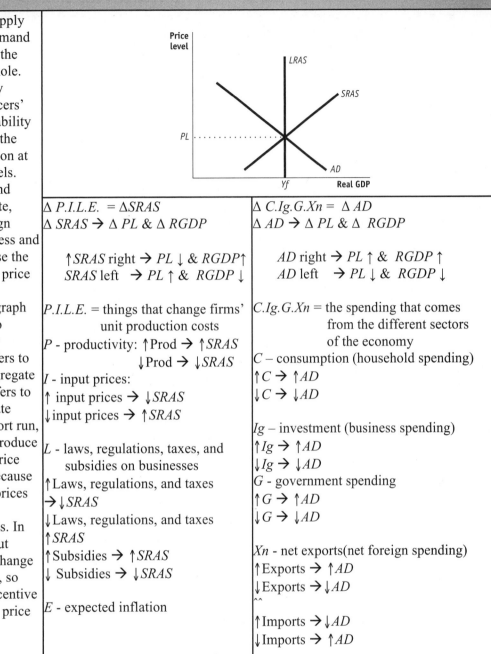

Δ *P.I.L.E.* = $\Delta SRAS$
Δ *SRAS* $\rightarrow$ Δ *PL* & Δ *RGDP*

$\uparrow$*SRAS* right $\rightarrow$ *PL* $\downarrow$ & *RGDP*$\uparrow$
SRAS left $\rightarrow$ *PL* $\uparrow$ & *RGDP* $\downarrow$

P.I.L.E. = things that change firms' unit production costs
P - productivity: $\uparrow$Prod $\rightarrow$ $\uparrow$*SRAS*
$\qquad\qquad\quad$ $\downarrow$Prod $\rightarrow$ $\downarrow$*SRAS*
I - input prices:
$\uparrow$ input prices $\rightarrow$ $\downarrow$*SRAS*
$\downarrow$input prices $\rightarrow$ $\uparrow$*SRAS*

L - laws, regulations, taxes, and subsidies on businesses
$\uparrow$Laws, regulations, and taxes
$\rightarrow$$\downarrow$*SRAS*
$\downarrow$Laws, regulations, and taxes
$\uparrow$*SRAS*
$\uparrow$Subsidies $\rightarrow$ $\uparrow$*SRAS*
$\downarrow$ Subsidies $\rightarrow$ $\downarrow$*SRAS*

E - expected inflation

Δ *C.Ig.G.Xn* = Δ *AD*
Δ *AD* $\rightarrow$ Δ *PL* & Δ *RGDP*

AD right $\rightarrow$ *PL* $\uparrow$ & *RGDP* $\uparrow$
AD left $\rightarrow$ *PL* $\downarrow$ & *RGDP* $\downarrow$

C.Ig.G.Xn = the spending that comes from the different sectors of the economy
C – consumption (household spending)
$\uparrow$*C* $\rightarrow$ $\uparrow$*AD*
$\downarrow$*C* $\rightarrow$ $\downarrow$*AD*

Ig – investment (business spending)
$\uparrow$*Ig* $\rightarrow$ $\uparrow$*AD*
$\downarrow$*Ig* $\rightarrow$ $\downarrow$*AD*
G - government spending
$\uparrow$*G* $\rightarrow$ $\uparrow$*AD*
$\downarrow$*G* $\rightarrow$ $\downarrow$*AD*

Xn - net exports(net foreign spending)
$\uparrow$Exports $\rightarrow$ $\uparrow$*AD*
$\downarrow$Exports $\rightarrow$$\downarrow$*AD*

$\uparrow$Imports $\rightarrow$$\downarrow$*AD*
$\downarrow$Imports $\rightarrow$ $\uparrow$*AD*

Helpful hints for the *AD-AS* model:
- Make sure your *LRAS* curve is vertical, your *AD* curve is downward-sloping, and your *SRAS* is upward-sloping.
- Use the correct labels to establish that you are in the *AD-AS* model: *AD, SRAS, LRAS, rGDP*, Price Level (NOT Price or P!!), *Y*, and *PL*.
- Use arrows to help clarify any shift.
- *LRAS* only shifts if there is economic growth. Economic growth only happens if *LRAS* has shifted.
- Remember to show equilibrium on the axes, not internally on the graph.

The Phillips Curve

The Phillips curve can be further divided into a short-run and long-run version. The short-run Phillips curve shows the trade-offs that exist between inflation (π%) and unemployment (u%)in the short run.

The long-run Phillips curve exists at an economy's natural rate of unemployment (natural u%) and shows that no relationship exists between inflation rates and unemployment rates in the long run.

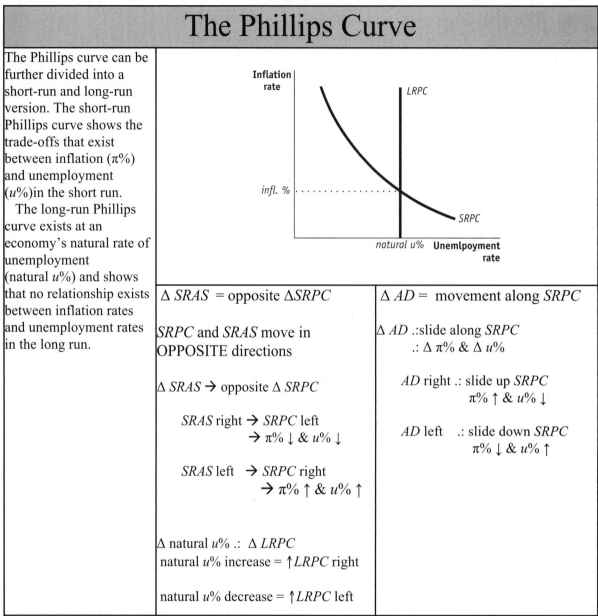

Δ *SRAS* = opposite Δ*SRPC*

SRPC and *SRAS* move in OPPOSITE directions

Δ *SRAS* $\rightarrow$ opposite Δ *SRPC*

    SRAS right $\rightarrow$ *SRPC* left
            $\rightarrow$ π% $\downarrow$ & u% $\downarrow$

    SRAS left $\rightarrow$ *SRPC* right
            $\rightarrow$ π% $\uparrow$ & u% $\uparrow$

Δ natural u% .: Δ *LRPC*
natural u% increase = $\uparrow$*LRPC* right

natural u% decrease = $\uparrow$*LRPC* left

Δ *AD* = movement along *SRPC*

Δ *AD* .:slide along *SRPC*
    .: Δ π% & Δ u%

    AD right .: slide up *SRPC*
          π% $\uparrow$ & u% $\downarrow$

    AD left .: slide down *SRPC*
          π% $\downarrow$ & u% $\uparrow$

Helpful hints for the Philips Curve graph:
- *LRPC* is vertical at the natural rate of unemployment (UR$_N$ or NAIRU).
- *SRPC* is downward-sloping.
- Be very careful in using abbreviations! Use INF or π for inflation. DO NOT USE i or I for inflation!
- Anytime the economy is operating at long-run equilibrium, the inflation rate and the unemployment rate will be at the points where the *LRPC* and the *SRPC* intersect.
- A short-run equilibrium might not be at the intersection of these two curves. If the two curves intersect, then the economy is in long-run equilibrium.

VI. TEST-TAKING TIPS

Once you have mastered all of the course material, you are ready to begin reviewing for the AP® Macroeconomics exam. Below is a description of the types of questions you will find on the exam, as well as tips and suggestions for how to answer these types of questions.

The Multiple-Choice Section

When you are taking the multiple-choice section of the exam, be careful that you do not spend too much time on any one question. Remember that you have 70 minutes to answer 60 questions, so don't get stuck on any one question. Skip and return to a difficult question or make a guess if you have no idea how to answer it. Also, be very careful that you fill in the correct bubble for your answer (be especially careful if you do skip a question) and that each bubble is filled in neatly.

Unlike tests that you might take in a class, the AP® exams do not use "all of the above," "none of the above," or true/false type questions. Instead, the multiple-choice questions you will encounter will come in several different formats. The most common question type asks you to either define or classify concepts learned in macroeconomics. The next most common question type is best described as cause and effect format. Far less common are questions that ask you to calculate an answer or interpret a graph.

Define/Classify Format
This format asks you to simply identify or classify information. These are often the simplest questions and require that you have read and understood the material. Read through each question carefully and then analyze the answer choices. Some of the answer choices will contain 'correct' information in them, but they may not be relevant to the question being asked, so avoid the temptation to skim the question and look for the first 'true' thing you see. Make sure the answer matches the question being asked.

Question: Which of the following would be classified as a debit to the current account in the balance of payments?
  a. Japanese investors purchase real estate in Hawaii.
  b. $20 million in medicine is exported from American pharmaceutical manufacturers to private hospitals in Australia.
  c. Argentine investors purchase $5 million worth of United States Treasury securities.
  d. United States corporations pay $400 million in dividends to foreign shareholders.
  e. United States gasoline producers import $1 billion worth of crude oil from foreign producers.

Cause and Effect Format
The cause and effect format questions are quite popular on the AP® Macroeconomics exam and can be a real challenge unless you have a strategy. The strategy that works well for many successful students is to analyze a single column and see what distractors you can eliminate.

Question: Which of the following is most likely to occur if the Federal Reserve conducts a contractionary monetary policy?

Open-Market Operation		*Nominal Interest Rate*	*$ Exchange Rate*	*Unemployment*
a.	Sell bonds	Increase	$ appreciates	Increase
b.	Sell bonds	Decrease	$ depreciates	Decrease
c.	Buy bonds	Decrease	$ depreciates	Decrease
d.	Buy bonds	Decrease	$ appreciates	Decrease
e.	Buy bonds	Increase	$ depreciates	Increase

How to think about it: I know that contractionary policy leads to an increase in the interest rate, so I can immediately eliminate b., c., and d. I remember that contractionary policy means sell bonds, so I think a. is correct. I go through the chain of events to double check: Sell Bonds → ↑ i → ↓AD. A ↓ in AD will cause the unemployment rate to increase, and as people buy less of all goods, including exports, they will supply fewer dollars on the foreign exchange market, causing the dollar to appreciate. Answer is a.

Calculation

When answering calculation questions, make sure to read the distractors carefully for clues as to the right answer. For instance, when given information about marginal propensity to consume, like in the question below, calculate the marginal propensity to save, the spending multiplier, and the tax multiplier, and jot them down on the test. That way you can 'test' the distractors until you find the correct answer.

Question: If consumers have a marginal propensity to consume of 0.8, then which of the following is true?

    a. A $4 billion increase in private investment will lead to a maximum economic expansion of $40 billion.

    b. An increase in income of $400 billion will result in an increase in $80 billion in savings.

    c. An increase in income of $400 billion will result in a decrease in consumption of $320 billion.

    d. The spending multiplier is equal to 4.

    e. The tax multiplier is equal to -3.

How to think about it: If the MPC = 0.8, then the spending multiplier is 1/1 – MPC = 5 and the tax multiplier = -MPC/(1 - MPC) = -4. So a $4 billion increase in private investment will lead to a $4 billion × 5 = $20 billion maximum expansion; an increase in income of $400 billion will lead to (1-MPC) × 400 billion = $80 billion in savings. Therefore b. is the correct answer.

Graphic Interpretation

AP® economics exams will frequently ask you to refer to a graph to answer questions. These questions require you to understand what is shown on the graph provided. Pay close attention to the specific information provided on the graph as you determine your answer – especially the labels on the axes of the graph.

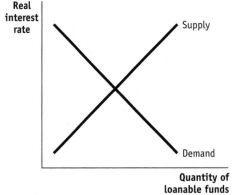

Question: Refer to the loanable funds diagram above; an increase in private borrowing is best shown as

    a. an increased demand for loanable funds.

    b. an increased supply of loanable funds.

    c. a decreased demand for loanable funds.

    d. a decreased supply of loanable funds.

    e. no change in the loanable funds market.

How to think about it: an increase in private borrowing means that people will demand more loanable funds. Therefore, to show an increase in private borrowing on the graph above, you would increase demand, so a. is the correct answer.

The Free-Response Section

The second section of the AP® Macroeconomics exam is made up of free-response questions. You are allowed 60 minutes to answer the free-response questions *where indicated* in the answer booklet. Make sure you use your time wisely. Consider outlining your answers and using graphs, symbols, and abbreviations where applicable.

Remember that someone will eventually read and score the answers that you write. The easier it is to find and follow your answers, the easier it is to give you points! Practice writing clear, concise, organized answers. Make sure you write the question in the space provided for that question. Denote which part of the question you are answering as you write your answer. Provide a clear, organized answer to each part of the question. Avoid including extraneous information – if it contradicts your answer, you may lose points. Use the scoring guides provided for the practice tests below as an example of a clear, complete, concise, organized response and strive to use a similar format for your answer.

But don't be concerned if you must answer questions out of order or cross out an answer and start again, etc. Exam readers will do their best to award you the points that you deserve – it is just in your best interest to make that as easy as possible for them!

You should also make sure that you answer each part of each question to the best of your ability. Even if you are unsure of the correct answer, write something. You may actually know more than you think. Also, make sure that you answer each part of the question even when you think your answer on an earlier part may not be correct. Each part of a free-response question is scored independently, so an incorrect answer on one part of a question does not mean you can't receive points for a subsequent part. For instance, suppose you are asked what the impact will be on the interest rate, and you answer incorrectly; you will not earn points for that part of the question. However, if the next question is based on the change in the interest rate you gave, you will receive points if your answer is consistent with what you answered for the interest rate. Consistency is key!

The free-response section is divided into three separate questions. The first question is the longest and most comprehensive and you should allocate roughly half of your time, about 25 minutes, to answering it. The second and third free-response questions are shorter and typically test a particular area of the course outline. You should allocate roughly a quarter of the time available, or about 12 - 13 minutes, to each of the shorter questions. Allocate and monitor your time carefully so that you are able to provide at least a basic response to each question. Each question usually has parts that require a simple "coin-flip" response, e.g. yes/no or increase/decrease. Make sure you take the time to at least answer these parts of every question. Under no circumstances should you leave a free-response question unanswered. Omission is a guarantee of no points.

On the free-response section, read each question carefully. Pay close attention to what each question is specifically asking. Remember those verbs you underlined during the planning period? As you answer each part of each question, cross out the corresponding verb so that you make sure you answer each part of the question. According to the experts, i.e. those who score your responses, one of the best ways to make sure you receive maximum points for your answer is to read the question and do EXACTLY what it says. Below are examples of some of the phrases and terms used in free response questions and the responses that should go with them.

'Draw a correctly labeled graph' - draw the required diagram and CORRECTLY LABEL the axes and curves on the graph!

Question: Draw a correctly labeled diagram of the short-run Phillips curve; label the curve *SRPC*.
Response:

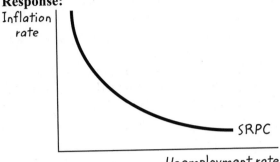

'Show' - This tells you to go back to a graph that you have previously drawn and clearly change that graph.

Question: Show the effect of an increase in inflationary expectations on the short-run Phillips curve from part a (i).
Response:

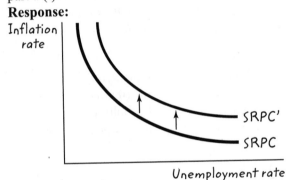

'Identify' - Make an assertion based on the information given in the question.

Question: Identify the effect of a decrease in consumption on output.
Response: Output decreases.

'Explain' - Go beyond the assertion and describe why the assertion you made happened.

Question: Identify the effect of a decrease in consumption on output. Explain.
Response: Output decreases because aggregate demand decreased.

'List' - Make a bulleted list of items.

Question: List three actions the Federal Reserve can undertake to change the money supply.
Response: Buy or sell Treasury securities
Change the reserve requirement
Change the discount rate

'Define' - Write a definition.

Question: Define discount rate.

Response: The interest rate charged when member banks borrow reserves from the Fed overnight

'Calculate' - Do some math and find a numerical answer. Show your work!

Question: Assume that the required reserve ratio is 10% and that banks hold no excess reserves. If the Federal Reserve purchases $50 million in Treasury securities on the open market, calculate the maximum possible change in loans throughout the banking system.

Response: Change in loans = Amt. single bank can lend X money multiplier

$50 million deposit - (10% X $50 million) = $45 million

$45 million X (1/10%) = $450 million <-- ANSWER!!!

VIII. PRACTICE TESTS

Use the following sample tests to help you prepare for your AP® Macroeconomics exam. Try to replicate the conditions you will have during the exam. Allow yourself 70 minutes to complete the multiple-choice section without using a calculator or any outside resources. There is no penalty for guessing, so attempt each question.

After you have completed the multiple-choice section, give yourself 10 minutes to plan your response to the three free-response questions that follow the multiple-choice section. After your 10 minute planning period, you should complete the free-response questions within 50 minutes. For the multiple-choice section, you are required to fill in the answer blanks on the answer document using a #2 pencil. You are required to answer the free-response section with a blue or black pen.

Answers and explanations, along with scoring guidelines for the free-response section, are available to your teacher on our website at bcs.worthpublishers.com/krugmanap2e.

Practice Test #1

Multiple-Choice Questions

1. Which monetary policy would be most appropriate for combating inflation?
   a. increase taxes and transfer payments
   b. raise the reserve requirement
   c. the open market purchase of Treasury securities by the Federal Reserve
   d. increase taxes and decrease government spending
   e. decrease taxes and decrease government spending

2. If the resources used in making consumer goods can be perfectly substituted for making capital goods, then the opportunity cost is
   a. increasing.
   b. zero.
   c. decreasing.
   d. constant.
   e. diminishing.

3. Depreciation of the United States dollar in the foreign exchange market could be caused by a decrease in which of the following?
   a. United States imports from Japan
   b. the United States price level
   c. demand for the British pound by U.S. investors
   d. the United States real interest rate
   e. Mexican exports to the United States

4. Assuming a system of flexible exchange rates, an open-market purchase of bonds by the United States Federal Reserve while other countries do nothing will most likely affect the rate of inflation and the international value of the United States dollar in which of the following ways?

	Inflation rate	*International value of the United States dollar*
a.	Decrease	Appreciate
b.	Decrease	Depreciate
c.	Increase	Appreciate
d.	Increase	Depreciate
e.	Increase	No change

5. The federal funds rate is
   a. the interest rate the Federal Reserve charges member banks for overnight loans.
   b. the interest rate banks charge their best commercial customers.
   c. the interest rate banks charge other banks for overnight loans.
   d. the percentage of demand deposits that banks may not lend to customers.
   e. the difference between the nominal interest rate and the real interest rate.

Labor Market in Parlin (in thousands of persons)	
Population	250
Labor Force	200
Employed	160

6. Study the information in the table above. If 20,000 discouraged workers are now reclassified as unemployed, what would be the new unemployment rate for Parlin?
   a. 20%
   b. 36%
   c. 18.2%
   d. 27.3%
   e. 40%

7. An increase in government spending combined with an open-market purchase of bonds will result in
   a. an increase in real gross domestic product and an increase in the interest rate.
   b. an increase in real gross domestic product and an indeterminate change in the interest rate.
   c. an indeterminate change in real gross domestic product and a decrease in the interest rate.
   d. a decrease in real gross domestic product and a decrease in the interest rate.
   e. a decrease in unemployment and an increase in the interest rate.

8. If a $50 billion increase in government spending results in a $200 billion increase in real output, then which of the following would be the marginal propensity to consume?
   a. 0.90
   b. 0.80
   c. 0.75
   d. 0.50
   e. 0.25

9. Money as measured by M1 functions primarily as a
   a. unit of account.
   b. store of value.
   c. medium of exchange.
   d. source of divisibility.
   e. source of durability.

10. A sudden increase in energy prices will most likely trigger
   a. cost-push inflation.
   b. demand-pull inflation.
   c. lower interest rates.
   d. decreases in the money supply.
   e. an immediate decrease in inventory.

11. Simultaneous increases in the rates of inflation and unemployment are best associated with which of the following?
    a. a leftward shift of the money demand curve
    b. a leftward shift of the aggregate demand curve
    c. a rightward shift of the short-run Phillips curve
    d. a rightward shift of the long-run Phillips curve
    e. a rightward shift of the short-run aggregate supply curve

12. Which is most likely to occur if the Federal Reserve increases the reserve requirement on demand deposits?
    a. Banks will be able to lend more excess reserves.
    b. Interest rates will decrease.
    c. The money supply will decrease.
    d. The discount rate will decrease.
    e. Aggregate demand will increase.

13. Which monetary policy action by the Federal Reserve will shift aggregate demand to the right?
    a. the open-market sale of bonds by the Federal Reserve
    b. a decrease in the discount rate
    c. a decrease in taxes
    d. an increase in government spending
    e. an increase in the reserve requirement

14. The net export effect is best described as
    a. an increase in capital investment at the expense of government spending.
    b. a decrease in net exports resulting from appreciation of the currency.
    c. an increase in both inflation and unemployment.
    d. a decrease in gross private investment resulting from government borrowing.
    e. a rightward shift of the money supply.

15. If the real interest rate in France decreases relative to that of the rest of the world, capital flow and currency should change in which of the following ways?

	Capital flow	*Currency*
a.	Out	Appreciate
b.	In	Appreciate
c.	In	Depreciate
d.	Out	Depreciate
e.	No change	No change

16. Which would be the appropriate fiscal policy to combat inflation?
    a. buy bonds
    b. sell bonds
    c. decrease taxes
    d. decrease government spending
    e. increase the reserve ratio

17. Which of the following best exemplifies frictional unemployment?
   a. Skilled workers are replaced by robots.
   b. Economic recession forces companies to layoff many workers.
   c. Workers lack the necessary skills to gain employment in the semiconductor industry.
   d. College graduates enter the labor force and seek employment.
   e. Men and women quit working to take care of their young children.

18. Which of the following best describes the sequence of events that occurs when the Federal Reserve buys Treasury securities on the open market?
   a. Money supply increases, interest rates decrease, consumption and investment increase, aggregate demand increases, output and price level increase
   b. Money supply increases, interest rates decrease, consumption and investment decrease, aggregate demand decreases, output and price level decrease
   c. Money supply decreases, interest rates increase, consumption and investment decrease, aggregate demand decreases, output and price level decrease
   d. Money supply decreases, interest rates decrease, consumption and investment decrease, aggregate demand decreases, output and price level decrease
   e. Money supply decreases, interest rates increase, consumption and investment increase, aggregate demand increases, output and price level increase

19. Assume that autonomous consumption is $500 and that the marginal propensity to save is 0.25. If disposable income increases by $1,000, then consumption spending will increase by
   a. $250.
   b. $125.
   c. $1,250.
   d. $750.
   e. $375.

20. Assume that all input prices are inflexible. An increase in the money supply will have which of the following effects on output, price level, and real wages?

	Output	*Price level*	*Real wages*
a.	Increase	Increase	Increase
b.	Increase	Decrease	Increase
c.	Decrease	Increase	Increase
d.	Increase	Increase	Decrease
e.	Increase	Decrease	Decrease

21. If the velocity of money is not changing, and the real output in an economy is growing 4% per year, what will happen if the central bank raises the money supply by 5%?
   a. deflation of 1% per year
   b. inflation of 1% per year
   c. inflation of 9% per year
   d. disinflation of 1% per year
   e. disinflation of 9% per year

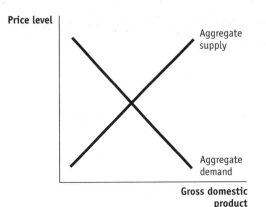

Price level

Aggregate supply

Aggregate demand

Gross domestic product

22. According to the graph above, an increase in consumers' wealth will most likely cause income and unemployment to change in which of the following ways?

	Income	Unemployment
a.	Increase	Increase
b.	Decrease	Increase
c.	Decrease	Decrease
d.	Increase	No change
e.	Increase	Decrease

23. If the price level in the United States increased relative to the price level in Belgium, then the U.S. dollar would
   a. appreciate, making Belgian exports to the United States more expensive.
   b. depreciate, making U.S. imports from Belgium more expensive.
   c. appreciate, making Belgian imports from the United States cheaper.
   d. appreciate, making U.S. imports from Belgium cheaper.
   e. depreciate, making U.S. exports to Belgium cheaper.

24. If an economy is currently operating below the natural rate of unemployment, then which of the following will cause both unemployment and interest rates to increase?
   a. The Federal Reserve raises the discount rate.
   b. The government reduces spending while raising taxes.
   c. The Federal Reserve buys Treasury securities on the open market.
   d. The Federal Reserve lowers the reserve requirement.
   e. The government increases spending and reduces taxes.

25. A decrease in which of the following would most likely lead to economic growth?
   a. personal savings
   b. gross private investment
   c. the real interest rate
   d. capital formation
   e. bond purchases by the Federal Reserve

26. Which of the following would cause a surplus in a competitive market?
   a. a price higher than the equilibrium price
   b. a price lower than the equilibrium price
   c. a price ceiling
   d. a quota
   e. a tariff

27. The inverse relationship between the real interest rate and the quantity of funds available for borrowing is shown by the
    a. aggregate demand curve.
    b. demand for loanable funds.
    c. short-run Phillips curve.
    d. supply of loanable funds.
    e. production possibilities curve.

28. $10 billion increase in government spending funded by a $10 billion increase in taxes will have which of the following effects on aggregate demand?
    a. increase aggregate demand by an amount greater than $10 billion
    b. increase aggregate demand by an amount of $10 billion
    c. no change in aggregate demand
    d. decrease aggregate demand by an amount greater than $9 billion
    e. decrease aggregate demand by an amount of $9 billion

29. An increase in the government's budget deficit will most likely result in
    a. increased tax revenues.
    b. decreased government spending.
    c. higher interest rates.
    d. a decrease in the international value of the dollar.
    e. an increase in unemployment.

30. Which of the following would cause the Canadian dollar to depreciate relative to the Mexican peso?
    a. an increase in Canadian household income
    b. a decrease in Mexican interest rates relative to Canadian interest rates
    c. an increase in Mexico's average price level
    d. a decrease in Canada's average price level
    e. an increase in Mexican household income

31. Deflation is caused by
    a. an increase in the money supply.
    b. decreased short-run aggregate supply.
    c. increased aggregate demand.
    d. decreased aggregate demand.
    e. a rightward shift of the short-run Phillips curve.

32. If the nominal interest rate increases from 6 percent to 8 percent while the real interest rate remains unchanged, then
    a. expected inflation remains unchanged.
    b. expected inflation decreases by 2%.
    c. expected deflation increases by 2%.
    d. disinflation occurs.
    e. expected inflation increases by 2%.

33. Which of the following would lead to a decrease in the United States' gross domestic product in the short run?
    a. There is a decrease in personal income taxes.
    b. Banks lend out all excess reserves.
    c. Households increase their savings.
    d. Businesses increase their investment in new capital.
    e. Government increases defense spending.

34. An increase in the population's educational attainment will cause the
   a. aggregate demand curve to shift left.
   b. aggregate demand curve to shift right.
   c. long-run aggregate supply curve to shift left.
   d. long-run aggregate supply curve to shift right.
   e. short-run aggregate supply curve to shift left.

35. Assume that private investors buy $100 billion worth of treasury securities on the open market from the Federal Reserve. If the required reserve ratio is 25 percent, the maximum increase in the money supply is
   a. $25 billion.
   b. $75 billion.
   c. $300 billion.
   d. $400 billion.
   e. $500 billion.

Questions 36 - 37 are based on the following diagram, which shows the choices in production of two countries, Zumbulu and Costa Del Rey, producing two goods, bananas and cocoa, using all of their available resources.

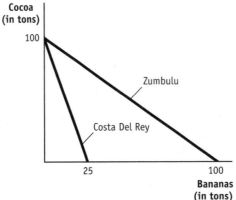

36. Before specialization and trade, the opportunity cost of producing 1 ton of bananas in Zumbulu and in Costa Del Rey is which of the following?

	Zumbulu	*Costa Del Rey*
a.	4 tons of cocoa	1 ton of cocoa
b.	1 ton of cocoa	1 ton of cocoa
c.	1 ton of cocoa	0.25 ton of cocoa
d.	1 ton of cocoa	4 tons of cocoa
e.	0.25 ton of cocoa	4 tons of cocoa

37. Which of the following statements best describes the absolute advantage or comparative advantage that each country has?
   a. Zumbulu has an absolute advantage in bananas, while Costa Del Rey has a comparative advantage in bananas.
   b. Neither has an absolute advantage in cocoa, while Costa Del Rey has a comparative advantage in bananas.
   c. Zumbulu has a comparative advantage in bananas, while Costa Del Rey has a comparative advantage in cocoa.
   d. Zumbulu has a comparative disadvantage in bananas, while Costa Del Rey has an absolute advantage in bananas.
   e. Neither has a comparative advantage in cocoa, while Zumbulu has a comparative advantage in bananas.

38. Max can make 10 cakes or 5 pounds of marshmallows in a day. Eli can make 6 cakes or 2 pounds of marshmallows in a day. Assuming that they both have constant opportunity costs, which of the following terms of trade would both of them find beneficial?

    a. No terms of trade will be beneficial to both since Max has absolute advantage in both goods.

    b. Max will trade 1 marshmallow for ½ of a cake.

    c. Max will trade 1 marshmallow for 2 ½ cakes.

    d. Max will trade 1 marshmallow for 3 ½ cakes.

    e. Max will trade one marshmallow for 4 cakes.

39. A decrease in government spending will most likely cause aggregate demand and short-run aggregate supply to change in which of the following ways?

	Aggregate demand	*Short-run aggregate supply*
a.	Increase	Increase
b.	Increase	No change
c.	Decrease	Increase
d.	Decrease	No change
e.	Decrease	Decrease

40. Which type of unemployment would decrease if computer-based social networking reduced the amount of time it took for job seekers to find jobs?

    a. frictional

    b. cyclical

    c. seasonal

    d. structural

    e. part-time

41. The marginal propensity to save is

    a. always equal to the marginal propensity to consume.

    b. equal to the tax multiplier.

    c. the percentage of the change in disposable income that is spent.

    d. used to calculate the money multiplier.

    e. equal to one minus the marginal propensity to consume.

42. If the marginal propensity to consume is 0.75 and there is a recessionary output gap of $200 million, which of the following actions would exactly close the output gap in the short run?

    a. Decrease government spending by $200 million.

    b. Decrease both taxes and government spending by $200 million.

    c. Increase taxes by $200 million with no change in government spending.

    d. Increase government spending by $50 million with no increase in taxes.

    e. Decrease taxes by $50 million and increase government spending by $25 million.

43. Which of the following combinations of fiscal and monetary policy would effectively increase capital investment while not increasing the price level?

	Fiscal policy	*Monetary policy*
a.	Expansionary	Contractionary
b.	Expansionary	Expansionary
c.	Contractionary	Expansionary
d.	Contractionary	Contractionary
e.	Contractionary	No change

This Year's Production	Last Year's Price	This Year's Price
100 consumer goods	$2 per good	$3 per good
50 capital goods	$10 per good	$10 per good
200 services	$1.50 per service	$2 per good

44. Based on the information in the table above, calculate this year's nominal gross domestic product (GDP) and the rate of inflation that occurred between last year and this year.

	This year's Nominal GDP	Inflation rate
a.	$1,000	50%
b.	$1,000	20%
c.	$1,200	20%
d.	$1,200	10%
e.	$750	10%

45. If firms are able to reduce their per unit production costs through increased productivity, then the short-run aggregate supply curve, short-run Phillips curve, and inflation will change in which of the following ways?

	Short-run aggregate supply curve	Short-run Phillips curve	Inflation
a.	shift to the right	shift to the right	increase
b.	shift to the right	shift to the left	decrease
c.	shift to the right	no change	increase
d.	shift to the left	shift to the left	decrease
e.	shift to the left	shift to the right	increase

46. Assuming that input prices are flexible, an economy operating above full employment will experience which of the following changes in output and price level in the long run?

	Output	Price level
a.	Increase	Increase
b.	No change	Increase
c.	Increase	No change
d.	Increase	Decrease
e.	Decrease	Increase

47. In the long run, increases in the money supply result in which of the following changes in the nominal and real gross domestic product (GDP)?

	Nominal GDP	Real GDP
a.	Increase	Increase
b.	Increase	Decrease
c.	Decrease	No change
d.	Increase	No change
e.	No change	Increase

48. An increase in resource prices will shift the
   a. short-run aggregate supply to the left.
   b. short-run aggregate supply to the right.
   c. aggregate demand to the right.
   d. aggregate demand to the left.
   e. long-run aggregate supply to the right.

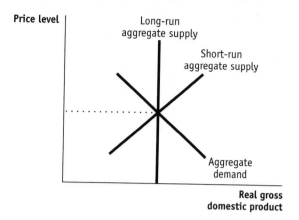

Price level

Long-run
aggregate supply

Short-run
aggregate supply

Aggregate
demand

Real gross
domestic product

49. According to the graph above, which of the following is true about this economy in the long run?
   a. Contractionary monetary policy will restore this economy to its long-run equilibrium.
   b. The long-run aggregate supply curve will shift to the left in order to restore the long-run equilibrium.
   c. The economy depicted is currently in a long-run equilibrium.
   d. A combination of increased government spending and an increase in the money supply could shift aggregate demand to the right and restore long-run equilibrium.
   e. Wages will increase as they adjust to the new price level and the short-run aggregate supply curve will shift to the left and restore long-run equilibrium.

50. In the long run, decreases in aggregate demand lead to which of the following changes in nominal and real gross domestic product (GDP)?

	Nominal GDP	Real GDP
a.	No change	Decrease
b.	Decrease	No change
c.	Decrease	Decrease
d.	Increase	Increase
e.	Increase	No change

51. Assume that the required reserve ratio is 5 percent and that the bank keeps an additional 5 percent in reserve. If Shayne deposits $100 in cash into her checking account, the amount this bank will lend from this deposit is
   a. $10.
   b. $2,000.
   c. $90.
   d. $900.
   e. $5.

52. If the United States dollar appreciates relative to the euro, then United States' imports and exports will most likely change in which of the following ways?

	Imports	Exports
a.	Increase	Decrease
b.	Decrease	Decrease
c.	Decrease	Increase
d.	Increase	Increase
e.	No change	No change

53. Which of the following would be included as current year consumption in calculating gross domestic product?
   a. the purchase of stock
   b. the sale of a treasury bond
   c. a professional manicure
   d. the purchase of a new construction crane by a corporation
   e. wages paid to employees for work performed this year

54. A shift in the short-run Phillips curve corresponds to
   a. a shift in long-run aggregate supply.
   b. a shift in short-run aggregate supply.
   c. a shift in aggregate demand.
   d. a shift in the long-run Phillips curve.
   e. an increase in the slope of the short-run aggregate supply curve.

55. Which of the following would cause a rightward shift in the aggregate demand curve?
   a. an increase in household saving
   b. an increase in expected profits
   c. an increase in interest rates
   d. an increase in the exchange rate
   e. an increase in taxes

56. Decreased business taxes would increase real gross domestic product by increasing which of the following?
   a. unemployment
   b. the M2
   c. aggregate supply only
   d. aggregate demand only
   e. aggregate supply and aggregate demand

57. An increase in the supply of loanable funds will have which of the following effects on the exchange rate and net exports?

	Exchange rate	Net exports
a.	Appreciate	Decrease
b.	Appreciate	Increase
c.	Appreciate	No change
d.	Depreciate	Increase
e.	Depreciate	Decrease

58. A point lying inside the production possibilities curve indicates that the combination of goods or services being produced is
   a. not possible given the available resources.
   b. both productively and allocatively efficient.
   c. the result of reduced trade barriers.
   d. an indication that resources are not being fully employed.
   e. desirable if economic efficiency is a primary economic goal.

59. Which would most likely gain from unanticipated inflation?
    a. renters who rent on a month-to-month basis
    b. banks that have issued many long-term loans at fixed interest rates
    c. individuals living off of fixed pensions
    d. governments running a budget deficit
    e. employees who have already agreed to a long-term wage contract

60. An increase in government spending in the United States will have what effect on the price level in the United States, output, and the value of the peso (the currency of a trading partner)?

	Price level	*Output*	*Value of peso*
a.	Decrease	Decrease	Increase
b.	Decrease	Increase	Increase
c.	Increase	Increase	Increase
d.	Decrease	Increase	Decrease
e.	Increase	Increase	Decrease

Free-Response Questions

On the actual AP® exam, you have 60 minutes to complete all three questions. The College Board requires that all free responses be completed in blue or black ink. Note that only answers written in the designated space in the answer booklet will be scored.

1. The economy of Alex is currently operating below the full employment output.

   a. Using a correctly labeled graph of the Phillips curve, show the current unemployment rate. Label the current short-run equilibrium point A and the long-run equilibrium point B.

   b. Using a correctly labeled graph of aggregate supply and aggregate demand, show each of the following:

   (i) The full employment output level, labeled Y_f
   (ii) The current output level, labeled Y_1 and the current price level, labeled PL_1.

   c. The Fed can conduct monetary policy to address the recession.

   (i) Identify the open-market operation that would correct the output gap.

   (ii) Using a correctly labeled graph of the money market, show the effect of the open-market operation identified in **b.** on the nominal interest rate.

(iii) As a result of the open-market operation you identify in part **c.(i)**, what will happen to aggregate demand? Explain.

d. As a result of the monetary policy you identified in part **c.(i)**, the output gap is corrected. However, the action undertaken by the Fed caused an inflationary gap instead of returning the economy to long-run equilibrium.

    (i) Show on the graph in **a.** the new unemployment rate as a result of causing an inflationary gap, labeled C.

    (ii) What effect will the change you describe in part **b.(ii)** have on short-run aggregate supply? Explain.

    (iii) What effect will the change you describe in part **c.(iii)** have on the long-run aggregate supply?

2. Assume the United States Federal Reserve requires banks to keep reserves of 10 percent against demand deposits only.

    a. If Roberto deposits $500 cash into his checking account, calculate the following:

        (i) the initial amount his bank can lend

        (ii) the maximum possible change in the money supply from his deposit

    b. Instead of depositing $500 cash into his checking account, Roberto deposits the cash into his savings account. Calculate the following:

        (i) the amount his bank must maintain as required reserve

        (ii) the value of the money multiplier on time deposits

    c. Explain why banks may try to avoid the required reserve ratio by temporarily treating demand deposits as time deposits.

3. Assume that the real interest rate in Brazil increases from 2 percent to 6 percent while the real interest rate in the United States has stayed at 2 percent.

a. Using a correctly labeled graph of the foreign exchange market for the United States dollar, show the effect of the increase in Brazil's real interest rate on the following:

(i) the supply of the United States dollar. Explain.

(ii) the value of the United States dollar

b. Using a correctly labeled graph of the loanable funds market in the United States, show how the increase in Albania's real interest rate affects the real interest rate in the United States.

This page left blank intentionally.

Practice Test #2

Multiple-Choice Questions

1. Which of the following is included in M2 but not M1?
   a. currency in circulation
   b. demand deposits
   c. money market mutual funds
   d. stocks and bonds
   e. savings accounts

2. An increase in government spending while the economy is fully employed will most likely result in
   a. cost-push inflation.
   b. stagflation.
   c. demand-pull inflation.
   d. lower interest rates.
   e. a decrease in the money supply.

3. In the long run, increases in the money supply result in which of the following changes in aggregate demand and the long-run aggregate supply?

	Aggregate demand	*Long-run aggregate supply*
a.	Increase	Increase
b.	Increase	Decrease
c.	Decrease	No change
d.	Increase	No change
e.	No change	Increase

4. A decrease in resource prices will shift the
   a. short-run aggregate supply to the left.
   b. short-run aggregate supply to the right.
   c. aggregate demand to the right.
   d. aggregate demand to the left.
   e. long-run aggregate supply to the left.

5. In the long run, decreases in aggregate demand lead to which of the following changes in nominal gross domestic product (GDP) and the price level?

	Nominal GDP	*Price level*
a.	No change	Decrease
b.	Decrease	No change
c.	Decrease	Decrease
d.	Increase	Increase
e.	Increase	No change

6. Assume that the required reserve ratio is 20 percent. If Coriander deposits $100 in cash into her checking account, the maximum amount of new loans the banking system can create is
   a. $20.
   b. $80.
   c. $400.
   d. $500.
   e. $5.

7. If exchange rates are fixed and the United States' rate of inflation decreases relative to its trade partners, then the United States' imports and exports will most likely change in which of the following ways?

	Imports	*Exports*
a.	Increase	Decrease
b.	Decrease	Decrease
c.	Decrease	Increase
d.	Increase	Increase
e.	No change	No change

8. Which of the following would be counted towards gross private investment in this year's gross domestic product?
   a. the purchase of corporate stock
   b. the sale of a Treasury bond
   c. the purchase of inventory
   d. the purchase of a new car
   e. the purchase of a college education

9. Movement along an existing short-run Phillips curve corresponds to
   a. a shift in long-run aggregate supply.
   b. a shift in short-run aggregate supply.
   c. a shift in aggregate demand.
   d. a shift in the long-run Phillips curve.
   e. an increase in the slope of the short-run aggregate supply curve.

10. Which of the following would cause a leftward shift in the aggregate demand curve?
    a. an increase in the expected price level
    b. a decrease in interest rates
    c. a decrease in the exchange rate
    d. a decrease in consumer confidence
    e. an increase in household wealth

11. Increased business taxes would decrease real gross domestic product by decreasing which of the following?
    a. unemployment
    b. the M2
    c. aggregate supply only
    d. aggregate demand only
    e. aggregate supply and aggregate demand

12. An increase in the demand for loanable funds will have which of the following effects on the exchange rate and net exports?

	Exchange rate	*Net exports*
a.	Appreciate	Decrease
b.	Appreciate	Increase
c.	Appreciate	No change
d.	Depreciate	Increase
e.	Depreciate	Decrease

13. A production possibilities curve with a constant slope indicates which of the following?
    a. Increasing opportunity cost is present.
    b. The combination of goods and services that lies on the production possibilities curve is unattainable given the current technology.
    c. The opportunity cost of production is decreasing.
    d. The opportunity cost of producing the first unit is the same as the opportunity cost of producing each successive unit.
    e. Resources are being used at a slower rate than they were in the past.

14. Which would most likely be harmed by unanticipated inflation?
    a. property owners who rent to occupants on a month-to-month basis
    b. a bank that has made many long-term loans at fixed interest rates
    c. an individual whose main source of income is stock dividends
    d. governments running a budget deficit
    e. an employer whose labor force is locked into a long-term wage contract

15. An increase in banks' willingness and ability to lend excess reserves will most likely result in which of the following?

	Nominal interest rate	*Quantity of money*
a.	Increase	Decrease
b.	Decrease	Increase
c.	No change	No change
d.	Increase	No change
e.	Increase	Increase

16. An increase in personal income taxes will most likely cause output and unemployment to change in which of the following ways?

	Output	*Unemployment*
a.	Increase	Increase
b.	Decrease	Increase
c.	Decrease	Decrease
d.	Increase	No change
e.	Increase	Decrease

17. If the real interest rate in France decreased relative to the real interest rate in the United States while domestic prices remained unchanged, then the euro would
    a. depreciate, making French exports to the United States more expensive.
    b. appreciate, making U.S. imports from France more expensive.
    c. depreciate, making French imports from the United States cheaper.
    d. depreciate, making U.S. imports from France cheaper.
    e. appreciate, making French exports to the United States more expensive.

18. If an economy is experiencing a significant recession, then which of the following will cause employment and interest rates to increase?
    a. The Federal Reserve raises the discount rate.
    b. The government reduces spending while raising taxes.
    c. The Federal Reserve buys Treasury securities on the open market.
    d. The Federal Reserve lowers the reserve requirement.
    e. The government increases spending and reduces taxes.

19. Which best describes the mechanism by which interest rates influence economic growth?
    a. Lower interest rates encourage increased consumption, which results in economic growth.
    b. Higher interest rates discourage private investment, which results in economic growth.
    c. Decreases in net investment and increases in depreciation result in economic growth.
    d. Lower interest rates encourage gross private investment, capital formation, and economic growth.
    e. Increased interest rates result in the currency appreciating, which leads to economic growth.

20. Which combination of monetary and fiscal policies would be appropriate for an economy experiencing a recession?
    a. The Federal Reserve purchases securities on the open market while government spending increases.
    b. The Federal Reserve purchases securities on the open market while government increases taxes.
    c. The Federal Reserve sells securities on the open market while government increases spending.
    d. The Federal Reserve sells securities on the open market while government increases taxes.
    e. The Federal Reserve lowers the discount rate while the government simultaneously decreases spending and raises taxes.

21. An economy produces capital goods and consumer goods. If the country can produce more consumer goods without giving up capital goods, which of the following statements is definitely true?
    a. The opportunity cost of capital goods is less than the opportunity cost of consumer goods.
    b. The economy is operating outside of its production possibilities frontier.
    c. The opportunity cost of consumer goods is zero.
    d. The economy is productively efficient.
    e. The opportunity cost of capital goods is equal to the opportunity cost of consumer goods.

22. Depreciation of the Japanese yen in the foreign exchange market could be caused by an increase in which of the following?
    a. U.S. imports from Japan
    b. the United States price level
    c. demand for the Japanese yen by U.S. investors
    d. the U.S. real interest rate
    e. Japanese exports to Mexico

23. Which of the following has occurred if there is a rightward shift of the Phillips curve in the long run?
    a. Expectations of inflation have decreased and the unemployment rate has increased above the natural rate of unemployment.
    b. Expectations of inflation have increased and the unemployment rate has decreased to less than the natural rate of unemployment.
    c. Expectations of inflation have decreased and the unemployment rate has decreased to less than the natural rate of unemployment.
    d. Expectations of inflation have increased and the unemployment rate has increased back to the natural rate of unemployment.
    e. The natural rate of unemployment has increased and inflation has decreased.

24. Which of the following is a combination of fiscal and monetary policy designed to reduce inflation in an economy?
    a. increase taxes and reduce government spending
    b. raise the discount rate and sell Treasury bonds
    c. sell treasury bonds and reduce taxes
    d. decrease government spending and the required reserve ratio
    e. increase taxes and sell Treasury bonds

25. Which of the following would cause an increase in the official unemployment rate?
    a. People quit working in order to attend school full-time.
    b. People working in the service industry are reclassified from full-time to part-time.
    c. College students begin actively applying for employment.
    d. People who were employed by the government start their own consulting business.
    e. People retire from their jobs and perform volunteer work for charitable organizations.

26. Which of the following best describes the sequence of events that occurs when the Federal Reserve increases the required reserve ratio?
    a. money supply increases, interest rates decrease, consumption and investment increase, aggregate demand increases, output and price level increases
    b. money supply increases, interest rates decrease, consumption and investment decrease, aggregate demand decreases, output and price level decreases
    c. money supply decreases, interest rates increase, consumption and investment decrease, aggregate demand decreases, output and price level decreases
    d. money supply decreases, interest rates decrease, consumption and investment decrease, aggregate demand decreases, output and price level decreases
    e. money supply decreases, interest rates increase, consumption and investment increase, aggregate demand increases, output and price level increases

27. Assume that autonomous consumption is $500 and the marginal propensity to save is 0.05. If disposable income is $2,000, total consumption equals which of the following?
    a. $100
    b. $25
    c. $600
    d. $2,400
    e. $2,575

28. Assume that all input prices are flexible. An increase in labor productivity will have which of the following effects on output, price level, and real wages?

	Output	*Price level*	*Real wages*
a.	Increase	Increase	Increase
b.	Increase	Decrease	Increase
c.	Decrease	Increase	Increase
d.	Decrease	Increase	Decrease
e.	Increase	Decrease	Decrease

29. If the aggregate price level is 1.1, the real gross domestic product is $10 trillion, and the income velocity of money is 2, then the money supply equals
    a. $11 trillion.
    b. $10 trillion.
    c. $20 trillion.
    d. $5 trillion.
    e. $5.5 trillion.

30. A binding price floor is imposed in the market for gems. What effect will this price floor have on the quantity supplied, the quantity demanded, and the amount of gems actually exchanged?

	Quantity supplied	*Quantity demanded*	*Quantity exchanged*
a.	Increase	Decrease	No change
b.	Decrease	Increase	No change
c.	Increase	Decrease	Decrease
d.	Decrease	No change	Decrease
e.	Increase	Increase	Increase

31. The inverse relationship between inflation and unemployment is shown by the
    a. aggregate demand curve.
    b. demand for loanable funds.
    c. short-run Phillips curve.
    d. long-run Phillips curve.
    e. production possibilities curve.

32. If government wants to increase spending by $100 billion without increasing the price level, then
    a. taxes must increase by exactly $100 billion.
    b. taxes must increase by more than $100 billion.
    c. taxes must decrease by exactly $100 billion.
    d. taxes must decrease by more than $100 billion.
    e. taxes must remain constant.

33. An increase in the government's budget surplus will most likely result in
    a. decreased tax revenues.
    b. increased government spending.
    c. higher interest rates.
    d. a decrease in the international value of the dollar.
    e. an increase in inflation.

34. Assume that the United States has a balance of trade deficit with China. What action by Chinese policymakers would offset the effects of the trade deficit on China's currency?
    a. increase exports to the United States
    b. decrease imports from the United States
    c. increase Chinese interest rates
    d. increase the purchase of United States' real and financial assets
    e. decrease the purchase of United States' real and financial assets

35. Cost-push inflation results in
    a. increased short-run aggregate supply.
    b. decreased short-run aggregate supply.
    c. increased aggregate demand.
    d. decreased aggregate demand.
    e. a leftward shift of the short-run Phillips curve.

36. If the real interest rate is 4 percent and expected inflation is 3 percent, then the nominal interest rate is
    a. 1%.
    b. -1%.
    c. 3%.
    d. 7%.
    e. 12%.

37. Which of the following would lead to an increase in the United States' gross domestic product in the short run?
    a. There is an increase in personal income taxes.
    b. Banks hold more excess reserves.
    c. Full-time employees are reclassified as part-time employees according to a new government definition.
    d. Households save less of their disposable income.
    e. A significant tax is placed on all capital investment in new technology.

38. A decrease in available technology will cause the
    a. aggregate demand curve to shift left.
    b. aggregate demand curve to shift right.
    c. long-run aggregate supply curve to shift left.
    d. long-run aggregate supply curve to shift right.
    e. short-run aggregate supply curve to shift right.

39. Assume that the Federal Reserve buys $1 billion worth of Treasury securities from a primary security dealer. If the required reserve ratio is 25 percent, then the initial change in excess reserves is
    a. $250 million.
    b. $750 million.
    c. $3 billion.
    d. $4 billion.
    e. $4.25 billion.

Questions 40 - 41 are based on the following diagram, which shows the choices in production of two countries, Ostrichalia and New Zebrand, producing two goods, cotton shirts and wool sweaters, using all of their available resources.

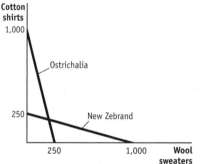

40. According to the theory of comparative advantage, Ostrichalia would find it advantageous to
    a. export cotton shirts and import wool sweaters.
    b. import both wool sweaters and cotton shirts.
    c. export both wool sweaters and cotton shirts.
    d. import cotton shirts and export wool sweaters.
    e. trade 1,000 cotton shirts for 200 wool sweaters.

41. Which of the following statements best describes the conditions for specialization in either Ostrichalia or New Zebrand?
    a. Ostrichalia should specialize in wool sweaters, according to its absolute advantage in them.
    b. Ostrichalia should specialize in wool sweaters, according to its comparative advantage in them.
    c. New Zebrand should specialize in wool sweaters, according to its absolute advantage in them.
    d. New Zebrand should specialize in wool sweaters, according to its comparative advantage in them.
    e. Neither country should specialize, but instead should avoid trade and become self-sufficient.

42. Amanda and Stuart are trading partners. In a single day, Amanda can produce 10 turkeys or 5 mugs, while Stuart can produce 3 turkeys or 9 mugs. Assuming that Amanda and Stuart both have constant opportunity costs, which of the following statements is true?
    a. Amanda should specialize in producing turkey because she has an absolute advantage in turkey production.
    b. Stuart should specialize in producing mugs because he has an absolute advantage in mug production.
    c. Amanda would be willing to trade with Stuart as long as she could purchase a mug for less than 2 turkeys.
    d. Stuart would be willing to trade with Amanda as long as he could purchase a turkey for less than 9 mugs.
    e. Since they both have absolute advantage in at least one good, they cannot be made better off through trade.

43. Which is most likely to occur if the Federal Reserve sells treasury bonds on the open market?
    a. Interest rates will decrease.
    b. The money supply will increase.
    c. Net exports will increase.
    d. Excess reserves in the banking system will decrease.
    e. Aggregate demand will increase.

44. Which fiscal policy action by government will shift aggregate demand to the left?
    a. the open-market sale of bonds by the Federal Reserve
    b. an increase in the discount rate
    c. an increase in taxes
    d. an increase in government spending
    e. an increase in the reserve requirement

45. Cost-push inflation occurs when there is
    a. an increase in capital investment at the expense of government spending.
    b. a decrease in net exports resulting from appreciation of the currency.
    c. an increase in both inflation and unemployment.
    d. a decrease in gross private investment resulting from government borrowing.
    e. a rightward shift of the money supply.

46. If the real interest rate in Argentina has increased from 5% to 6% and the real interest rate in Brazil has increased from 4% to 6%, Brazilian capital flow and currency should change in which of the following ways?

	Capital flow	Currency
a.	Out	Appreciate
b.	In	Appreciate
c.	In	Depreciate
d.	Out	Depreciate
e.	No change	No change

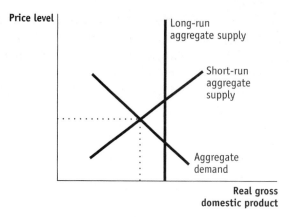

Price level

Long-run aggregate supply

Short-run aggregate supply

Aggregate demand

Real gross domestic product

47. According to the graph above, which of the following is true about this economy in the long run?
    a. Contractionary monetary policy will restore this economy to its long-run equilibrium.
    b. The long-run aggregate supply curve will shift to the left in order to restore the long-run equilibrium.
    c. The economy depicted is currently in a long-run equilibrium.
    d. A combination of increased government spending and an increase in the money supply could shift aggregate demand to the right and restore long-run equilibrium.
    e. Wages will increase as they adjust to the new price level and the short-run aggregate supply curve will shift to the left and restore long-run equilibrium.

48. An increase in government spending combined with a decrease in personal income taxes will most likely cause aggregate demand and short-run aggregate supply to change in which of the following ways?

	Aggregate demand	*Short-run aggregate supply*
a.	Increase	Decrease
b.	Increase	No change
c.	Decrease	Increase
d.	Decrease	No change
e.	Decrease	Decrease

49. Which type of unemployment would increase if robot technology were widely adopted in manufacturing?
    a. frictional
    b. cyclical
    c. seasonal
    d. structural
    e. part-time

50. The spending multiplier increases as
    a. the tax multiplier decreases.
    b. the marginal propensity to save increases.
    c. the average propensity to consume decreases.
    d. the balanced budget multiplier increases.
    e. the marginal propensity to consume increases.

51. If the nominal interest rate is equal to 0%, which of the following statements is true?
   a. The Federal Reserve cannot use open-market operations to increase the money supply.
   b. The real rate of interest will be positive as long as inflation is positive.
   c. The quantity of money supplied is also equal to zero.
   d. The Federal Reserve cannot use open-market operations to decrease the money supply.
   e. The real interest rate is less than the rate of inflation.

52. Which of the following combinations of fiscal and monetary policy would effectively reduce net exports and capital investment?

	Fiscal policy	*Monetary policy*
a.	Expansionary	Contractionary
b.	Expansionary	Expansionary
c.	Contractionary	No change
d.	Contractionary	Contractionary
e.	Contractionary	Expansionary

Last Year's & This Year's Production	Last Year's Price	This Year's Price
100 consumer goods	$2 per good	$2 per good
50 capital goods	$10 per good	$10 per good
200 services	$0.50 per service	$1.50 per service

53. Based on the information in the table above, if you use this year as the base year, what was the GDP deflator for last year?
   a. 75
   b. 80
   c. 100
   d. 120
   e. 125

54. If households experience an increase in disposable income, then aggregate demand, the short-run Phillips curve, and unemployment will change in which of the following ways in the short run?

	Aggregate demand curve	*Short-run Phillips curve*	*Unemployment*
a.	Shift to the right	Shift to the right	Increase
b.	Shift to the right	Shift to the left	Decrease
c.	Shift to the right	No change	Decrease
d.	Shift to the left	No change	Decrease
e.	Shift to the left	Shift to the right	Increase

55. Assuming that input prices are flexible, an economy operating above the natural rate of unemployment will experience which of the following changes in output and price level in the long run?

	Output	*Price level*
a.	Increase	Increase
b.	No change	Increase
c.	Increase	No change
d.	Increase	Decrease
e.	Decrease	Increase

56. Assuming a system of flexible exchange rates, an open-market purchase of bonds by the United States Federal Reserve while Japan does nothing will most likely affect the United States' rate of inflation and the international value of the Japanese yen in which of the following ways?

	Inflation rate	*International value of the Japanese yen*
a.	Decrease	Appreciate
b.	Decrease	Depreciate
c.	Increase	Appreciate
d.	Increase	Depreciate
e.	Increase	No change

57. In order to increase the federal funds rate, the Federal Reserve
  a. raises the discount rate.
  b. raises the reserve requirement.
  c. lowers the reserve requirement.
  d. buys bonds on the open market.
  e. sells bonds on the open market.

Labor Market in Anselia (in thousands of persons)	
Population	600
Not interested in working at all	100
Interested in working, but not looking because they believe there are no jobs	100
Looking for work and not working	100
Part-time workers	100
Full-time workers	200

58. Based on the information in the table above, what is the unemployment rate?
  a. 20%
  b. 25%
  c. 50%
  d. 75%
  e. 16.67%

59. A decrease in taxes with an increase in the required reserve ratio will result in
  a. an increase in real gross domestic product and an increase in the interest rate.
  b. an increase in unemployment and an indeterminate change in the interest rate.
  c. an indeterminate change in real gross domestic product and an increase in the interest rate.
  d. a decrease in real gross domestic product and a decrease in the interest rate.
  e. a decrease in unemployment and an increase in the inflation rate.

60. If the marginal propensity to consume is 0.8, then the largest change in consumption that would happen as a result of a $100 million decrease in taxes is
  a. a decrease of $80 million.
  b. an increase of $80 million.
  c. a decrease of $100 million.
  d. an increase of $400 million.
  e. a decrease of $400 million.

Free-Response Questions

On the actual AP® exam, you have 60 minutes to complete all three questions. The College Board requires that all free responses be completed in blue or black ink. Note that only answers written in the designated spaces of the answer booklet will be scored.

1. Assume that the United States economy is in long-run equilibrium.
   a. Assume that the United States only produces two goods, clothing and gems. Draw a correctly labeled graph of the production possibilities curve for the United States. Show a point that could represent current production and label it X.

   b. Draw a correctly labeled graph of the aggregate demand and aggregate supply for the United States showing the economy in long-run equilibrium. Label current output Y_0, the current price level PL_0, and the full employment rate of output Y_f.

   c. Bulgaria is a trading partner of the United States. The currency of Bulgaria is the lev. Draw a graph of the foreign exchange market for the currency of Bulgaria. Label the equilibrium exchange rate E_1 and the quantity of lev exchanged Q_1.

   d. Assume that the marginal propensity to consume in the United States is 0.75.

      (i) Suppose that government spending decreases by $100 million. Calculate the impact of the decrease in government spending on output.

(ii) On your graph of the aggregate demand and aggregate supply in part **b.**, show the effect of the decrease in government spending on the output and price level in the United States. Label the new output Y_1 and the new price level PL_1.

(iii) On your graph of the production possibilities curve in part **a.**, show a new point that would represent the current level of production in the United States. Label this point Z.

e. On your graph of the foreign exchange market for lev, show the effect of the change you showed in **d.(ii)** on the exchange rate. Label the new exchange rate E_2.

(i) Identify if the lev has appreciated or depreciated.

(ii) What impact will the change in the value of the lev have on aggregate demand in the United States? Explain.

2. Assume that households increase their savings.

a. Using a correctly labeled graph of the loanable funds market, show how the increase in savings affects the real interest rate.

b. Indicate how the change in the real interest rate you identified in part **a.** will affect gross private investment.

c. Explain how the change in investment you identified in **b.** will affect the rate of economic growth.

3. Because of political turmoil in Europe, foreign investors have been purchasing financial assets in the United States.

a. Using a correctly labeled graph of the U. S. dollar, show the effect of the increase in the purchase of U. S. financial assets on the following:

(i) the demand for the dollar

(ii) the international value of the dollar

b. Explain how the change in the international value of the dollar you identified in **a.(ii)** will affect U. S. net exports.

c. Using a correctly labeled graph of the short-run Phillips curve with a point labeled A on the curve, show how the change in net exports you identified in **b.** will affect the following:

(i) inflation

(ii) unemployment